SLOUCHING ΤΟ...

MW01030743

Nina Coltart is a distinguished member of the Independent Group of the British Psycho-Analytical Society, and a greatly admired speaker and supervisor. In her talks and essays, she explores the parameters of the psychoanalytic relationship against a background of broader issues in morality and culture.

Her work is direct, honest, moving and illuminating. *Slouching Towards Bethlehem* is the first collection of her writings, and shows the consistency and breadth of her interests over many years of psychoanalytic practice. Among the topics which she considers are love, religion, Buddhism, and moral responsibility. She employs a broad range of techniques – from assessment and the special place of 'attention' in the analytic process, to the silent or the elderly patient. The title essay is justly famous – an account of an apparently hopeless analysis, in which Dr Coltart's dramatic intervention produced remarkable results. Something analogous can be said of practically all her writings.

NINA COLTART took her first degree in Modern Languages at Oxford before beginning her medical training. She became a training analyst in 1972. A former Vice-President of the British Psycho-Analytical Society, she was Director of the London Clinic of Psycho-Analysis for ten years, and has played an important role in the recent development of psychotherapy training in London.

Slouching Towards Bethlehem ...
and further psychoanalytical explorations

NINA COLTART

FREE ASSOCIATION BOOKS / LONDON

First published in Great Britain in 1993 by
FREE ASSOCIATION BOOKS
57 Warren Street, London W1P 5PA

2002 2001 2000 1999   10 9 8 7 6 5 4

A CIP catalogue record for this book is available
from the British Library

ISBN 1 85343 186 9

Printed in the EC by J.W. Arrowsmith Ltd, Bristol

Contents

Acknowledgements

My special thanks are due to the friends and colleagues who have invited me to speak in a variety of places during the last decade, thus providing the only incentive which ever stimulates me to write a paper at all. Among them are Neville Symington in Sydney, Gregorio Kohon in Brisbane, Polly Lind in New Zealand, Joe Berke in London, and, rather specially, Kit Bollas, who has facilitated many enjoyable encounters with new colleagues in different parts of the United States.

I would like to thank Bob Young for his patient, relentless pursuit of the idea of collecting my papers for publication. Without his encouragement, I doubt whether I would have thought of it, and it might not have come about. And also I would like to thank Ann Scott for her sympathetic help and skilful editing.

The real hard work has always been done by my friend of over thirty years, Isabel Vincent. She has turned my many (longhand) versions into word-processed ones with reliable speed and accuracy; and moreover with a lively critical interest in their subject matter which has been of constant value to me. I am deeply grateful to her.

My most grateful thanks to Ruth Levitt for compiling the index.

Some of these papers are reproduced by kind permission of the following journals: *International Journal of Psycho-Analysis* for 'The analysis of an elderly patient', 72(2); *British Journal of Psychotherapy* for 'Diagnosis and assessment for suitability for psychoanalytic psychotherapy', 4(2), and 'Attention', 7(2); *Psychoanalytic Dialogues* for 'The silent patient', 1(3); and *Psychoanalytic Psychotherapy* for 'The treatment of a transvestite', 1(1).

I would also like to thank the following: Gregorio Kohon who edited *The British School of Psychoanalysis: The Independent Tradition*, Free Association Books, and included my first paper, 'Slouching towards Bethlehem'; and Dame Iris Murdoch, Chatto & Windus and Ed Victor Ltd for kind permission to quote from the novel *The Black Prince*.

1

SLOUCHING TOWARDS BETHLEHEM ... OR THINKING THE UNTHINKABLE IN PSYCHOANALYSIS

This paper was first given as a contribution to the English-speaking Conference of Psychoanalysts in 1982. The Conference was in the form of a symposium, whose overall title was simply 'Beyond Words'. This is an expanded version of my original paper.

After I had agreed to write this paper, my mind went blank for quite a long time. Then I began to realize that a paper for a symposium whose overall title was 'Beyond Words' appropriately had to be generated in that very area, namely, where blankness seemed to be. After a while, the title for the paper announced itself. I was wary of it, since it seemed both eccentric and religious. But it stuck tenaciously. For those of you who do not know it, it is taken from a short poem by W. B. Yeats called 'The Second Coming' (1919). It occurred to me when I reread it closely that it is a poem about breakdown and the possibility of healing, or could be seen as such. It is mysterious, but then so is our subject. It goes like this (my final italics):

> Turning and turning in the widening gyre
> The falcon cannot hear the falconer;
> Things fall apart; the centre cannot hold;
> Mere anarchy is loosed upon the world,
> The blood-dimmed tide is loosed, and everywhere
> The ceremony of innocence is drowned;
> The best lack all conviction, while the worst
> Are full of passionate intensity.

First published in *The British School of Psychoanalysis: The Independent Tradition*, edited by Gregorio Kohon. London: Free Association Books, 1986.

Surely some revelation is at hand;
Surely the Second Coming is at hand.
The Second Coming! Hardly are those words out
When a vast image out of *Spiritus Mundi*
Troubles my sight: somewhere in sands of the desert
A shape with lion body and the head of a man,
A gaze blank and pitiless as the sun,
Is moving its slow thighs, while all about it
Reel shadows of the indignant desert birds.
The darkness drops again; but now I know
That twenty centuries of stony sleep
Were vexed to nightmare by a rocking cradle,
And what rough beast, its hour come round at last,
Slouches towards Bethlehem to be born?

This is not a paper on religion. It does not look to Messianic
dogma, nor to Christian symbol to help us out of the anarchic
depths of the unconscious. What caught my attention was the idea
that there is a distinct metaphor for us in the poem which speaks
to the whole of what analysis is about. We can move the metaphor
of the poem from the religious to the analytical. Some people have
seen this metaphor as pessimistic; you will gather that I have seen
it differently.

It is of the essence of our impossible profession that in a very
singular way we do not know what we are doing. Do not be
distracted by random associations to this idea. I am not undermin-
ing our deep, exacting training; nor discounting the ways in which
– unlike many people who master a subject and then just do it, or
teach it – we have to keep at ourselves, our literature and our
clinical crosstalk with colleagues. All these daily operations are the
efficient, skilful and thinkable tools with which we constantly
approach the heart of our work, which is a mystery.

The day that one qualifies as an analyst, the analyst that one is
going to be is a mystery. Ten years later, we may just about be able
to look back and discern the shape of the rough beast – ourselves
as analysts in embryo – as it slouches along under the months and
years until, its hour come round at last, there is some clearer sense
of ourselves as analysts. The process of doing analysis has slowly
given birth to an identity which we now more or less recognize as
an analyst, or at least the identity which we have become, and are
still becoming, which for us approximates to the notion of 'being

an analyst'. This may be very different from that which we long ago had visualized or hoped for.

It is my belief that something very similar obtains also for our work with our patients. However much we gain confidence, refine our technique, decide more creatively when and how and what to interpret, each hour with each patient is also in its way an act of faith; faith in ourselves, in the process, and faith in the secret, unknown, unthinkable things in our patients which, in the space which is the analysis, are slouching towards the time when their hour comes round at last. When that hour comes, by dint of all our long, thoughtful, interpretative attempts to familiarize ourselves with the patient's inner world, we begin to see shaping up things that we may have guessed at; or predicted, or theoretically constructed or relied on; or even, almost like byproducts of months of careful, steady work, things that take us by suprise. We have been waiting attentively, in Freud's own words, 'for the pattern to emerge'. Those of us who were fortunate enough to be taught by the late Dr Bion value the stress which he laid on the need to develop the ability to tolerate not knowing; the capacity to sit it out with a patient, often for long periods, without any real precision as to where we are, relying on our regular tools and our faith in the process to carry us through the obfuscating darkness of resistance, complex defences, and the sheer unconsciousness of the unconscious.

In parenthesis, there is a possible solution or definition here of that controversial problem, the difference between psychotherapy and psychoanalysis. Although I am currently stressing our ignorance, there is always something going on that we more or less know something about; the daily *tabula rasa* of the analytic session produces a mass of information, and for a patient who comes once or twice a week it may well be constructive and ego-supportive to get on to a track indicated by one of these signposts. In analysis we can afford to ignore them, in the slow, attentive working towards a deeper nexus of feeling, fantasy and wordless experience, that is slouching along in a yet unthinkable form. Clues we note and store away, but need not, often must not, hear them as distracting sirens' songs to be fallen for and followed.

I want to say something here about the act of faith. It is to do with Wilfred Bion. I have to confess that at the time I wrote my

short paragraph above about being taught by Bion, it was pretty
well a summary of what I knew about him. Of course, I knew he
had invented a Grid (1963) and I had never talked to anyone who
could make real sense of it. But since writing my original paper, I
felt a strong urge to read all the works of Bion, and have done so. I
was both delighted and horrifed by what I found. Delighted because
some of it expressed so clearly some of my own ideas; horrified
because it began to look as though I have been plagiarizing. But I do
not think I can have been. I have concluded that, apart from perhaps
being more influenced by the few seminars that I had with him than
I had realized, we had simply developed individually along similar
lines in *some ways*. I stress this because I do not wish time or
imaginative conjecture to be wasted in thinking that I am seriously
comparing myself to any extent with him. Wilfred Bion was a
widely cultured man and I think probably a mystic and a genius.
Certain clues in his writings suggest that, in the most modest and
dispassionate way, he thought the same. And I am not. Also he did
invent that Grid, and he constantly refers to it, and even now I have
read him word for word, it makes little sense to me, and I cannot
use it. This may be because Bion was, amongst other things,
mathematically minded, and I am innumerate.

   To return to the act of faith. I found that Bion *uses* this phrase
and by it intends to signify the most highly desirable stance of the
psychoanalyst. He says that the act of faith is peculiar to scientific
procedure and must be distinguished from the religious meaning
with which it is invested in common usage. The essence of its
creation – and Bion sees it, as I do, as a positive, willed act – is
refraining from memory and desire, a phrase which many people
do loosely associate with what they know of Bion. He says in
Attention and Interpretation (1970):

> It may be wondered what state of mind is welcome if desires and
> memories are not. A term that would express approximately what I
> need to express is 'faith' – faith that there is an ultimate reality and
> truth – the unknown, unknowable, 'formless infinite'. This must be
> believed of every object of which the personality can be aware . . .
> (p. 31)

The channel for the transformation of the apprehension of the
ultimate reality, or a bit of it, is the analyst's direct attention and

perception, and the capacity to bring together hitherto meaningless fragments of the patient's mental and verbal elements into a thinking process, and communicate this back to the patient. Bion says that this form of attention, this act of faith, must be what he calls 'unstained by any element of memory or desire' (p. 33). He means in the analyst, of course.

> The more the analyst occupies himself with memory and desire, the more his facility for harbouring them increases and the nearer he comes to undermining his capacity for [the act of faith] . . . if his mind is preoccupied with what is or is not said, or with what he does or does not hope, it means that he cannot allow the experience to obtrude . . . (p. 41) No one who denudes himself of memory and desire, and of all those elements of sense impression ordinarily present, can have any doubt of the reality of psycho-analytical experience which remains ineffable. (p. 35)

It will be seen that Bion has intuition very high in his hierarchy of the tools at our disposal, and is advocating a constant sternly self-disciplined practice. Indeed, at one point, he actually equates intuition with analytic observations.

It must be emphasized, however, in case it is not clear enough already, that Bion is not advocating random speculative commentary unrooted in a huge reservoir of experience, thought and theoretical knowledge, and in the capacity to draw upon and correlate all these, in the intervals between the dark experiencing of the act of faith, in the interests of making the evolution of the total experience comprehensively available to the patient. The philosopher Immanuel Kant said: 'Intuition without concept is blind: concept without intuition is empty.' It seems to me that Bion, and I in my way in this paper, are striving for the merging of the two.

Before I move on from this section on Bion's thought, I just want to quote from a question-and-answer seminar recorded when Bion was in São Paulo in 1977 (Bion, 1980). It says with such simplicity so much that elsewhere in his writings Bion goes over repetitively at length and in a complex way. The questioner asks: 'How did you come to realize the advantages of suppressing memory and desire during an analytic session?' and Bion replies: 'I found I could experience a flash of the obvious. One is usually so busy looking for something out of the ordinary that one ignores the obvious as if it were of no importance.' Whereas, again in *Attention and Interpretation*, he says, unhelpfully if challengingly: 'There can be no rules about the nature of the emotional experience that will show that the emotional experience is ripe for interpretation' (1970, p. 32). Here I would add that faith and self-reliance are indeed needed!

The crucial thing about our technical development is that it hinges on a paradox. There is a delicate balance between our reliance on our theories and on our knowledge of human nature in many of its dimensions – (and experience tells us that human nature continually reveals similar patterns, and that generates good theory) – the balance, I repeat, is between this reliance, and our willingness to be continually open to the emergence of the unexpected. 'Plus ça change, plus c'est la même chose' may be a good truism for analysts; but it is only true in a restricted sense; it is the changes that are rung that are the essentials of individual humanity. There is a grim stage when we are learning to be analysts when we are endangered by our own templates, our theories, and our teachers. We may detect the faint shuffle of the slouching beast, and be tempted to throw a set of grappling irons into the darkness, seize it, label it, hang it round with words, and haul it prematurely to birth. We may then often be stuck with a deformed monster that we have largely created by our own precipitate verbosity: we may then proceed laboriously onwards with a sort of analytic mistake, while the true creature who is not yet ready for the light of day retreats backwards into the darkness again.

The use of the metaphor of the poem here says what I want to say, but perhaps I should explain it a little, and less poetically. The seductive impulse to use the power of one's thinking and theorizing to take possession of our patients too soon can be great, but will, as suggested, be of little ultimate value to them. Precipitate control of the material may lead to a sense of satisfaction in the analyst, and often appeal to quite conscious layers of the patient, whose resistance to exposing his or her true unknown reality to the light will have been served by it.

Heisenberg's Uncertainty Principle is a hard taskmaster in the everyday life of the consulting room; it seems to me undesirable that one should communicate certainty about a patient to a patient, or, at least, one should do so only very occasionally. The whole of our subject, psychoanalysis, can be, and often is, attacked on the grounds that it is unscientific and cannot be supported by any scientific evidence. The most that can be claimed for it is that it is *probable*, and what we use is not rigorous scientific investigation, but the act of faith, supported by rational and imaginative conjectures, themselves inevitably conditioned by our learning and our experience. The act of faith may feel like a spontaneous regression to complete unknowing, and may well be accompanied by dread; it can be disturbing to the analyst and seem like a serious self-induced attack on his ego, which in a way it is. To quote Bion again – from my memory of one of his seminars – with particular reference to trying to capture the rough beast too soon: 'Such depths of ignorance are difficult to dare to contemplate, though I am bound to feel a wish to believe how Godlike I am, how intelligent, as a change from being appalled by my ignorance.' But it may be at the expense of the *true* pattern emerging that we do this.

I am sure I am not saying anything heretical or unfamiliar to analysts at least, if I confess that I sometimes wish ardently, as I settle down for the opening sessions of what promises to be a long analysis, that the first year were already over. This is part of the paradoxical nature of our work. I would not for the world pass up that first year with all its subtle demands on the technique of getting the patient rooted in the analysis, feeling for the available transferences, learning history, and doing first aid, which is often so necessary when things have fallen apart and anarchy has been loosed upon the world.

But after this preliminary work there comes a time which is exhilarating, when the pace quickens and the gears change. Paradoxically again, this is often the time when darkness begins to close in, but it is a darkness having that special quality of the unknown which is moving towards being known. Freud was speaking of a time like this, I imagine, when he said that sometimes he had to blind himself in order to focus on the light in one dark spot. There is a textural richness which begins to draw deeper analysis out of one's own darkness, and stretch oneself towards the limit of ingenuity, technique, and a rapid use of identifications and intuition, combined with imaginative intensity. During phases like this in analysis it is true to say that one does not *think* at all during some sessions, at least in the ordinary cognitive use of the word. Indeed, one of the most satisfying elements about entering the stage of doing an analysis when the anxiety of the early years is left behind and senility has not yet come, is this freedom from actually thinking while one is actively engaged in working; that is, when the act of faith is becoming easier. Of course, to say this is not to detract from the high value attaching to the power of attention and total concern with the patient. In fact there is plenty of evidence, not only in our literature, but in that of philosophy and religion, that the attention is more total when temporarily freed from concurrent cognitive processes. This switch into fifth gear cannot exactly be legislated for, although Bion's advice that we should rigorously practise for it is relevant, and it does not by any means always happen. Then we fall back again on thinking, and theorizing, and trying things out in our heads, or just waiting. But in the fifth-gear phases, when the act of faith is most fully deployed, when our listening ear seems to be directly connected with our tongue and speech, interpretative dialogue is not a process which I would regard as being under everyday conscious control. Fascinating data derived from bio-feedback experiments show that the nature of the brainwaves actually changes in the states to which I am referring and predominantly alpha rhythm on the EEG takes over from normal waking mixed beta and theta waves. When I gave this paper at the 1982 conference, one of the analysts in the discussion took up what I have just said and asked me rather peevishly what I meant by saying that this was fascinating. I fear I was unable to answer satisfactorily. I had myself participated in bio-feedback experiments and had learned to alter my brainwaves, blood pressure and skin resistance. If the phenomenon I have just described is not self-evidently fascinating, then we are on different wavelengths and I cannot justify the use of such a personalized word.

Certain recurring problems in analytic work give valuable encouragement to our reliance on the process that I have just attempted to describe. These are problems which may be rather specially regarded as falling into the arena entitled 'beyond words'. One of them is silence. Any silence of more than about forty minutes in analysis begins to have its own peculiar interest. But there is a very particular challenge issued by profoundly silent patients, who are often, by the way, not diagnosable as such during a careful assessment interview. I make this point because it indicates that profound silence itself, as well as what it conceals, can be a rough beast which is slouching along in the depths of a communicative, articulate patient and whose time may need to come round and be *endured* in the analysis.

I have treated eight patients in twenty-five years who have been deeply silent for long periods during the analysis. One for nearly a year, several for months or weeks.

One of these was a man who was in his mid-fifties when he started treatment with the complaint of near-suicidal depression. He was unmarried, sexually virginal, powerful, charismatic, and a successful captain of industry. He was not, I decided in the first year, a False Self personality, nor was he, apparently, homosexual or perverse. He had a huge number of acquaintances, but no really close friends. He was a clubbable man. The very fact of starting analysis, and that he had never really talked deeply to anyone about himself meant that, in his case, the first couple of years were full of interchange and improvement. But I was suspicious that something else was gathering its forces in the depths of his inner world. He slowly made an eroticized transference, and was somewhat elated for months. I could not exactly predict what the shape of the beast was going to be, but that there was something completely different that had to emerge in time if the analysis was going to work, I did not doubt. He had come to me with his centre not holding, and with things falling apart, and the initial improvement had not truly touched that. In his second year, he suddenly ground to a halt, and fell violently silent, exuding ever-stronger black waves of hatred and despair. I slowly tried out the various technical manoeuvres that I had learned over the years for approaching and entering silence. To no avail. The change in him from late midlife-crisis neurosis to something which breathed psychosis was heavy in the atmosphere. He never failed to attend, but his body movements and even his shape seemed to have altered. Very close attention to these things is of the essence when faced with such a massive 'beyond words' challenge. He slouched and humped himself grimly and disjointedly up and down my stairs and in and out of my room. His gaze, when he glanced at me, was shifty, evil, and terrified. He was as if possessed. When I spoke about what I saw and felt, he glowered, grunted and sank further into an ungainly heap. He had never wanted to lie on the couch, so all this was face to face. I carried dark and heavy projective identifications, to put it one way, which I tried in vain to decode to him, until I was almost as saturated in despair as he was.

One day, without really thinking it out clearly, I suddenly demonstrated an example of what Neville Symington has called 'the analyst's act of freedom' (1983). I simply and suddenly became furious and bawled him out for his prolonged lethal attack on me and on the analysis. I wasn't going to stand for it a second longer, I shouted, without the remotest idea at that moment of what alternative I was proposing! This outburst of mine changed the course of the analysis. I subsequently wrote about this man more fully, under the title 'The analysis of an elderly patient' (1991a; this volume, Ch. 10).

It was only in the subsequent interpretative understanding of that parameter, as my outburst would be called, and of the preceding black months, that we came to see how much, to his own suprise and horror, this man had needed to live out, and have experienced and endured by another person without retaliation, his primary hatred of a genuinely powerful mother. He had, so to speak, lost her to his only brother who was born when he was eighteen months old, and he had been required by her throughout his life to love and revere her unstintingly. He had solved this first great problem of his life by remaining unswervingly loyal to her and it had nearly cost *him* his life. You will see that the act of freedom arose from the exercise of an act of faith. I had given up trying to 'understand' this patient, given up theorizing and just sat there day after day without memory or desire in a state of suspension, attending only with an empty mind to him and the unknowable truth of himself, which had shaped his life, until such a moment as I was so at one with it that I knew it for the murderous hatred it was, and had to make a jump for freedom – his as well as mine, though I did not think that out at the time – by shouting. These acts of faith can feel dangerous.

I would like to speak briefly here for a moment of another thing that is often, I have the distinct impression, felt to be dangerous in psychoanalysis, albeit in a different way from the encounter with the murderous hatred via the act of faith. This is laughing. You hardly ever hear analysts talk about laughing in sessions, and you do not find papers written about it either. Again I return to Bion for a comment though he nowhere has developed it as much as I could have wished. In one of his São Paulo seminars, he is talking about how psychoanalysis has changed and developed; he wonders would Freud even understand what some of us are doing now? Then, apparently at random, he goes straight on to say: 'I wonder if it is within the rules of psychoanalysis to be able to laugh at ourselves? Is it according to the rules of psychoanalysis that we should be amused and find things funny? Is it permissible to enjoy a psychoanalytic meeting? I suggest that, having broken through in this revolutionary matter of being amused in the sacred process of psychoanalysis, we might as well continue to see where that more joyous state of mind might take us' (1980, pp. 94–5). Then, rather maddeningly, but very characteristically, he says no more about this explicitly, but I think it is significant that he goes straight into a short passage which ends like this:

> I sometimes think that analysts are sunk in this same Oedipean gloom; so much so that they are often taken by suprise when they discover that there is such a thing as mental pain. One feels that they have only learnt that there is a *theory* that there is mental pain, but that they don't believe it exists, or that psychoanalysis is a method of treating it. So when a patient gets 'better' they are suprised; they don't believe it has anything to do with the work they are doing. But if we are to go on growing and developing, I believe that the psychoanalytical procedure does a great deal to help that development to take place . . . Psychoanalysis helps the spirit, or soul . . . to continue . . . we help the soul or the psyche to be born, and even help it to continue to develop *after* it is born. (pp. 96–7)

Now the immediate juxtaposition of those two passages makes me think that implicit in the second passage is the message of the first; to put it very simply, that laughter and enjoyment can be therapeutic factors in psychoanalysis. Certainly I believe that one not only can but should enjoy psychoanalytical sessions.

I once thought about writing a paper on laughing in psychoanalysis and perhaps this is the nearest I shall get. I suppose there is a fear that I may be deluding myself, and not noticing that what it really means is that my technique has got sloppy, or that I have developed a special sort of defence, or both, or many more horrendous things, but certainly with advancing age laughter seems to occur more often than it did. Of course, it is important to try to continue to analyse and monitor what is happening. I remember that when I was still training, I started to treat a patient in what had to be called five-times-a-week psychotherapy, because I was not yet an analyst. He was not one of my training cases. He was a man who could make people laugh. He was quite ill, but he was really extremely amusing. I was so serious about my training and what I thought were the sacred rules of psychoanalysis that I used to use a lot of energy trying not to laugh. Of course I analysed the aggression in his jokes, and there was plenty of it, and what was defensive, distracting and seductive about it all. And so I would now. But I also think now that I would laugh first if I felt like it. I am now of the opinion that I deprived both him and me unnecessarily by being so prim. I think I might have got nearer to some true shape or pattern in him *faster*, by responding with a natural reaction and *then* talking about it. If we are too protective of our self-presentation and of what we consider grimly to be the sacred rules of True Psychoanalysis, then we may suffocate something in the patient, in ourselves, and in the process.

Another category of patients who present one with specific 'beyond words' problems are those with psychosomatic symptoms. In this I include, of course, the fairly straightforward, pure, and now relatively rare hysterical conversions. The overlap between these and some psychosomatic symptoms of different aetiology can be extending and confusing. For example, I have had the opportunity to treat five cases of asthma of late onset in adults, two in analysis, and three in focal analytic psychotherapy. They could not exactly be classified as hysterics, because I believe hysterical symptoms are rooted in a pathological disablement of the will, and willing and breathing, which is what goes wrong in asthma, do not connect up properly in a psychological sense, that is, we do not breathe at will. A paralysed limb where the voluntary muscles cease to work hysterically is a different matter. But they were certainly conveying a message of conflict through their asthma atacks, and this *is* what hysterics do. They were also threatening life itself, and two of them very nearly did die in *status asthmaticus*. If I were to condense into one sentence what the hidden central dynamic was, I would say it was pre-verbal, never thinkable, never expressible rage with the mother, rooted in a period before attainment of the depressive position. In silence, eventually, I had to experience this rage directly myself as raged at, before being able to evolve this shape into suitable words.

The special interest of psychosomatic symptoms, to pick up the main metaphor of this paper, is that the rough beast whose hour is not yet come is holed up in the body. There is a lovely quotation from the poet John Donne, in his poem 'Progress of the Soul', which refers to the non-pathological aspect of this:

> her pure and eloquent blood
> Spoke in her cheeks, and so distinctly wrought,
> That one might almost say her body thought. (lines 244–6)

The beast has crossed that mysterious barrier whose location eludes us, and moved over into a stronghold from which it is only on rare occasions easy to be delivered. Mostly, the beast seems inaccessible, and we perceive that part of the mind has lodged on a psychotic island in the body. This image arises from a paper by Herbert Rosenfeld (1985), which sheds light on the treatment of women who not infrequently select the uterus as their psychotic island. We could say that a psychosomatic symptom represents that which is determined to remain unconscious, or unknowable, but which at the same time has actually made itself conscious in a very heavy disguise; it is speakable about only in a dense and enigmatic code. In terms of the metaphor of my paper, we have to ask what is the unthinkable content slouching along in the darkness of the psychosomatic symptom? How do we build a bridge which really *holds* over the secret area of the body–mind divide? Can the unthinkable become thinkable? Can we possibly devise words which have enough compatibility with the physical track chosen by the mind, so that we can send some sort of message down back along that same track via the body to the mind? By ordinary, careful analysis laced with inspiration one may at length interpret the psychosomatic symptom so irresistibly that it yields. A rush of new affects may appear. The now more verbal material may be enriched by new–old memories. Or the symptom may just quietly fade away. Nevertheless, there is a certain mystery which we do well not to ignore. It would be unwise to conclude that because we have apparently cured a genuine psychosomatic symptom by dynamic interpretation we actually *know* how it was *done*. We may be able to derive further theory from it. We may even be able to repeat the performance with another patient with a similar problem. But we do not quite know how it was done. Where and how did our laboriously evolved words and thoughts meet and capture the resolutely unthinkable beast in the unconscious process?

There is a way of visualizing analysis as a spiral process. The seemingly same ground is ploughed over and over again. And yet there is always something new about it. I refer to this spiral effect here because it has a special relevance to our work with psychosomatic symptoms. We may have undermined such a symptom to the point of its yielding. The patient may be in completely different territory, a long way up the spiral. Suddenly the symptom returns. It requires investigation all over again. The original understanding does not influence it in the same way. The mind is so protean that it can colonize the body in a new spirit and skilfully enlist the symptom under a new banner in the ongoing war of resistance in the transference.

Perhaps I may end here by saying that patients with such symptoms, and silent patients, teach us most vividly and memorably that there is always in our work a dimension that is beyond words. Some people *suffer* more from the unthinkable than others, and for these we have to do all in our power to help towards the therapeutic transformation, to bring thought to the unthinkable and words to the inexpressible. Gradually the rough beast may, within the framework of the analytic relationship, slouch towards being born, and the new creature emerging from the birth is the increased happiness and peace of mind of the patient. But in all of us there are some things which will never be within our reach; there is always a mystery at the heart of every person, and therefore in our job as analysts.

2

DIAGNOSIS AND ASSESSMENT FOR SUITABILITY FOR PSYCHOANALYTIC PSYCHOTHERAPY

In day-to-day work, we draw partly on unconscious skills, knowledge and intuition. But the situation in which we need to be consciously in touch with a whole range of ideas and concepts is the diagnostic interview. Here I would stress *diagnostic* in conjunction with assessment for analytical psychotherapy; we have to be getting at some sort of diagnostic picture, in order to think about patients coherently and, if necessary, to be able to discuss them with colleagues to whom we may be referring.

My main qualification for giving this paper is the amount of consultation I do in private practice. The diagnostic interviews at the London Clinic of Psycho-Analysis of which I was Director for ten years were pretty specialized and it is in private practice, where for many years I have done an average of three consultations a week, that my experience of diagnosis and assessment for analysis and psychotherapy mainly lies. Of these consultations, only about 10 per cent turn out to be 'therapeutic consultations' in their own right, that is, do not require referral for therapy, and only about 5 per cent are subsequently placed in full five-times-a-week psychoanalysis. The therapeutic consultation is a special event which is not necessarily predictable at the point of referral. Winnicott wrote and taught about it. It is very rewarding for both patient and therapist, and really does not fall within the scope of this paper. I will just say that it occurs when you can focus on a main, or presenting problem, and say or interpret something mutative; or

First published in the *British Journal of Psychotherapy*, Volume 4, Part 2, (1987).

when the very act of self-exploration in this special atmosphere, enables the patient to reach a solution which is satisfying.

First, we must consider the 'real' role of the psychoanalytic diagnostician in contrast to the mythical role which often exists somewhere around the edge of many people's half-conscious fantasy. I am of the opinion that a good solid block of experience in general psychiatry early along the line of one's own development is a real help; this is principally linked to the fact that I myself had that and, therefore, my view immediately underlines another factor, which is that we cannot expect or even desire that subjectivity be absent from our work in this field. I do not want to imply that one simply does a sort of extended psychiatric interview, or that one operates exactly as one used to in the acute admission wards; this would be to imply that people without psychiatric experience cannot assess a patient with a view to deciding about analytical therapy, which is not true; but I think it will be found that those who have had long psychiatric experience *are* the people who do much of the day-to-day assessment work within the body of those who practise as analysts and therapists in London and certainly in the British Psycho-Analytical Society, and are the main sources of referral within that body. Also it is a help if one has a full practice and is therefore usually not assessing with oneself as analyst or therapist in mind; one is facilitated by a somewhat increased mobility of objectivity if one is not personally looking for a patient.

The 'real' assessors rely to a certain extent on intuition. They have their own theoretical, philosophical and experiential framework, both personal and clinical. They may hold quite strong opinions – reasonably well thought out, we would hope – on some things such as 'the widening scope of psychoanalysis' (Stone, 1954) or alternatively 'the need to limit the scope of psychoanalysis' (Kuiper, 1968); or the effects of certain specific traumata; or the possibility of working with a phase of transference psychosis. They should have a working knowledge of alternative therapies and avenues of placement for people who are not suitable for full classical analysis (Baker, 1980) so that there is no pressure at all to opt for analysis as a sort of last ditch and only solution; this is often a despairing view held by non-analysts rather than analysts. Actually, it takes a long time to build up a consultation practice in which all the joints in the machine are working smoothly, and it is a continuous process to keep them oiled. I refer particularly to the need to maintain an up-to-date list of colleagues, both analysts and therapists, with vacancies, preferably with details of how many times a week, and what sorts of patient are or are not required. The only way to maintain such a list efficiently is to do it yourself. Attempts are made from time to time, usually by enthusiastic newly-qualified analysts, to collate such a list, and keep in touch with colleagues about it, both referrers and patient-seekers. In my time, I have witnessed the rise and fall of this phenomenon at least seven times. I now keep in touch myself with a large number of people and their vacancy situations; thus, on doing a consultation, I know there is a choice of therapists ready and waiting, and I would reckon to place any patient requiring analysis or therapy within a week. It is distressing to patients to be kept waiting for weeks or months once they have geared themselves up for consultation, which may well have been exposing and anxiety-provoking, and although waiting cannot be helped at the Clinic, in private practice I believe that rapid and appropriate placement is part of what I am paid for. Finally, consultants should have somes idea, again grounded in experience, of how and why the odd process of analysis works, and why it may be desirable and appropriate for some people. It has been only too truly said that an expert is someone who knows everything about a subject except what it is for.

The mythical assessor, who does not exist, has an omniscient knowledge of all possible criteria of analysability, a peculiar capacity to predict the full course of treatment, a clairvoyant power to read the whole personal history and potential, both conscious and unconscious, of someone whom he or she is meeting once in a lifetime for two hours, and a God's eye view of the details of this person's therapeutic relationship for the next five years. This may sound ludicrous when spelt out, but if you examine your own half-conscious expectations, I think you will find that this creature exists somewhere on the fringe of them.

It is important to remember what a momentous thing you are saying to a patient when you seriously and thoughtfully advise analytical psychotherapy or, even more so, full psychoanalysis as the treatment of choice. You are 'involving him in an adventure which is not comparable with any other medical treatment [and yet which curiously falls somewhere in the outer boundaries of that category] and the way in which such advice is presented shows very clearly that it is no ordinary prescription' (Diatkine, 1968, p. 266). In the consultation, you try to help patients to see and feel some psychodynamic aspects of their problem. You convey to them your own considered beliefs on how and why analytic therapy might help them; you tell them something of the basic rules; you give no guarantee either of 'cure' or of length of treatment and, having been as explicit as you can, you leave the ultimate choice and responsibility to them. As a referral source, however, you will probably be instrumental in 'matching' them with a therapist. I would stress here that matching is not twinning. It is not necessarily advisable to place, say, the obsessional patient with an obsessional colleague; this is also rather particularly true of quite schizoid individuals. These examples need not be multiplied; the implication is that a good referrer needs a good working knowledge of colleagues' capabilities and special talents. I do, however, believe in the validity of the process I am calling matching. There is a sort of idea floating about, which has one foot in theory and one in wishful thinking, that, once a good training is internalized, any therapist can treat any patient. I could spend some time on this idea, but perhaps it is most important to say that I believe that some therapists have gifts for some sorts of patients, and others for others. I rely strongly on assistance from my unconscious at this stage, which, usually while with a patient or soon thereafter, throws up a name or two with force and clarity. This is a condensed statement, of course, and one of its main implications is that one has to know something about the colleagues on one's list, and have assessed and discussed with them briefly how they work and what they are good at.

And now to criteria: perhaps we should start with certain features which are not exactly controversial, but which in an odd way tend to get left out of discussion, and out of literature; it is almost as though it is thought not quite nice to acknowledge them. It may be that in ignoring them we underline our own high-mindedness and nobility of purpose; here, as so often, we find that Freud is an exception. I refer specifically to the features of intelligence, moral character and money. However ethically Utopian or politically idealistic your views, it is no good pretending that these things do not matter, because they do. A case may be argued for the widening scope of psychoanalysis, but we must not ignore the voice of experience and the dictates of our culture. Shortly after the war, before the London Clinic of Psycho-Analysis became organized and structured as it is now, the waiting list there was over 400; this was due to a shortage of experienced consultants, a lack of selection technique and perhaps to a kind of naive enthusiasm about the potential of psychoanalysis. All that it led to was hopeless confusion amongst students taking on cases, endless disappointments among people languishing on the waiting list for years, and interminable analyses for many of those chosen. During my time as Director, I had several ongoing correspondences with ex-patients of the Clinic who should never have gone into analysis in the first place, and whose disastrous treatments had left them with their last state apparently worse than their first. One was from a patient who could predict future events, mostly bad, from cracks in the walls and ceilings. I discovered that his analyst had gone abroad immediately on finishing his training and had then quite rapidly died. As to cause and effect, of course I cannot say. The patient was chronically mad, and his long complaining letters to me were, naturally, that his analyst had been mad. In 1895 Freud wrote that there was no point embarking on the treatment of 'anyone who struck me as low-minded and repellent, and who, on closer acquaintance, would not be capable of arousing human sympathy' (1895a, p. 265). In 1905 he was of the opinion that the prerequisites for psychoanalysis include ethical development and reliable character, adding, rather mysteriously but evocatively, 'it must not be forgotten that there are healthy people as well as unhealthy ones who are good for nothing in this life' (1905a, p. 263). Neither intelligence nor ethical development are very easy to define or measure in the sort of interview we are discussing; the fact remains that a good measure of both is a necessary ingredient for the prescription of a workable analytical therapy. Intelligence of the sort I mean is fairly easy to assess in a diagnostic interview; it does not necessarily equate with intellectual brilliance, which can be a formidable defence and a nuisance. The intelligence has to be fairly quick and fairly verbal (but not excessively so – slow thinkers often make good patients) and, above all, it has to be linked to two other features which I will come to in a moment. Ethical reliability is not so easy to assess accurately although experience helps to develop a feeling for it. By this time, my experience includes a few memorable horrors. A man who turned out to be a criminal psychopath bluffed his way right through his interview with me, during which I continued to think he was a senior registrar, into being placed by me with a respected colleague, and presented a hideous problem to her, lying, stealing, involved in fraudulent behaviour of monumental proportions. In my own defence, I can only add that, when I spoke to her on the telephone about the referral, I *did* say: 'There's something very odd about him; he did tell me he was capable of lying, and I'm sure he was, but I couldn't get at it.' Incidentally, he was a hairdresser, not a psychiatric registrar! But do not be put off by this piece of evidence of my gullibility; mostly one *can* ascertain if there are degrees of moral awareness and integrity.

Thirdly, money. It may be a sad state of affairs, but generally speaking a certain amount of money is needed to undertake analytical therapy at present. I believe that the most that therapists can do about this is not to be too rigid about set fees, but to work on a sliding scale which correlates with patients' capacity to pay. I should add that I am of the opinion that it is psychologically much more effective and beneficial to treatment for a patient to pay what he possibly can: I do not propose to explore this statement at length, but I am confident that it is one with which most experienced practitioners would agree. I am certainly not recommending that therapists in a full-time practice should be masochistic or sentimental. It is quite a slow business, mastering all the many issues surrounding money. For the clarity and comfort of the treatment on both parts, one should, if possible, charge what accords with one's self-esteem as well as with the patient's resources. It is no good ever thinking, however, that our profession is one in which you get rich quick, or even slowly. There is a lot of public misconception and mythology about us, too: someone said to me only the other day, 'Everyone knows analysts charge £70 per session!'

To return to the two criteria which I linked with intelligence, and for which one listens and searches in assessment. One is the 'will to be analysed'. Namnum, in an interesting paper in the *International Journal of Psycho-Analysis* (1968) refers this vital feature to what he calls the 'autonomous ego' (p. 272) and it will be seen on a moment's reflection that this must join up with the important concept of the possibility of a *treatment alliance* being formed, and put alongside the need to assess the possibility of the creation of a transference neurosis. The will to be analysed is not by any means the same thing as the more random, changeable and drive-motivated 'wish for recovery', although in initial interviews they may appear to be the same thing. One should listen with the third ear in an initial interview to search for this potential function of the autonomous ego because it will be what ultimately keeps the therapeutic alliance alive, and keeps the analytical therapy an open and going concern; the will to be analysed in the therapeutic alliance will be of vital importance when the transference *neurosis* becomes active and resistant, and opposes treatment, and when the early wish for recovery is forgotten in the day-to-day work of the therapy. A brief way of assessing this potential function in an initial interview is by temporarily going against the flow of the patient's thought and feeling for you at some well-judged dynamic moment, often late in the interview. For example, by a sudden confrontation with an uglier or more hidden part of himself when he is settled into feeling comfortable with you. This ploy is helpful in several ways, one of which is that it facilitates the patient leaving you without too much regret. It is all too easy, if you conduct a consultation along the lines I am suggesting, for a quite strong positive transference state to be evoked in the patient. It helps if, when someone telephones in the first instance to make an appointment, you make it clear *then* that you will not be treating him or her yourself, but making an assessment for purposes of referral to a suitable colleague.

The other criterion which I was linking with intelligence is what has been called psychological-mindedness. This feature is very much easier to pick up in a diagnostic interview than is the true will to be analysed. There are various ingredients of psychological-mindedness which can be roughly defined and located and with this aim one can usefully hold the following queries in one's own mind while doing an assessment interview:

1   Is there the capacity in the patient to take a distance from his own emotional experience? This must be nicely judged, as

obviously it should not be such a distance that one senses there is a great chasm, as in very severe denial, splitting, or repression.
2   If one listens beyond the full stops in a narrative can the patient go on, and begin to reflect on himself, perhaps in a new way *as a result of* being listened to in this particularly attentive way? If there are no signs of elaboration or extension by the patient on trains of thought, there may be severe inhibitions and/or anxieties, or extreme passive dependency, and a valuable capacity for free association may never develop.
3   Are various memories brought forward with different qualities and charges of affect? And are the affects, so far as one can tell, more or less appropriate? If not, a flat and uninflected history may bode ill for analytical therapy and indicate severe affective splitting and blunting. In other words, a lot of memories with very little feeling are suspect.
4   Is there a capacity to perceive relationships between sections of history, and details that are recounted, and the patient's prevailing sense of discomfort? If the patient starts by complaining of one or more symptoms or states of mind, but shows no sense or related significance when he goes into his history, then again there should be a warning signal in the assessor's mind.
5   Is there some capacity to recognize and tolerate internal reality, with its wishes and conflicts, and to distinguish it from external reality? You will see that this connects up directly with the continuing assessment in the interviewer's mind about the possibilities of maintaining a therapeutic alliance in conjunction with a transference neurosis. Does the patient show some facility in interview to move between the two, that is, internal and external reality, in a way which shows a certain cathexis for the value and the enjoyment of introspection and the taking of psychic responsibility for the self?
6   Does the patient show a lively curiosity and a genuine concern about this internal reality, if he has already shown that he got a good glimpse of it? This is a crucial point. Psychoanalytical therapy has nothing to offer a patient who only wishes to be relieved of his suffering. If he can make even a tenuous link between the idea of relief from psychic pain, and an increase in self-knowledge, and if he then shows some real pleasure in finding out some tiny thing about himself in the initial interview,

this is one of the best criteria for the analytical approach. This kind of drive and interest about the sources of pain in oneself is the greatest possible help in therapy, and is a sustaining tributary to the therapeutic alliance. It can help to counteract even more severe pathology, including acting-out.

7   Is there some capacity for the use of the imagination? Fantasies may be present in a diagnostic interview (though not often), but even small signs, such as striking use of metaphor, are positive indicators. The voluntary reporting of a dream the night or so before the interview is a real bonus, and should always be worked on.

8   Are there signs of a capacity to recognize the existence of an unconscious mental life? Is there some acknowledgement that in some way the patient is in a state of involuntary self-deception? By this, I mean that he may have a true sense of the existence of the unconscious, and know that he is holding it off and not letting himself know more about it, and needs skilful help to do so. Are there some signs of a willingness to undo this state of affairs?

9   Does the patient show signs of success or achievement in some, even if limited, area of his life and some degree of proper self-esteem in relation to this? It is an important truism that he who fails at everything will fail at analysis. Here I would emphasize the areas of study or work and one or more important relationships.

So much for some of the vital questions which are part of one's active inner processes during a diagnostic interview.

Now we must consider briefly some of the more or less labelled categories which, by a sort of long-term consensus of experience, seem to be either more suitable for dynamic psychotherapy, or less suitable. Here again we are up against the fact that much of this labelling derives from psychiatry; this need not be unhelpful or constricting so long as we ourselves do not feel too wedded to our labels or categorizations. It should be remembered that we are using every method at our disposal to marshal information on all sorts of levels in one single interview. I propose to make two quotations, in order that they may be reflected upon in this context. The first is by Glover writing in 1954 about signs of analysability and, in decreasing order of appropriateness, he said they were hysteria, compulsion neurosis, pregenital conversion states, neurotic disturbance, character disturbance, perversions, addictions, impulsiveness, and psychosis. There is room for discussion of many of these categories and Glover's placing of them in the hierachy of treatability. For example, the phrase 'neurotic disturbance' is almost too vague to be useful. Personal choices also play a part; some therapists would far rather treat a character disturbance or a perversion, than a compulsion neurosis. There is a most valuable and readable paper in the *International Journal of Psycho-Analysis* of 1968, written as part of a symposium on criteria for analysability; this is Elizabeth Zetzel's paper 'The so-called good hysteric'. Zetzel's four categories of diagnosable hysteria (pp. 256–7) and their potential for response to analysis are most helpful for a diagnostician. If at the end of an interview you feel that, more or less accurately, you can say, 'This patient is something like a Zetzel Group One or a Zetzel Group Two', then most of the questions outlined earlier will have been answered in the affirmative and you can go ahead with the analytic prescription. An experienced practitioner would also willingly take on a Zetzel Group Three patient. Sooner or later, usually by mistake, one finds oneself referring or treating a Zetzel Group Four patient and this is a difficult, often disastrous, good learning experience!

I would like to refer momentarily back to Glover's list, with special reference to 'character disorder'. Since 1954, when the paper was written, extensive and helpful advances both in theory and technique of understanding and treating severe narcissism have been made. These advances bring a whole category of character disorders into a more accessible treatment arena. Deep narcissistic character disorders are, however, extraordinarily difficult to treat and, furthermore, they are sometimes difficult to locate in diagnostic assessment; depression allied with a kind of affective flatness, allied again with subtle projective mechanisms, should make one suspicious of the concealed narcissistic disorder. So also should a tentative diagnosis of a False Self, however coherent or engaging. All of Winnicott's perceptive writings on the understanding and treatment of the False Self personality would not be thought today to go far enough, since the True Self concealed therein is now realized to be most often a severely disordered narcissistic character.

The other quotation containing compressed information comes from a paper by Knapp in the *International Journal of Psycho-Analysis* of 1960 which is subtitled 'A review of one hundred supervised analytic cases'. In this paper Knapp considers the following categories to be very difficult or unsuitable for psychoanalysis: psychosomatic states, delinquents, psychotic signs or behaviour trends, adverse life situations, schizoid borderline psychotics, too long periods of previous treatment, very high levels of anxiety and tension, and some patients older than the analyst. This list should also be reflected upon and reconsidered by each individual diagnostician and therapist. Some therapists like working with psychosomatic states, and recently analysts such as Murray Jackson and Joyce McDougall have extended our knowledge of them; they often get better almost in passing, without too much direct focus on the symptom and even if they do not, the whole cathexis of the somatic symptoms may change. 'A high level of anxiety and tension' may be tackled and contained if the two-pronged therapeutic alliance and transference neurosis can be rapidly established. Many dynamic psychotherapists in recent years have been exploring the treatment of patients older than themselves, and this is not nearly such a closed field as it was. Freud himself was really rather odd about older patients, apparently forgetting that in the 1920s he was still at the peak of his power, *and* in his sixties. The attractive feature of the older patient is the degree of motivation. It is quite unlike that encountered in young people and compensates for some of the more embedded resistances.

To close, I want to consider the style in which one conducts this particular and specialized form of interview – the diagnostic assessment. I would like to quote from a paper by Adam Limentani in the *International Journal of Psycho-Analysis* (1972):

> The accurate forecast of the patient's behaviour before therapy has begun is a challenge to the diagnostician, who *nevertheless* has the means of eliciting evidence of the prospective analysand's capacity to move freely within his psyche. But he will be able to do this only if *he* is prepared to *move freely within the interview situation*, so that he can induce fluid responses in the interviewee. The silent and inactive evaluator, who clings faithfully to the psychoanalytic model of behaviour, will obtain only a partial if not distorted picture of what he is meant to observe. (p. 358, my italics)

I would like to stress the important point being made here. Interviewers should not behave, in my opinion, like a caricature of an analyst; such an interviewer does not help to start the patient off, does not ask any questions, does not comment, may write notes during the interview, makes no intervention or summing up, and at the end may mysteriously advise long-term treatment with someone who will be presumed to be like the very cartoon model that has been presented. I cannot emphasize enough how counter-productive and to some extent actively sadistic I think this is. In an assessment interview one has to *work*. All the attitudes listed just now may be appropriate to a session when a patient is settled in treatment – all except taking notes that is, which in my opinion should never happen in a patient's presence. Consultant diagnosticians must draw on all their skills and use their whole personalities with confidence and concern to meet the patients' personalities at every possible point in the short time available to them. It seems to me narcissistic and uncreative to sit and do nothing; it more often happens in younger assessors and is, of course, at a charitable estimate, a defence against anxiety. But it is not good enough, and not helpful to the patient, for whom this may be one of the momentous days of his or her life, and whose anxiety level can be guaranteed at the very least to be higher than that of the interviewer. On the other hand, you are not required to make the patient particularly comfortable, nor to seduce the patient into liking or appreciating you, either in a diagnostic interview or, come to that, in treatment. You need to establish a certain rapport and keep it going, and within that framework, think about and learn to deploy all the skills you have to find out about this stranger's inner world. This may involve some questioning, some interpretation, some link-making comments, sympathy expressed only in your whole attitude of extremely attentive listening, and some concise summarizing of your own views towards the end of the interview.

It should always be remembered that if you are prescribing psychotherapy on a long-term basis you are making a powerful statement, and your respect for patients should entail that you give them your own insight into their needs and their character, and your reasons for making the prescription.

3

THE TREATMENT OF A TRANSVESTITE

The analytical psychotherapy of this man lasted for just on three years – thirty-five months to be exact. It fell fairly distinctly into three phases, which I will try to present, and I will also try to incorporate my theoretical understanding of what was happening as we go along. He was referred to me by his general practitioner, and from him I have been able to obtain follow-up information which would not otherwise have been possible, but which, after an eventful treatment, is of great interest to me.

The patient consulted his GP at the wish of his wife, and made this fact quite clear from the beginning. After five years, the marriage was unconsummated, and the wife, having presented for a while with mild psychosomatic symptoms, eventually told the GP this. My patient had concealed his transvestism from his wife, so straight away we see that he falls into a minority category of married transvestites. This may seem somewhat surprising, but a little research at the time revealed it to be so. There was an anonymous paper in the medical press some years later by a transvestite physiologist, which advocated telling the wife, but advising against having children. One might, however, infer that the mutual pathology of the couples who know, in most of which the wife actively co-operates, is likely to be different from those where the secret is kept. My patient's wife, an intelligent working woman, had come to the conclusion that he was perhaps a latent homosexual; she said she did not think he was having an affair

First published in *Psychoanalytic Psychotherapy*, Volume 1, Part 1 (1985).

with another woman. It may sound rather mysterious to say so, but in this view, as it transpired, she was both right and wrong.

However, the patient told the GP about his transvestism, and said that he had no wish to be cured of it; he did, nevertheless, want to consummate the marriage, and felt guilty and frustrated that he could not, and anyway, he said, both he and his wife wanted a baby. He was willing, on these grounds, to acccept a referral for analytical psychotherapy. He therefore came to me in an ambivalent frame of mind, to say the least; he came under pressure from another person, and he wanted a part-cure without symptom removal; as to character change, he was aware of some motivation towards what he called 'self-improvement', and in this respect, he said he was lazy, frightened of authority figures, and selfish about his wife; he said he and she often quarrelled, and that a lot of it was unnecessary and childish, and he would like to get over it. During our first interview, I asked him if he loved his wife, and he said he thought he did, and I thought then, and continued to think, that this was substantially true, in his own terms.

He was aged thirty when he came, a big, masculine, good-looking man, with beautiful dark blue eyes fringed with long, thick lashes, over which he wore rather thick spectacles. He was a professional worker in the communications industry. He used the images and symbols of his job constantly in dreams.

The first phase of the treatment, which lasted approximately a year, was characterized by extraordinarily intense analytic dialogue. He came three times a week, and preferred to sit facing me, a feature which became more thoroughly understood later. From the first, he showed a considerable capacity for dynamic understanding; he was quite unfamiliar with jargon, and came from a distant suburban milieu refreshingly free of people in treatment and analytic clichés. Perhaps I need hardly add that I often felt uneasy and rather suspicious of the subtle flair he demonstrated for the work, his easily translatable dreams, and the apparent rapid development of his insight. I frequently had the feeling, and interpreted it to him, that his intense desire to fuse with, and please, me, as the mother/'other woman', facilitated the depth and rapidity of understanding that he showed. It was also, I began to think, a sign of deep splits in his ego, and I often felt impelled to point out to him that the acuity of his insights left his pathology intact. However, when confronted by a patient capable of this type of response, one cannot simply change it, or affect it much by interpretation, at least in the early months, even should one think such a manoeuvre desirable, which I did not. One can only work along with it, and use it as best one may. A close watch on the countertransference is essential, since the way in which this sort of patient-work can seduce therapists into thinking they are being rather brilliant, and thus missing the pitfalls and resistances, is quite powerful. Interpretation should include work on the meaning of this seductive attempt to wield power.

The patient's early history had dramatic and traumatic features. He was an only child, his father worked in a capacity not unlike his own present profession, and his mother had worked in the same field as his wife did. His birth was said to have caused a 'terrible tear' in his mother, which is alleged to have kept her in hospital for three months after the birth, and which necessitated her return to hospital for another three months when the patient was six months old. It seems that the story of his damage to his mother played a vivid part in the legends of his childhood, that is to say he was told about 'the tear' quite early, he thought, but in a mysterious way which left the locality and aetiology of the tear very obscure and a source of dark fantasy. During the early separations from the mother, he was looked after by the maternal grandparents, and he described the grandmother as 'deaf and rather tyrannical'. His parents separated when he was two-and-a-half, for reasons unknown: it was felt and conveyed by the mother that the father had left her (them). The mother and the patient henceforth lived with the maternal grandparents. Nevertheless, they still seem to have visited the father from time to time until the patient was three, at which point father went into the armed services during the war. The patient had no memory of these meetings, or of his father at all. There was one 'event' which sounded more like a dream or a myth than a memory, which ran thus: a man came to the door of the grandparents' house when the patient was five, and *he* thought it was his father, and is said to have run screaming to his grandmother, saying: 'There's father at the door . . . get an axe.' The patient *thought* that this was true, and we could see how this belief nurtured or contained a formless terror, and a feeling that violence must be resorted to, or was the prerogative of the father.

Subsequent legend, told him by his grandfather when he was about seven, was that father, after a couple of years in the Forces, was dismissed with dishonour, and that this was 'something to do with an act of violence'. No more was ever elicited about this, and some of my later attempts to get the patient to find out something, anything at all, about father from the mother, failed completely. Either he could not bring himself to ask, or mother would not tell. That is to say, both these things actually occurred. On two occasions, the patient nerved himself to ask, and then his nerve failed, and on the one occasion when he succeeded, his mother became both vague and secretive, a combination for which I imagined her to have a talent, and changed the subject. The patient, whom I shall refer to as B, invented, from the age of five onwards, his own myth about his father, which was that he had been killed gloriously in battle at sea. This sustained him in competition with his peers throughout his childhood and adolescence, and he more than half came to believe it. Indeed part, if only part, of his resistance to finding out more about his father while he was in therapy, stemmed from this. One of the worst moments of his therapy, in fact, was when I suddenly said to him one day, trying to undermine a semi-delusional defence, 'You do realize, don't you, that your father is quite likely alive and well and living somewhere *today*?' B was stunned and took some time to recover.

The two previous paragraphs serve to demonstrate that from very early on in B's life, there were Mysteries, and especially a Mystery surrounding his father, and we came to see how this atmosphere had been sustained by the combined efforts of the mother, the maternal grandparents, and B himself. Perhaps one should add, by the father as well, but although theoretically justifiable, this is somewhat abstract. It seems appropriate here to introduce the first dream that B brought to the therapy, in his sixteenth session. It followed my having made a simple but classical interpretation when in the previous session he had told me of two of his main childhood fears; one was that there was a frightening man hiding in the wardrobe, and the other was that there was a great snake under the bed. I had said (albeit with the rather wary, suspicious feeling already described) that these fears could have been about a terrifying father, and of his frightening big penis. In the next session, B told me that he had dreamt the following: he had had a dream and then realized this, and come to a session and we had started to analyse it. We were in a very cosy understanding relationship. Then two men, one older, and one a younger colleague of mine, came in, and took over the analysis, *against B's will*, and forced him down and gave him an injection in his bottom. This was the end of the dream, and when I asked him what thoughts it now brought into his head, his associations were that though he hated injections, he now remembered that in the dream he had wanted to show me the mess they had made of his backside. He then recalled that one of his strongest childhood daydreams had been of being in a specially cosy, tender relationship with quite a lot of women, in which he specifically played the role of comforter. Then he said he thought the younger man was perhaps a rival to him, and that the older one was maybe my boss. Putting this together with other things I already knew about B, I said that I thought that he experienced therapy as being very cosy between him and me, and that he had already linked it with his childhood daydream, which on the surface looked rather tender and innocuous; but that this served to conceal a much more violent and sexualized fantasy, where he as the woman is attacked, or raped, by men, probably his father and his male self. It is for this assault, hidden from the daydream, that he then comforts the women; a gently loveable creature who would never, of course, do anything like that to them himself. After some digestion of this view, B said that the dream looked as if it was 'rather homosexual'. So it did, I agreed, but in the first place, I did not think that was the significant concealed message; and in the second place, we then re-discussed his strong *conscious* repudiation of homosexual interest, wishes or fears. This attitude, incidentally, recurs in the literature on transvestism; it is very common that the only conscious reaction to homosexuality is one of aversion. This was again confirmed in a recent television programme, *Phantom Ladies* on BBC 1, which presented interviews with three transvestites. Later on, I hope to show that B *did* have unconscious homosexual wishes and anxiety, and that he managed them in a rather special way. At that stage, we developed the theme no further, but I did comment on the element of coercion present in the dream, that is, that he is forced away from the cosy relationship to me, and that neither he nor I can prevent it. This led to a revelation about his interest in

pornography, and in fantasies which he elaborated in which the
woman did have to be coerced into various situations. The point
of attending to this dream in some detail here, however, is really to
show how early in the therapy, the lovely cosy therapy with me, a
fierce and violently sexualized father/male self appeared.

Of the grandparents, the grandmother was dominant, and the
grandfather was more of a playfellow, loved, but never experienced
as a satisfactory father surrogate. Stoller's theory, presented in *Sex
and Gender* (1968), that the mothers of transvestites feminize their
boy children, either deliberately or unconsciously, is borne out by
inference and reconstruction, rather than by direct data, in B's
case. He slept in his mother's room until adolescence, and this does
not seem to have been because the accommodation was so sparse.
He went to boarding school, but could only do so because the
mother already worked there, and his fees were reduced. B had
many early memories of seeing her undress when *he* thought *she*
thought he was asleep. Alongside his fears of a man in the wardrobe
and a snake under the bed, he suffered a great and constant terror
that the grandparents and his mother would go out at night and
not come back. He found a way to relieve the fear, at the age of
five, which was secretly taking a pair of his mother's silk knickers
to bed with him.

Phyllis Greenacre, in her paper 'Certain relationships between
fetishism and faulty development of the body image' (1953),
states:

> In a number of the patients developing later fetishism . . . the boy
> child has been in very close visual contact with a female . . . and it
> appears that there may have been a state of primary identification
> which resembles that seen in twins, with a well forecast bisexual
> splitting of the body image even antecedent to the phallic phase.
> (p. 92)

She goes on to say that there is uncertainty and anxiety regarding
the genitals, instead of consolidation of the body image, in the
phallic phase, and she concludes: 'These children hardly solve their
Oedipal problem at all' (p. 94). This I feel to be exactly true about
B, although I am aware that there is only a cetrain amount of
overlap between the categories of fetishist and transvestite. B was
not, as some transvestites have been, dressed as a girl in childhood,

but there does seem to be evidence of the mother's need to keep him very close to her, to expose herself to him, and to stimulate his potential capacity for a fantasy of fusion with her body, reinforced by the comforting and sexual gratifications of his surreptitious use of her clothes. Rather than developing into a normal Oedipal fantasy range, he became feminized. It also began to become much clearer to me that there was extensive denial of things noticed by the mother. Denial, dissociation, disavowal ... all these concepts convey something of the perceptual milieu in which B lived, and here I should add that his wife demonstrated the same qualities to a remarkable degree. An example of what I mean, between B and his mother: at the age of twelve, with an effort which still made him sweat to recall, he had told his mother that he had been dressing in her knickers and slip, and that the feeling of wanting to do so worried and frightened him, and what should he do about it? He reports his mother as not seeming surprised, disturbed or interested, but looking into the distance and telling him that if he prayed to God about the feeling, it would probably go away. God played no part in the ordinary life of the household, indeed was as mysterious and remote as father; and it seems as if B condensed this answer of his mother's and heard it something like: 'If you put on my clothes, you'll have to go away to your father' which, I should add, was in any event one of the threats which the adults used from time to time throughout B's childhood.

The two dominant fantasies of B's childhood life were first to become a fairy, or sometimes a mermaid, and second, as already stated, to be the comforter of a harem of older women who in some way were unhappy or damaged. We came to understand these very specifically. The fairy is a girl, but can fly, that is, can have an erection. She is also magical and omnipotent. She can, in B's own very revealing language, 'always get out of a tight corner;' the mermaid, too, is a girl with a penis. The harem fantasy was somewhat more complex, and brought in early manifestations of sadomasochism as well as his castration anxiety. It took a lot of working through, including the use of dreams in which I appeared, to bring home to him that in his 'Beauty and the Beast' fantasy, as he called this daydream about the women (in which he comforted the beauty who had been harmed by the beast), there must *of necessity* be lurking somewhere in the shadows the beast who has harmed the beauty; in other words, that although he always presented himself as the hero-comforter, it was *his* fantasy, and he must also therefore be the beast. The second phase of the treatment, one of increased aggression and acting-out, was ushered in by his real recognition of this; and with this acknowledgement, some integration of his split-off, hidden and hitherto projected aggression began to take place.

This was about a year into the therapy, and he had an important dream at this point, after the recognition as described above. He dreamt that he saw a man in the garden with his back to the house. B felt that the man was sinister or intending an aggressive act of some sort, but in fact added that 'the man looked at home there'. He was dressed casually, rather as B does himself. 'Seeing him from behind,' he said 'it could have been me.' But the man had sandy hair, which he was told his father had. His wife came into the kitchen, and B feared she might scream because she was frightened of the strange man's aggression. B peered through the window glass at him, and then as the man turned round and came nearer the window, B became completely paralyzed. This was the end of the dream. We talked about the obvious associations with the father, and the frightened feeling in B himself, projected into the wife. He said, apparently at random, that this had been a morning dream, and he had been increasingly worried recently by waking with an erection and trying to hide it from his wife. I then interpreted the dream as follows: the garden man is his male sexual self, at first only seen from behind, that is, with his penis hidden, perhaps because this character has some features of his frightening father; but this sexual self is, after all, 'at home' there, and makes a move to be more so; he 'arranges' for his wife to be afraid of his approaching sexual aggression – she 'deserves' to be, since he wants to frighten and upset his mother; but then so is *he* frightened of it, and as it threatens to come nearer – the man comes up the garden – all he can do is become paralyzed, that is, impotent, in a desperate attempt to keep his male self at bay, and protect the woman from his destructive power.

It was at this point in the therapy that B really began to gain insight, not only into his own aggression, even a little way into his sadism, but also into the enormous importance to him of having a penis; even though he felt forbidden to use it with his wife because of the great power for destruction with which he invested it, which in turn, through the talion law, led to severe castration anxiety. Painstaking work on the unravelling of this between us led to more detailed revelation of his cross-dressing and masturbatory activity. Use of the transference at this stage was not predominant in the work, and I strove to avoid covert or colourful invitations to get caught into what I felt, mostly by intuition, would be fascinating, but essentially perverse blind alleys. Relying for that period on the therapeutic alliance, and on his mobile capacity for identifying with the therapeutic process (= me = mother), we worked out an understanding which has been so well expressed by Stoller (1968) that I would like to quote him for a paragraph:

> Transvestism is in great part a defensive structure raised to protect a threatened but desired sense of masculinity and maleness, and the corollary, to preserve a badly threatened potency. One should not be fooled by the apparent paradox that he does this via the detour of dressing like a woman (p. 180)... Transvestism is in fact a rather efficient method of handling very strong female identifications without the patient having to succumb to the feeling that his sense of masculinity is being submerged by feminine wishes. The transvestite fights this battle against being destroyed by his feminine desires, first, by alternating his masculinity with the feminine behavior, and thus reassuring himself even when feminine that it isn't permanent; and, second, *by being always aware even at the height of the feminine behaviour – when he is fully dressed in women's clothes – that he has the absolute insignia of maleness, a penis.* And there is no more acute awareness of its presence than when he is reassuringly experiencing it with an erection. (p. 186; my italics)

I only wish to add here to this succinct theoretical statement something which was very important for B and that is that in the 'defensive structure' there is a wish to protect the woman from (as well as submit her to) the sadism of which the penis is felt to be capable.

To return to and continue with some of B's history. He became more aware of transvestite activity and fantasy at the age of about fifteen, and was only desultorily interested in the usual homosexual culture at his boarding school. He was aware of ordinary heterosexual attraction and wishes from the age of about eighteen and, like many transvestites, hoped that marriage would eliminate that part of himself. He lived with his wife for a year before they got married, but without having intercourse (which first made me wonder about the wife's psychopathology and unconscious collusion). He described her as 'very attractive, chic, tight belts, good legs, slim'. All this is true. I saw her once. Their honeymoon was somewhat marred by his impotence, but in a curiously ambivalent way she continued to play along with him. During the five years of the marriage, he often took what might be seen as great risks, seen, that is, from any angle other than that of his unconsciously wishing her to find out about him. He kept pornography in his briefcase which was left lying about, he kept his female clothes in an unlocked suitcase in the attic, he dressed up when she was out at work, but might be expected back at any minute. Nevertheless, overtly, the secret was kept. I gradually formed the opinion, partly through tiny signs within the therapeutic process, that their sexuality was enacted between them in a form of sadomasochism. Thus: she would become angry and tearful because he wouldn't make love to her; he would then become mute, sullen and impotent; she would become angrier, crying and accusing; he would then, ultimately – his sadism up to now having consisted in *not* responding to her hysterical pleas – become very angry and do something quite violent, but to an object, for example, he would throw a chair or break a clock; she then seemed to become first frightened, then satisfied, as if an orgasm had been achieved, and they would then have a reconciliation, with mutual tenderness and comforting cuddling. This part of the process was very important to them both, and thus the beauty and the beast/comforter fantasy reached its climax.

Phase two of the treatment was really divided into two: that is, there was an active aggressive period, followed by several months of great difficulty and inertia. As his aggression became more available to him, he used it constructively at work, where terror of authoritarian father-figures had hitherto constricted him considerably. This seemed to improve and stay improved, but the tempestuous stasis in the marital situation remained. One of the early insignia of phase two was a marked strengthening of the transference, greatly welcomed by me, as it brought me on to firmer ground, and considerably reduced the rather eerie suspicious feeling I had had for over a year that we were engaged in some project that was more like making an intricate, elegant, perverse film than having a therapy going on between two people. The strengthened transference had distinctly eroticized features. It first showed itself in what seemed to be a sort of strong resistance, expressed by B as feeling there was a sheet of glass between him and me, and his finding much more difficulty and reluctance to speak, as it were, from behind it. The description, of course, immediately put me in mind of depersonalization, but I had had some experience of that with previous patients, and the rest of what he said and conveyed did not feel like that. Then he began to tell me (perhaps because he was a bit shielded from me, I suggested) quite a lot more about his masturbation fantasies and practices – which up until then I had not heard very much about, and certainly not in detail. A cardinal feature was that after he had dressed fully as a woman, he would scrutinize himself closely, long and lovingly in the mirror; this adoration of a beautiful woman seen there was followed by a strong fantasy of taking her off to bed, coercing her into having intercourse until, in some way against her conscious will, she came to like it, or reluctantly acknowledge that she half-liked it; then, having won her fully over, he would heal and comfort her by further intercourse, in which his having the penis was of prime importance, and in which he achieved a sense of ecstatic union between his male and his female self. I eventually understood that the sheet of glass between us was the mirror, and I was the mirror-woman; with this as the central interpretation, the implications of it, and the elucidation of complex details of the fantasies which it facilitated, the therapy became more dynamic, and, though clearer, in some way more difficult. It will be recalled that he had always refused to lie down, and although this was an overdetermined phenomenon, it became obvious that if I were to be successfully enlisted to play the part of the mirror-woman in the secret sexualization of the therapeutic process, then I would always have had to be facing him. I found that construction and delivery of interpretations in that position and at that time was a slow and tricky job. B was excited, resistant and frightened, by turns and often all at once. But on looking back, I think that the slow gain that was made during this laborious psychoanalytical disentangling of a dense, perverse transference situation was that *he became more consistently and self-identifiably a man*. Fortunately, B managed to continue to report more or less articulately his experiences both of his fantasy world, and of the sessions. I used for a while to wonder whether he made heroic efforts to overcome shame and self-consciousness in his communications, but I came to the conclusion that he did not suffer much from shame, and that what there was, was to some degree countered by a kind of vanity, a narcissistic gratification in revealing his hitherto entirely secret and solipsistic world to a real audience/mirror.

Much of our dialogue at that time, if transcribed directly, would sound quite mad; sometimes he was a man, and I was his female self, sometimes he was a man and I was a separate woman (this, of course, was more frightening to him), and sometimes I was a phallic woman, or it was not clear where the penis was, sometimes we were both women. This last situation revealed something of how he defended against his homosexuality to which I made reference earlier – he projected it into a fantasy of two lesbian women coming together. At all times, however, my own experience of the therapy was *not* like working with a psychotic.

As this phase developed, it became characterized by some intermittent heavy drinking on B's part, and towards the end of it by intercourse with his wife. Thus one of the conscious aims of treatment was achieved. The two activities were not unconnected, as he managed intercourse, aggressively, when rather drunk, and thus achieved several aims at once: he was able to say, as it were, 'There, I've given you what you want', and at the same time he maintained the sadomasochistic quality of their relationship, because the wife complained about his behaviour, although 'giving in', apparently somewhat against her will, like the coerced woman of his fantasy. His very first intercourse with her followed a drunken evening when his local soccer club, for whom he played, had their annual stag evening and there was a cabaret which included a stripper. There was not time or opportunity, nor did it seem of prior importance, to go into the obvious homosexual aspects of this, especially when he produced this dream immediately following these two events. He dreamt that he was in a train, and his mother was sitting opposite to him, naked; at first, he was surprised, but thought to himself in the dream that he liked it, or that at least he could accept it; then he became very angry at what he thought other people would think of her, and he yelled at her, and she became small and shrivelled and very old and ugly. I said that I thought this dream contained a violent wish, and its anxiety, as to what his aggressive sexuality could do to the figure repre-sented by the woman sitting opposite to him (me), and the original 'stripper' in his life (his mother).

B's new-found capacity for intercourse made him think more seriously about the whole business of being a father; he was not cross-dressing nearly as often, he seemed to lose interest in pornography – both these events were experienced as bereave-ments, and he felt angry and bitter towards me about that; he began to be quite seriously depressed, to which he was not in the least accustomed. A particular feature of the depression was getting in touch with feelings of helplessness in himself, and we tried to trace their origin, and meaning to him in childhood. He realized that he might well have thought that with his mother he had 'won' as a child, that he was 'king of the castle'. The more he contem-plated this, the more he realised that huge and powerful fantasies about what he and his penis could do evolved from feelings of smallness and 'not being up to much'. He ceased to be potent with his wife, he lost the sense of being powerfully and excitingly in charge with me and the therapy, and described a feeling of being 'shattered'. We realized that this was an appropriate word also for a broken mirror. However, it seemed to be about then that he began to grasp a quite simple idea that in the end meant most to him, and shifted some of the inner weights and balances which had kept him so immobilized in the perverse state. The idea, not new in the therapy, which gradually came to assume mutative force for B was of the extent to which he had made women/his wife into a/ his mother, and therefore made them not only objects of extreme ambivalence, but also sexually taboo; and how he protected himself from the castration anxiety of being an adult sexual male not only by being a woman, but also by remaining what he called 'the little lad', playing his fantasy games all alone.

The therapeutic work was slow and sluggish, and B continued low and shattered. He ruminated depressively over a pair of alternatives: he felt he had to choose either to give up transvestism and all it meant to him, entirely, or that he had to give up his wife entirely, and along with her any hope of ever being a potent man and father, both of which he consciously wanted. At the same

time, he began to see that not only might he have difficulties in
actually being a father because of his own distorted paternal
introject and fantasies, but also that he as 'the little lad' might be
jealous or envious of his own child. I felt oppressed by his sense of
defeat and his heavy depression, and the summer term of that year
ended on a sombre note.

But after that summer holiday, his mood changed. He and his
wife had very nearly split up, apparently at her insistence, but so
far they were just managing to stay together, though in a constant
state of argumentative tension. B became far more aggressive and
defiant to me, both in general, and also with a special method
which was of particular interest. He began to use his brain to
devour books on psychology and psychiatry, to try to show me up
as wrong, misguided, and, as I added, castrated and helpless. He
was no longer depressed, and to me he exhibited a cheerful
contempt and superiority. It was not so difficult to explore this
interpretatively, and I thought to myself that it might be correct to
welcome this development into a male chauvinist pig as a sign of
slight progress. By his reading and his use of it, he started becoming
me in order to do battle with me; I drew parallels with his early
fusional experience with his mother and noted his intention to
incorporate a new version of a female self. However, what seemed
more important was to understand how phallic I and my knowledge had seemed to him, and how much he needed to take over
this phallic function and use it aggressively with me, sometimes in
an all-male fight, sometimes to test out how I as the castrated, or
more helpless, female person, would survive; and to see what I
would then do to him, and whether and how *he* would survive.

A month after the summer holiday he had to be away on a
course for two weeks, and when he came back, he had grown a
moustache. My instant thought was that this must do something
rather drastic to the beautiful woman in the mirror, but some deep
caution about a too literal mirroring of B made me not refer to it
at all until he did. Then he announced one day that he had been to
see his mother over the weekend, and she had said how awful he
looked, and why didn't he shave it off; and he added that although
he felt defiant to her, he also felt frightened of her, and he described
himself as being 'all at sixes and sevens'. I said that that was just
the trouble with the 'little lad', he was about six or seven and he

couldn't possibly have a moustache and be a big powerful man when he also so much wanted to be close to his big powerful mother.

Another difficult phase of about three months set in almost at once. Really the prospect, or experience, of working through disidentification (as Greenson [1966] has called it) from his mother, and perhaps therefore also from his female self and his whole secret way of life, was extraordinarily tough going for this man, and I will say he really worked, in his therapy, on it. He became depressed again and what he called lethargic and inert, and he told me at this point how often projects which he started as a boy or young man had come to grief through his inability to carry them through. The worst and latest example, of course, was his marriage, and the real test faced us now as to whether the treatment was going to come to grief on the same rocks. Often in those months around Christmas it did seem possible that the therapy might founder – one could not even say in spite of his conscious wishes to the contrary, because his conscious attitude had, if anything, become more ambivalent as therapy had progressed.

In February he was sent on a long residential management course far from home which necessitated us reducing to once-weekly sessions for six weeks. Suddenly everything took a dramatic turn. He met a girl there, with the same name as his wife, and fell violently, romantically, and thank goodness, transiently, in love with her. She refused to have sex with him. His mood now approached hypomania, and in this mood he would return home each weekend, and have prolonged sexual interludes with his wife, unsustained, so far as I could make out, by any perverse fantasy, use of pornography, or cross-dressing, although my interpretation that he was transforming her from the forbidden mother into the new strange girl was accepted. In a real and peculiar sense, he was using the girl as a transitional object. In this hypomanic state, he was overtly planning to leave his wife, although sexually by now very involved with her, and to try to force the other girl to come away with him. He ruminated violently on this course of action. I said I thought he was trying to leave a powerful possessive aspect of his mother *in* his wife, and that his thinking and behaviour seemed somewhat dislocated, although it began to come together with the use of the transitional-object concept in the interpretative

work. In the last but one session of those six weeks, I said he must
be considering that he could make his wife pregnant. He was
treating me with jaunty scorn at the time, and dismissed the idea,
so I had to restrain myself as a good therapist from saying 'I told
you so' when he announced the week after the course was over
that his wife had had a positive pregnancy test.

B instantly left home. He gave up the girl he had met, and he
brought a few things from his own home and took a bedsitter not
a mile away from my home, which is many miles from his own
home. I blanched inwardly at such a massive piece of acting-out,
particularly since it took me by surprise and I was not easily able
to begin to interpret it to him. However, that slowly improved
with time. B embarked on a curious, promiscuous, largely non-
transvestite life for the next six months, acting out a whole lot of
adolescent fantasy; he came regularly for his sessions, occasionally
drunk, but not very, and not often; I saw this self-presentation in
sessions as an overdetermined phenomenon. It was certainly
aggressive and dismissive towards me, but it was also a form of
defence, an attempt to blur his anxiety about what he was doing;
and furthermore it was symbolic of a sort of oral regression *with*
me in which he was trying to establish a pre-perverse relationship
as a foundation for work on separation, dis-identification and
further disentanglement from the perversion.

He went home every weekend, when his relationship with his
wife seemed to be remarkably good. One might wonder at her
collusive psychopathology, but at the same time there was no
doubt that a rather masochistic long-suffering quality about her
was a strong ingredient in sustaining the marriage over a difficult
period. Their sexual relationship improved and became enjoyable,
although B did not keep me informed about the degree to which
he was assisted by fantasy. He visited prostitutes during his
London life, but I got the impression that this was more for the
purposes of practising fairly straight sex, rather than for exploring
perverse varieties. He treated me with a mixture of infantile
dependence and verbal violence at this time; there was a marked
split between his physical acting-out, and his fantasy life, and both
the latter, and the splitting, continued to be worked on in the
transference.

As his frenetic activities died down, he became more depressed, more lonely and more realistic. Work in the therapy included the positive aspects of using both his wife and me, in different ways, as good objects, stabilizing, containing, with a reduction in persecutory feelings, which in turn led to reductions in the needs for splitting and denial. The real confrontation with becoming a father had to be worked on. There was a strengthening of his wish to grow through his solipsistic transvestite world, and become a more complete man in his own right. I deliberately did focal work on the consolidation of a self-experience which, as he used and emerged from the regression, could be freed from two extensive aspects of himself – the protective, yet so constrictive, little lad, and, even more importantly, the seductive and dominating female. Towards the end of that summer, B told me that he thought it unlikely that he would return to treatment after the end of the summer break. I was somewhat disconcerted by this, as the work had been, and was, so intense, and furthermore, if he adhered to it (the decision to leave, that is) there was not a lot of time to work on it between us. I saw it primarily as an attempt at a final acting-out from the transference, as if one woman, myself, who was essentially a combination of the mother and the fantasy-female self, had to be summarily rejected if he were to achieve more sense of autonomy; as if I and all I stood for could not be maintained – almost could hardly continue to exist – if he were to make any sort of a go of his relationship with his wife, which he was still as clear as his ambivalence would allow that he wanted to do. I reminded him of his vague but strong hope in early youth that marriage would cure him of all his secret powerful fantasy-life. He said a lot had happened since then, with which I could hardly disagree. I thought then, and still think, that a marked attempt by me to deploy techniques to hold him in treatment would inevitably have become counterproductively coloured by feelings of coercion. He was less depressed and less rivalrous and scornful of me, so we used what now really seemed to be the limited time at our disposal to try to overview the therapy, gather up some loose ends, and get some more solid impression of what the leaving meant. In essence, it seemed as though he experienced me as a store cupboard, in which he proposed to pack away as thoroughly as possible fragments, and larger pieces of fabric, of his 'old self'.

He still had not returned home to live, and although he felt that 'important decision-making processes' were going on in him, I could not feel any strong conviction that he would do so; however, this was to some extent countered by a theme which had run consciously through the treatment from the beginning, namely, that they both wanted a baby, and his wife was by now in the fifth month of her pregnancy. The therapy ended in early August, with me feeling uncertain, unsatisfied, and yet attentive to the future, as B said he would let me know what happened. I wrote a long closing note on the therapy, the seriousness of which lapsed at the end, thus: 'I suppose I might say that from a withdrawn, impotent, fantasy-ridden transvestite, B has changed into an aggressive, potent, alcoholic sex-maniac.' One may deduce that I did not regard a therapy which ended thus as an unqualified success.

The day after my return from holiday, which he had obviously carefully noted, B requested two more sessions. I found I was unable to predict their content, and I recalled the element of mystery which had flavoured the atmosphere of B's childhood, and realized he was making me experience something of the same. What transpired in these sessions was that B had decided to return home, to continue to try to abstain from cross-dressing and from reading pornography – neither of which he had cathected so strongly as before in the last six months – and to try to build something more stable, if less exciting, on the foundations of an increased appreciation of his wife as a separate individual. These sessions were in October, and a few days later I had a note from him, from home, enclosing his cheque, and saying: 'My wife's pregnancy is going very well, and we are both awaiting the baby's arrival with considerable awe.'

He rang me two days after their daughter was born, and seemed delighted.

I did not hear anything for three years, when B wrote me a brief letter, saying that he and his wife had recently had a son. He filled in a little on his own life: he enjoyed his children, his wife and he still argued a lot, and he still sometimes drank too much; his interest in 'all the things we talked about so much' was still 'sporadically intense' but no longer such a powerful and constant feature of his life.

The general practitioner told me some years later that they seemd to him to be 'a normal family'. But then about two years ago, the GP told me that the wife had told him that B had left home, after greatly increased rows and dissension, and that they were selling the house, and she was moving out of the district, with the children. This sounded a sad outcome, and not entirely unpredictable; at the same time, the wife said that she and B got on better now they were apart, and when he visited the children. She still maintained that she did not know why B had come to me, or what had been the matter. She said she did not know whether B had left home for another woman, but she did not think so. At this point I was reminded of the rather 'mysterious' thing I said in the second paragraph of this paper; that in thinking B might have another woman, she was both right and wrong. There *was* 'another woman' always. I do not know, of course, whether it was the lure of this other woman which finally triumphed. I have a hunch that it may have been a real other woman to whom he went in the end, and not his fantastic other self. But this may be a narcissistic sop to me as his therapist.

4

THE SUPEREGO, ANXIETY AND GUILT

We all know something about guilt and anxiety. We have all experienced both, and perhaps realized that there can be links between them. We may have a rather fuzzy feeling at times that we become anxious because of a fear of becoming guilty and we may have noticed that this small, fleeting apprehension can lead to avoiding a moment of guilt. We notice the prickings of conscience which may accompany an aggressive idea or fantasy, and which may well inhibit us from turning it into a reality. We have a direct awareness of the existence of the conscience, and we can sense causality between its ways of telling us things and the arousal of anxiety, and we know for sure the intimate bonds between it and the experience of guilt. It may be said that we could all have a stab at writing an essay in personal or cultural terms on the subject of this paper. While I was reading for it, I came across a sentence in one of Freud's *New Introductory Lectures on Psycho-Analysis*, in which he says: 'For analysts I am saying too little and nothing at all that is new; but for you I am saying too much and saying things which are not in your province' (1932b, p. 112). So if I may use that as my introduction, I ask you to forgive me if either of these things is true.

Perhaps the first thing we must try to get clear is that the conscience is not a synonym for the superego. Generally speaking, the conscience is held to be available to conscious inspection, and to conscious response; we may nurture it, attend to it, ignore it, or

Given annually as number 8 of 10 introductory public lectures at the Institute of Psycho-Analysis, London, 1985–91.

coexist uneasily at times with its promptings. A lot of the time it is *preconscious*, but that only means that though we are not always aware of it, it can be made conscious by focusing our attention, or having our thoughts drawn in its direction. Most religious systems confirm this, indeed rely on it. I think nevertheless, anyone who is at all self-reflective must at times *wonder* about his own conscience; in some people there is an uneasy awareness of an irrational, tyrannical quality to it. Roman Catholics who have been brought up from the cradle in the faith ascribe this, to an extent quite properly, to the thoroughness of early indoctrination; it is a well-recognized fact among analysts that to analyse even a long-lapsed Catholic presents one with a certain harsh and unrelenting set of problems connected with the tyranny of the conscience. But the oddity of this self-observable fact – that the conscience may have twists and powers that seem inexplicable in terms of conscious awareness and recall of early life – also occurs frequently in people from non-religious backgrounds.

Likewise, with guilt; generally this is held to be a conscious affect. Its existence is central to the teaching of the theistic religions, and by some of them, grossly exploited and reinforced. Freud has a lot to say about this in two of his late, long papers, *The Future of an Illusion* (1927), and *Civilization and its Discontents* (1930). These are enormously readable even to those who know little or nothing of previous analytical theory development, and I can most heartily recommend them. Some people, especially those designated 'scrupulous' in Catholic language, are only too well aware of the complex chains of feeling and behaviour into which the sense of guilt can lead them: placation, expiation, reparation, sacrifice, major life changes, flight, trickery, bluffing, dishonesty – once you start to think about it, the list is endless. I introduce the phrase 'sense of guilt' here, because that is primarily what psychoanalysis concerns itself with. Realistic and appropriate guilt cannot itself be analysed away, and nor should it be, in spite of some potent but half-baked myths about analysis which have developed during this century. It is where the sense of guilt begins to be inappropriate, excessive, irrational that analysis comes into its own. Furthermore, I should add here, it is still one of the more difficult dynamics of psychoanalytical understanding that there exists, most influentially, an 'unconscious sense of guilt' (Freud, 1923, p. 27). Freud himself, up against the difficulty when he started working on it fully in the 1920s, also thought of this as an unconscious need for punishment, aware that it is marginally easier for people to cotton on to this latter idea and that it could be more easily demonstrated to them about themselves. In *The Ego and the Id*, a long seminal paper written in 1923, to which I shall return, Freud refers to a certain state encountered in patients who cannot seem to respond to a positive piece of analytic work, though appreciating its value intellectually. He says they are not just being defiant or trying to be superior, though these possibilities have to be examined to be discounted, but he adds it is as if, and I quote, there is:

> a 'moral' factor, a sense of guilt, which is finding its satisfaction in the illness and refuses to give up the punishment of suffering . . . But as far as the patient is concerned this sense of guilt is dumb; it does not tell him he is guilty; he does not feel guilty, he feels *ill*. This sense of guilt expresses itself only as a resistance to recovery which is extremely difficult to overcome. (pp. 49–50)

I have jumped the gun a bit because I really want to tell you something about the development of the analytical theory of the superego, guilt and anxiety, but is seemed to me rather more engaging to talk a little first about some experiences common to all of us, and some puzzlements we may have had.

In referring above to *The Ego and the Id*, I am taking us into the era of a great surge of work and writing from Freud when, within the space of five years, he constructed a whole new, more coherent, more comprehensive theory of personality than any that had gone before. He tackled the problem of anxiety head on, reorganized and added to his earlier thinking on the structure and function of the ego, brought together and tied in various threads and ideas which had been running rather randomly through his works for many years, and, with his usual honesty, abandoned one or two concepts to which he had faithfully adhered over a long period. Re-reading these some half-dozen huge rich papers was rather like going through an old cupboard in which treasures of the years had piled up. I kept finding myself digging further back to see what had gone before, to trace the scattered history of some of the concepts which now he was bringing together and welding into a whole.

Passing references, or the beginnings of trains of thought, on the subject matter of our paper, are already evident as far back as his *Project for a Scientific Psychology* (1895b) in the *Three Essays on the Theory of Sexuality* (1905b) and in some short papers between 1907 and 1912; these trickled temporarily into the sand, but years later emerged again as tributaries flowing together into the great river of his thinking in the 1920s.

For example, he was always fascinated by obsessional neurosis in which the superego is so pathologically active, and was already writing about it in some detail by 1908. Phobias (that is, irrational fears and anxieties) begin to be studied in the case of 'Little Hans' in 1909 and Freud was thinking about the 'ideal ego' *before* the first great watershed of his thinking, which to my mind is the paper 'On narcissism' (1914a).

For many years though, Freud had enough to do in studying the clinical evidence for what was *in* the unconscious and how it was manifested; in shaping up his theories on sexuality and the instincts; in thinking about the concept of defence, by which for a long while he mainly meant repression; in sitting with his patients, writing clinical papers and developing technique; and in charting huge new areas on the two lines of human development, libidinal and narcissistic. Then he finally turned his attention to the field of the ego, the superego, guilt and anxiety, and I would now like to quote you a passage from *The Ego and the Id*, still fresh, apposite and quirky in his inimitable style:

> Psycho-analysis has been reproached time after time with ignoring the higher, moral, supra-personal side of human nature. The reproach is doubly unjust, both historically and methodologically. For, in the first place, we have from the very beginning attributed the function of instigating repression to the moral and aesthetic trends in the ego, and secondly, there has been a general refusal to recognize that psycho-analytic research could not, like a philosophical system, produce a complete and ready-made theoretical structure, but had to find its way step by step along the path towards understanding the intricacies of the mind by making an analytic dissection of both normal and abnormal phenomena. So long as we had to concern ourselves with the study of what is repressed in mental life, there was no need for us to share in any agitated apprehension as to the whereabouts of the higher side of man. But now that we have embarked on the analysis of the ego, we can give an answer to all those whose moral sense has been shocked and who have complained

that there must surely be a higher nature in man: 'Very true,' we can
say, 'and here we have that higher nature, in this ego ideal or superego, the representative of our relation to our parents. When we were
little children we knew these higher natures, we admired them and
feared them; and later we took them into ourselves.' . . . What has
belonged to the lowest part of the mental life of each of us is changed,
through the formation of the ideal, into what is highest in the human
mind by our scale of values. (Freud, 1923, pp. 35–6)

This wonderful passage does give the game away a bit. Freud is
referring to his growing understanding of how the superego comes
into existence. The name superego came fully into use only in this
paper, after which incidentally he almost entirely abandoned the
notion of the ego ideal, which throughout his life he equated
completely with the superego. It has been left to later generations
to refine distinctions between the two, both in affective components and in function. In Freud's view, then, the superego is seen
to be a special agency developed in and by the ego at the time of
one of the earliest of life's great critical requirements, namely the
overcoming of the Oedipus complex. The strong libidinal attachment to the parent of the opposite sex, and the accompanying
hostile rivalry to the same-sex parent have to be survived, surmounted and changed. This is a kind of basic *given*, if mankind is
going to survive through the nurturing medium of the family. A
special process is undertaken whereby the father is *identified with*
by the son, as an alternative to maintaining the aggressive wish for
his elimination; he is taken into the self, and thereafter related to
as a special inner object. Freud was insistent that, although later
authority figures – teachers, priests and the like – can be added
on to the superego, in its origin it is a unique, new creation,
primarily constituted by the parental imagos. An imago, incidentally, is not the same as an image. It is an image which is elaborated
by one's own fantasy additions. We can see in retrospect how even
more momentous than it appeared *then* this concept of the
superego in fact was and, incidentally, it is the true beginning
of sound object-relations theory: Freud's psychological thinking
hitherto had been more of a one-person event, all about the drives,
the fantasies, the symptoms of the individual. With the installa-
tion of this great new wing of the ego-house, object-relations
dynamics really come into existence: by this I mean, that two-

person psychology, our feelings about and reactions to, other people began to assume its importance, and the beginnings of its shape.

Melanie Klein and her followers later pulled back the chronology of the building of the superego, and saw the baby as object-related, at least to the breast, from the beginning of life, and soon embarking on the internalization of primitive superego part-objects too. But with this very major difference, the inner world can be seen in much the same light both in classical Freudian and later theory. The ego, which was to some extent synonymous with the sense of Self or 'I', now lived under the reign of these internalized figures, who were moved from the outer to the inner world. During the 1920s Freud finally developed the tripartite or structural view of the personality, which he described as the id, ego and superego. This idea was both enormously valuable, and misleading. It was valuable because it enabled further ideas to be developed in a vivid interactive way; mental phenomena could be described because contained within the framework of a psychic apparatus; functions could be, so to speak, located; dynamic interrelations and causes and effects could be thought about and discussed in a language which became one of the common tools of our profession. However it is misleading because it is also fiction. Freud was aware of this, and warned against too much credulity in what were the necessary artifices if a toolkit were to be constructed. Mental processes were seen as functions of a hypothetical *thing*, the psychic structure. One of the drawbacks to this was the conditioning to the visual impact of the concept. I myself have always suffered from a sort of hangover from this type of conditioning, whereby I *see* the id, ego and superego as a kind of hydraulic system, staffed by large mythic figures, who operate channels in which various valves and outlets are developed, and through which different sorts of energy flow. One of the fresh pieces of understanding which came into being was that a large section of the superego (and here we begin to see differences from the traditional conscience) is of necessity *unconscious*, more closely related to the id – which is the great source of instinctual energy – than is much of the ego, and most of the superego's power derives from that source. This is because it was the libidinal longing for the mother by the son which had to be brought under control as

well as the destructive wishes towards the father, and as this
solution was reached by bringing these characters inside, into the
new ego-compound called the superego, the id energies, fuelling
both libido and aggression, were channelled into it too. The
superego could in effect offer itself as an inner object of love, fear
and respect to the ego, or self, and it could also use all the power
the parental figures had, strongly reinforced by the child's *own*
aggressive power, now thus turned in on himself, to keep his
drives, intentions, wishes and behaviour in order. It will readily be
seen therefore that the superego has a close functional relationship
with the id, as the source of energy; in the hydraulic image, a huge
channel runs from id straight into superego; and conflict between
the wishes of the id, and the forbidding laws of the superego, the
now internalized authorities of childhood, is of course *experienced*
by the ego, which is the seat of awareness of feelings. The ego is
both very strong and very bossed about. The ego is the only part
of us that has *organizational* power, and after all, it did organize
the setting up of the superego in the first place. Having done so, I
think it must at times feel a bit like the Sorcerer's Apprentice, after
his piece of cleverness got out of hand. From then on it is always
more or less at the mercy of the tempestuous id and the judgmental
superego, trying to keep the peace, and get what it can out of life,
and continue to manage the external world as well.

Here we may think for a moment on two regularly observable
clinical facts. One is that those people who lead the most saintly
and moral lives often have the most chronically nagging, harsh
consciences. One might expect that this would not be so. Freud
talks about this at some length in those two works of his that I
mentioned: *The Future of an Illusion* (1927) and *Civilization and
its Discontents* (1930). He points out that very saintly people often
have to manage strong, flowing instinctual impulses, both of
aggression and sensuality; their force is directed into the superego
which continually marshalls the ego in a dictatorial way, and these
people's goodness is maintained at the cost of unceasing instinctual
inhibition. The other clinical phenomenon that we very often
encounter is that of the individual who protests that his upbringing
was not strict, his parents were gentle and indulgent; he does not
know *why* his conscience treats him with such severity. We see
now where the answer lies: it is the strength of his *own* aggression,

his own innate capacity for violent, even sadistic fantasy, usually held under repression, which flows into his internalized agencies, distorting, strengthening and arming them – and thus his superego – out of all recognition, when compared with what his parents were 'really' like.

Freud had long since got the hang of the fact that somehow or other the ego was doing the damming up and repression of strong, unacceptable emotional drives; since for over twenty years, he thought that these were mainly sexual, he thought that *anxiety* itself was what repressed sexual feelings turned into. As if, being squashed back and held down, they nevertheless gave off a cloudy, uncomfortable miasma which pervaded the ego from somewhere within or below. This was more or less 'the theory of anxiety' until he began to reconsider fully the psychology of the ego. There was plenty to support his early idea, and he gave it up reluctantly; but give it up he did, with a full renunciation, repeated for the last time very clearly in one of his *New Introductory Lectures on Psycho-Analysis* (1932a). He began to see that the ego, albeit so weak and helpless in some way in its relations to the superego and the id, both of them thundering at it from all inward sides, had two supreme advantages: one was its organizational powers, and the other was that it was learning continually from its position as the mediator with external reality. It gradually came to know about what it could manage in the way of excitement, stimulus, pressure – or at least in good-enough environmental circumstances it had a fair idea. Freud thought on about anxiety, as he had for so long, and so had many other analysts, and he was not satisfied. Adler thought it all arose from what he called organ inferiority, but his theory simply bypassed so much established analytic understanding that Freud soon dismissed it. Rank thought all anxiety arose from the trauma of birth and continually trying to repeat and master that. Freud quite liked this idea for a while, largely, I suspect, because he actually thought of it first, as with so many things that appear to have cropped up *de novo* elsewhere; he never really left it entirely, because although he didn't believe in anything like 'memories' of the womb or birth, he did hold on to the idea that *separation* in its manifold forms is the deepest form of anxiety, and biologically birth must be the first and perhaps the greatest experience of separation undergone by the human organism.

But in the 1920s we see Freud digging away at the idea that anxiety is fear, and fear is danger. So anxiety is the manifestation which suggests the approach of danger. The ego runs up a flag, which he calls signal anxiety, to tell itself that danger is felt to be around, and then proceeds to *do* something, as near as possible appropriate. Danger may *really* come from without, in which case there are realistic steps to be taken, sometimes literally, as when you actually do need to run away from something in order to survive. But what came to interest Freud, as it must all concerned with human psychic dis-ease, was danger from *within*, or very minor danger from without which was being magnified or distorted by fantasy or traumatic memory (and later we would add by projection). Now with his pliant, manageable theory of the psychic apparatus, he could see how the ego could become aware of *sensual* danger from onslaughts by the primitive, un-law-abiding part of itself, the id. Then it organizes defences, such as denial, repression, somatization, (and now we would add splitting). Or it can sense punishing danger from the shadowy ruler, the superego; then it organizes defences such as further identification with good objects, displacement, projection, avoidance or placation. All these may be within normal limits. But they may not be fully efficient and then there occurs a spillover into *symptoms* when ordinary signal anxiety gets much stronger. Semi-frustrated strong emotional drives may find the cracks in the ego's often imperfect defensive systems, and become symptoms, frequently bearing in heavy disguise a coded message as to their meaning, and sometimes so appealing to the ego's need to protect itself from the direct danger that the ego falls half in love with them and maintains them with unconscious vigour. This phenomenon is not at all uncommon. On the face of it we would think that unpleasure *must* be dominant, but the *hidden* message is that the ego is relieved and protected by the symptom and may get special attention – in itself a kind of *pleasure*. This is known as the 'secondary gain from illness'.

We learn much about inner-world structure from the analytic study of symptoms. The very first and absolutely memorable way in which I began to learn about hysteria was when I was a psychiatric registrar in the acute admissions ward of a big hospital, and a nun came in with a paralysed right arm. There was nothing wrong neurologically, indeed the paralysis did not match the neurological distribution of nerves, and this finding is often true of hysteria. We treated conversion hysteria with hypnosis then – after all, this was only sixty-five years after Freud had given up doing so! She was blandly indifferent to her symptom which was, in fact, incapacitating. Not only had she to eat, and so on, with her left hand, but she was the scribe in her convent and she could not now write. But it was no wonder that she was serene with it; she was a very sensual woman and under hypnosis we found that it was far less of a problem to eat and scrawl with her left hand, than to admit to her confessor that she wished to masturbate with her right. Her ego had sensed the danger of the wish, had repressed it, and with it the anxiety about the danger of shame and guilt, and thus it had satisfied her threatening superego and was sitting back quite pleased with itself.

This patient and her symptom were very instructive; the symptom was clear-cut, localized and dramatic. Her condition also served to point up an understanding of the origins of the development of the psychoanalytic method by Freud; it is *not enough*, in terms of a successful treatment outcome, simply to locate the unconscious wish (in her case the sexual one); this in itself does not 'give permission' to the ego to elaborate a sexual fantasy, let alone enact a piece of sexual behaviour, without anxiety and guilt. On the contrary, a sudden exposure to the conscious ego of this piece of the unconscious self may only serve to shock, and to reinforce the structures of the superego, thus increasing denial, splitting and symptom maintenance. Unfortunately, one of the myths about psychoanalysis which still flourishes today is that the omnipotent, amoral analyst *does* give this sort of permission by his methods, and that if it were not for the critical weight of most right-minded citizens opposing our devious machinations, sexual promiscuity would be rife in people who have the misfortune to cross our path. A variation of this view is also present in the active existence of therapists who still use the hypnotic and suggestion methods which Freud abandoned early in this century. The true analytic unravelling of such a symptom as this nun presented involved attention to her anxiety, to the pressures of her superego prohibitions, to the acknowledgement of a self which has a hidden sexual side, and the positive value to her of her defences; this latter then leads to a deeper understanding of, say, the place of sublimation in her particular profession, and a gradual ego-sense of the capacity to make more *choices*, consciously, about the management of her inner world.

Hysteria on the whole was easier to understand, and to treat, and still is, than obsessional neurosis, which nevertheless had held Freud's interest from the very earliest times. It was only when he got the understanding of the role of the superego, its responses to aggressive wishes from the id – and a more detailed view of the agility of the ego in trying to manipulate its two great masters – that he really began to understand obsessional neurosis. The painful thing about obsessional neurosis is that the guilt, or readiness for it, is much more conscious than in most other psychopathology – excepting melancholia, that is, which Freud had wrestled with in 1917, in 'Mourning and melancholia'. Or perhaps one should say that there is a constant anxiety in obsessional neurosis, which is about the *fear* of aggression, and the fear of the guilt for the aggression, an anxiety only temporarily allayed by the various defences organized by the ego – undoing, isolating, placating, and ritual magic. The symptoms, though bringing little in the way of conscious satisfaction, are themselves tormenting to endure and thus the unconscious guilt or need for punishment referred to above is satisfied. Freud had *guessed* at the unconscious sense of guilt years before, indeed had written about it in his 1916 paper 'Some character-types met with in psycho-analytic work', but it was only now that he *fully* understood that 'the ego' was not the same as 'the consciousness' but that on the contrary an enormous part of the ego, including most of the superego, is unconscious. He saw that anxiety and guilt, though both, in this part of his theorizing, *experienced by* the ego, can be deeply *un*conscious in their origins, as huge dynamic interactions take place in the recesses of the mind, and he began to grasp and therefore to be able to analyse accurately the pathways to these dark places.

As so often happens in a general medical training, and there are all sort of different clinical examples of this, the first case of obsessional neurosis I ever treated with psychotherapy stands out in my mind with great clarity. This may be partly because I was working in a big psychiatric hospital when I began my analytic training, and patients with neuroses who qualify for admission have to be pretty severely ill. This was a gentle, timid, courteous

man of forty, a bachelor who had become too incapacitated by his
symptoms to continue to live on his own. When he was brought
to my office for his first session, he took twenty-five minutes to
cross the threshold. I watched in alarmed fascination as he hovered
at the line made by the floorboards, lost in his trance of indecision.
I was aware of having to deal with a reaction in myself which is
common to many non-obsessional people, of a sort of impatience;
I should add that provoking this feeling in others is one of the
obsessional's most powerful ways of expressing aggression while
dissociating from the conscious intention to do so. I had my first
experience of how, to an observer, a severe obsessional symptom
can *seem* to be a lot madder than many of the signs exhibited by a
true psychotic. Indeed, it is sometimes an effort to remember that
the frail dividing line is simply that obsessional neurotics at all
times are, or can be, aware of just how mad and irrational their
behaviour is, however much they may be temporarily caught up in
serious performance of their ritualized magical activity. This man
was the unsuccessful youngest son of fiercely Orthodox Jewish
parents: he was unsuccessful by reason of the interference of his
symptoms in his everyday life. His manifold symptoms were
permeated by Talmudic significance. They made me think of a
phrase from the Cranmer Anglican *Book of Common Prayer*
(1672), when the penitent Christian, in the General Confession,
begs absolution for his 'manifold sins and wickedness' – thus is the
power of the Old Testament God carried forward into the Father-
Person of the New Testament Trinity God. But for this patient,
there was no saving belief in Christ to take upon Himself the sins
of the world, through the doctrine of Atonement, and shrive him;
thus he was continually attempting to ward off inner danger and
to expiate for his badness with a complicated series of repetitive
magical actions. He only partially responded to a slow attempt to
undo his causal chains, and to give him a greater emphasis on
choice and a reduced one on submissive enslavement to his
superego. To some extent my own beginning status must have
contributed to this, but also I think that the tenacity and power of
his unconscious guilt required him not altogether to yield up the
punishing suffering of his illness. His deeply unconscious aggressive wishes against both his parents, and particularly his father, to
whom he was overtly a dependent and obedient son, were of

course the source of this guilt: he demonstrated thus that it is the strength of the unconscious which is most often the generator of obsessional neurosis. His sexual drive was not strong, and such as it was, was throughout his worst days capable of sublimation through his always available talent for playing the piano.

This patient's self-inflicted misery leads me to recall that Freud was also welding into his new patterns of structure the place of the pleasure principle, and some of the 1920s writing attends to the problem of masochism. Long ago, I decided that as far as I understood masochism, it could usefully, if loosely, be described as 'making the best of a bad job'. I still do think this is a good working definition. The intensification of one's own aggression as it turns on oneself in its channelling through the superego can become sadistic, and as there is a strongly sexual component in sadistic excitation, so also there is a sexualization of the submission to the punishment which is wished for by the guilt for the unconscious aggression. An inhibited sexual wish also may still gain pleasure through masochistic compensations under the heavy hand of the prohibiting tyrant. This process is almost entirely unconscious and the unconscious sense of guilt is assuaged. Here we see the poor ego yet again managing the powers within, obeying the superego, giving space to the sexual drives, mixing them with the aggressive drives which are also fighting for expression, trying to accommodate to reality demands, and – usually with some success – hanging on to the experience of a bit of the crude pleasure principle. When the structural complexity of an obsessional symptom is fully dissected out by analysis, it really comes as small suprise that sometimes the ego thinks it can also walk on water: by this I mean that some of its manoeuvres to keep the self going are so complex that the ego can be forgiven for occasionally feeling rather specially clever and pleased with itself. We should note clearly here that the main source of the pleasure may have to be *renunciation*, and the more self-indulgent affect of *gratification* must be kept secret and unconscious for the sake of a benign smile from the superego.

We have thought rather a lot about the tyrannies of the superego; this is because their origin and elucidation are so much in the field of psychoanalysis. But of course it has numerous neutral and benign functions which approximate more closely and more mildly to what is called the conscience; self-observation, self-reflection, kindly as well as destructive criticism, appreciation, esteem, love. It does have a smiling face, and our maintenance of a reasonable self-esteem depends on the encouragement of that smile. The ego-ideal has, of recent years, and particularly in a very readable book called *The Ego Ideal* by Janine Chasseguet-Smirgel (1985), received much attention in its own right. It has become clearer that while it is certainly part of the same general agency as the superego, its development and functions are rather different, and some regard it alone as the part of the mind which enables humanity to transcend nature and achieve its greatest heights. It derives from primary narcissism and stands for the human longing to achieve blissful union – with nature, with God, with a supra-judgmental sense of self; maybe the prototype was union with the mother, and maybe the primary standard was the omnipotent, gratified, successful, infantile self. A brief summary clarification which I find useful is to remember that to fall below the standards of the *ego-ideal* is to produce *shame*; to fall below the standards of the *superego* is to produce *guilt*. The criticism of the ego ideal is to pronounce 'failure': of the superego 'badness'. Of course the two often overlap.

A few last words on anxiety itself. Freud clung for a long time, and never quite gave up, the idea that all anxiety at heart is castration anxiety; within his own framework, he made a good case for it. Much has evolved since then, including the knowledge, which Freud himself was more or less aware of, that Freud knew very little about female psychology – a sidelight on this is that obsessional neurosis which intrigued him so much for so long is commoner in men. This links up with Freud's theory that in men the superego is harsher and stronger than in women; this in turn arises from his view that the superego of men and of women have rather different formation patterns, dependent upon the quite marked differences of the Oedipus complex and its path to resolution in the two sexes. All this stuff he works out more clearly in the papers he wrote in the 1920s, including one with the unwieldy but clear title of 'Some psychical consequences of the anatomical distinction between the sexes' (1925).

All symptoms can safely be said to be anxiety symptoms at root, though the anxiety itself, arising in the vigilant ego and responded

to by it, may have been subsumed in the symptoms. But trying to
probe for the level and meaning of the hidden anxiety is always a
good reliable way of doing analysis, whatever imponderables one
may seem to be faced with. Primary anxiety represents a failure,
more or less extensive, on the part of the ego and its striving for
defence measures. The ego is the seat of anxiety, and if it cannot
defend itself from dangers, it will continue to suffer anxiety, dread,
helplessness, panic, and fear, often seemingly as irrational as are
the inner *provocateurs*. Signal anxiety has been described, and may
be fleeting. Separation anxiety is diversely and widely manifest,
and most often relates to fear of the loss of a loved or needed
person. Freud came to include castration anxiety in this category,
and indeed to see separation anxiety as the greatest category overall.

As I said earlier, the work of Melanie Klein and her school not
only opened up our understanding of the early pre-Oedipal
beginnings of superego development, but also gave us two new
concepts: that of persecutory anxiety, which is provoked by the
fear of being attacked by one's bad objects, outer or inner or
projected; and, when object-relationship capacity has developed
further, that of depressive anxiety, which is provoked by the fear
of what one's own hostility and badness can do to one's good
objects. The last one in my closing collection is objective anxiety;
this more or less refers to real things out there which it would be
silly not to be afraid of and do something about; the trouble with
this sort, as with practically anything else in the world, is that it
can be coloured by fantasy projected from within us, and the
object of fear may become so invested with symbolic or fantastic
input that the anxiety ceases to be objective or realistic, and
becomes neurotic, or is called phobic. It is realistic to be afraid of
a lion which is charging at you, but neurotic to be afraid, as some
people are, that a cat who lives in the street may come near you
when you go for a walk.

I hope I have shown you something of the theory of the
devlopment of the superego, and its intimate relationship with the
id and of how anxiety and guilt originate and grow, in our inner
world, and how the ego copes. I like occasional quotes from Freud,
as you know, and so I will end with one from *The Ego and the Id*
as we began:

If anyone were inclined to put forward the paradoxical proposition that the normal man is not only far more immoral than he believes but also far more moral than he knows, psycho-analysis, on whose finding the first half of the assertion rests, would have no objection to raise against the second half. (p. 52)

5

SIN AND THE SUPEREGO: MAN AND HIS CONSCIENCE IN SOCIETY

William Boyd, in his novel *Brazzaville Beach*, quotes a philosopher whom he does not name, as saying: 'There are three questions that every human being everywhere at any time, of any creed or colour, wants the answers to: What can I know? What ought I to do? What may I hope for?' (1990, p. 5). Supposing that one accepts that there is some truth in this, then there is an overall question, which is evoked by the trio: Why do we seek so deeply for these answers? I think this may be only partly answerable, and then in terms both of existential views, and of psychoanalysis. We find ourselves in this mysterious event called Life, and we are thrown into a world, that is mostly beyond our comprehension, to live our lives. Our human faculties include the capacity to make sense of some things, to understand some shreds of meaning, and it seems that we have a natural restlessness until we have tried to make sense of ourselves living our lives, with the one and only one thing that is knowable about them, namely, that we shall die. The questions, in the order they were asked, seem to fall naturally in accord with the developmental logic of life. 'What can I know?' is the question of youth. 'What ought I to do?' is the preoccupation of the more mature mind trying to sort out right from wrong. 'What may I hope for?' could be seen as a later-life question, when people turn to the contemplation of last things – and I too will return to this later. When I reflect on the subject matter of these lectures, the question 'What ought I to do?' seems to rise to the

This was the first of the eight Tavistock Public Lectures in London in 1990, under the overall title of 'The Seven Deadly Sins'.

surface first; and yet, before long, we see that what we think about what we ought to do is conditioned by what we can know; also that what we do is influenced by teleology, that is, it has a purpose, maybe a hidden one. In other words we are expressing hope when we choose to act.

All the world's religions, philosophies, ideologies and cults try to find the answers to these questions, and some feel that they have succeeded, and many people accept them. Uniquely among sentient beings, we look for answers to give meaning to our lives, and as this search progressed over the years, the conscience appeared, its shape and emphases shifting as cultures changed through the centuries; and with more or less success, it tried to tell us what we ought to do, and just as importantly, what we ought not to do; and the ought-nots became sins. Eventually Freud came along, and complicated matters, finding that the superego in some ways was worse than the simple conscience, but holding out also a hope of increased freedom from the tyrants within.

I thought I would take a brief historical overview of sin and the superego, and to linger with Freud here would be to look at the end first. So let us go far back in time.

'Man is born to trouble as the sparks fly upward' (Job 5:7) – this was Job's view of life, and indeed his troubles were so catastrophic and each fresh one came so hard on the heels of the last, that the account becomes almost hilarious if read at a sitting. In modern slang one might say, 'you name it – Job had it'. But the common feature of the troubles is that they represent what we would now call bad luck. The story, which is, I am sure, intended to carry a moral message, never truly clarifies whether Job had been a sinner, and thus had logically drawn the punishing wrath of the Lord on him, or whether he had led a blameless life and God simply selected him as a warning, an object lesson, to demonstrate the mysterious omnipotence of which he was capable. Job's comforters, a priggish trio called Zophar, Eliphaz and Bildad, certainly thought and frequently said that Job must have deserved it all, for sins against the Lord, and I am inclined to think that, though obscure, this is the intended moral. But Job certainly does not think so, at least consciously; he considers himself to be well above average good and holy, and he intends us to hear in great detail his side of things. However, in a manner that we now might consider significant, he includes several ranting, dismissive references to 'hypocrites', as for example when he says: 'Let mine enemy be as the wicked, and he that riseth up against me as the unrighteous. For what is the hope of the hypocrite, though he hath gained, when God taketh away his soul? Will God hear his cry when trouble cometh upon him?' (Job 27:7–9). Already many troubles have battered Job, and there hasn't been a sound out of the Lord, so one feels that this attempt by Job at splitting and projection of a doubt and a self-view is perilously near to insight. Job justifies himself ever more wildly, and eventually, in the nick of time, the Lord 'spake out of a whirlwind', whereupon Job makes a scrappy, half-hearted act of repentance, saying cravenly 'I have uttered that which I understand not' (Job 42:3), and then everything takes a turn for the better, Job is restored in God's sight, lavished with good things, and the comforters are packed off, discomforted at last.

My point in telling this story is to underline its ambiguity. Ambiguity was a feature that I noticed so increasingly frequently while attempting to explore the history of sin and the conscience in society, that I came to see that it is virtually inseparable from the moral systems of mankind. I finally concluded that it was Freud who shed light on this in the end, when he showed that the ambiguities are the true cultural expression of psychic dramas of conflict – between the conscious and the unconscious ego, the id and the superego, the life and death instincts, the passions and the rational will.

We cannot abandon our own conditioning, and of necessity we look back through the prism of psychoanalysis on the story of a man struggling with morality. We have Freud's structural theory as one of the cornerstones of our thinking, but we are not bound by holy law to 'believe' in it or in the existence of the dynamic unconscious; we are shown constant evidence of their existence, and of a vivid, conflictual psychic life going on in everyone all the time, often beyond the bounds of subjective awareness. Willingly we would agree that man is born to trouble; anxiety, tension, irrational misery and guilt, strong unassuageable longings – of such is suffering made, and human beings are the animals who are born to worry and to wonder and to suffer. We have developed skilful tools for assisting in the troubles; but we do not have a working concept of sin. On the contrary, Freud always stoutly maintained that he had no intention of providing either a coherent philosophy of life, nor a moral system; in *The Ego and the Id* in 1923 he spelt this out clearly (pp. 35–6). Nevertheless, there is a robust argument which can be maintained, that psychoanalysis is a moral activity in itself, tending as it does towards greater freedom both in the making of moral choices, and in the use of the rational will in implementing the potential of those choices. Many modern theologians such as Paul Tillich and Hans Kung have grasped psychoanalysis eagerly, claiming that increased psychic health is potentially synonymous with greater moral strength. Sin itself may be an alien word to us, and our way of making judgements about people does not lend itself to use of the concept. Yet sins are about how human beings live their lives and suffer: neither sin nor spirituality exists only in some other quite different branch of humanity. Neither sin nor spiritual striving can come about apart from the usual psycho-biological processes that occur in all of us. We deal with sin and its ramifying effects as surely as did a monk taking confession in his cell in the twelfth century; and we are the current representatives of a long tradition of those who worked for the cure of souls, and who, in so doing, tried to bring not only insight but also transformation to the suffering sinner.

The earliest mythology on record shows mankind in anxiety, and embryonic forms of guilt, which it attempted to alleviate by magic. There was a notion of expiation and of placating unseen powers; magical reparations to the numinous forces of the cosmos, however, cannot truly be said to have arisen out of awareness of what were later called sins, but rather from a sense of transgression, of taboos and animistic order. Humans were not punished for violations of moral codes, so much as for manipulations or breaking taboos, or for defilements, which may well have occurred accidentally. Cosmic order, not divine beings, was disturbed, though in some cases pacifiable, even at the terrible cost of massive human sacrifice. The notion of free will hardly existed, and it was almost impossible to choose to avoid defilement all the time. Numinous objects had tyrannical requirements; there was little heed paid to anything approaching sinful intentions in the mind of a subject.

It was the invention of theism, more particularly monotheism, which the Jews regard as their greatest contribution to the world, which enabled the concept of sin to develop. Strictly speaking, the long-term definition of sin concerns man in his special relationship to God; in the time of Moses, this was ratified as a covenant, a sort of contract which each individual felt to be between him and God, although, strictly, the covenant was between God and Israel, itself made up of all these individuals; God required of mankind observance of, and obedience to, his laws, supposedly handed to Moses on Mt Sinai, and in return for contractual obedience the Israelites were to receive special love, security and attention from God, who had chosen them to further his kingdom on earth. I have recently learnt, from working in a group with some rabbis of the Lubavitch Hasidim, that the Messianic idea is with them all the time, it is the detailed building of a holier state of things on earth, not just waiting for a new person to be born.

Sin was a breach in the law, therefore a deficit in a positive order of things. Man was told he was made in the image of God, and from being helpless creatures under the sway of cosmic caprice, with only uncertain magic to assist them, they now became transformed into ethical beings, with responsibilities, divinely enjoined, towards God and their neighbour. The Judaeo–Christian tradition created God and the laws, and therefore we can say they invented sin; curiously, though, Original Sin, the evil innate in us all, did not become a theological doctrine until the time of St Paul, even though Adam and Eve, and their inquisitiveness and their sexual rebellion against God, were then used as its exemplar. The rabbinic tradition held, more benignly, that though man is capable of falling away from God, and sinning, he was not inherently evil. I shall therefore explore that tradition further forward into history; but first, it is refreshing to take a moment for the comparison of monotheistic evolution with Greek and Far Eastern philosophical thought, already far advanced in sophistication by the time of Moses.

In the East, Buddhism, which grew nearly 3000 years BC, as the ethical, philosophical branch of Hinduism, is the only world religion which is completely a-theistic; it is not concerned with sin as such, and does not employ the word, or an equivalent, in Pali or Sanskrit. Indeed, it could not be concerned with it, by the definition I have proposed, namely that sin is a breach in a covenant with a personal God. Nor does Buddhism attach special weight to guilt, except as one among many conditioned responses in the individual, in which it also notes 'guilt-feelings' and the irrational power of the unconscious. Since there is no divine being, there is no external divine law, and of course, no penances or punishments, nor saving grace from above, nor transcendent offers of redemption. All morality depends on man alone working on himself. The philosophy and metapsychology are different from those of the Western traditions, but they repay study, as their psychological subtlety renders them congenial to the findings and techniques of psychoanalysis. This may account for their recent increased acceptance in the West. Gotama the Buddha did not say: Sin exists, and here's what you must do to be saved. He said: Suffering exists, and is dependent on your attitudes of mind, so here is a method, which you may choose to practise, to attain peace of mind. The practical emphasis is on techniques for deepening the awareness of what we are capable of doing with our minds, and how they are conditioned, in order to achieve detachment from their irrational powers.

The Greeks, however, appeal to us in a particular way, and via the Platonic and Aristotelian traditions, which influenced Western theology for many centuries, can still be found in liturgy and doctrine today. I think their appeal is in their love of drama and of heroes, and almost paradoxically, of rationality at the same time; or perhaps, considering drama, I should call it logicality. Tragedy may be said to be a Greek invention, and it was the preoccupation with the dramatic potential of moral situations which produced the great tragedies. They thought, however, within these contexts, that it was a fatal sort of blindness, a capacity for making mistakes on a huge scale, which was more of a moral challenge to mankind than ordinary, obvious sinning; and some of the appeal to us of this view is that it so clearly allows for an appreciation of the unconscious. Their heroes make dreadful blunders, which grip our attention with their mix of sin, crime and only too easily recognizable human faults. They portray the sorts of error which we know do get made, driven as humanity is by the dark forces of lust and greed and need and yearning for power: these were the kind of things that the Church later labelled sins. These Greek heroes are sensitive to what people think of them; they suffer from hubris, and then from shame, rather than guilt. Often one sees that there is an anxious narcissistic relationship to the ego-ideal rather than a humble guilt-ridden straight link with a harsh superego. The Greek heroes of tragedy and their predicaments do not very much resemble everyday life as we know it: there is a more immediate empathy with, say, Lear or Othello, than with the Greeks. But they extend our moral sense, they make us think about things that matter, and we feel moved and grateful that they have enacted psychic struggle on such a grand scale. In the philosophical field, Socrates and Plato, if I may oversimplify for a moment, had a somewhat simple ideal view that if one recognized the Good, one would choose it, and would see that to do otherwise, to fall into sin, would be an error of judgement. It is refreshing to encounter this respect for the human will, especially as it later became increasingly disabled and impotent in the dark ages of the Christian tradition. Aristotle did take issue with the idea that no-one would sin voluntarily if his moral choices were free; in other words he was more sceptical about just how free they were. He does allow for the use of the will as a moral agent, but he saw the difficulties as greater. He emphasized the power of the passions, and also of ignorance. Ignorance he seemed to conceive of as to an extent willed in itself – a willed unconsciousness, or what we might call denial, or what I think John Steiner meant by 'turning a blind eye' (1982, p. 247). In this Aristotle was followed by the Roman Catholic Fathers of the Church centuries later, when they came to hold that ignorance is not an ultimate excuse for falling into sin. Although sin, according to the definition of breaking a law of God, was not a Greek concept, nevertheless, there was an approxima-tion; universal laws which could be apprehended by human intellect were called divine laws. And in the time when Greek philosophy was in the ascendant, the superego was enhanced in significance in that it was the crux, the functional agent, of the tragic heroic tradition.

Returning from the dramatic conflicts of the Greeks to the Mosaic tradition, as developed and taught by the rabbis, one is struck by the absence of inner struggle there. The accepted definition of sin in theology, from the Torah onwards, was 'the purposeful disobedience of a creature to the known will of God'. The word purposeful implies that the will must be involved, but psychic dramas do not appear. Sin, especially in the early days of Mosaic law, and then throughout the Old Testament and, as far as

I can tell, into orthodoxy today, is a constant factor. Enshrined in the Torah, and as time went by, in the Talmudic commentaries, are the details of the theocratic moral system, with hundreds, if not thousands, of prescriptions about what must and must not be done. There is little sense of moral conflict: dramas do occur, in real life events – floods and walls falling down and so on – but there is little or no sense of anguished reflection on the stages of the theatres of the mind.

To be sure, many of the Prophets, especially Ezekiel and Jeremiah, proclaim the personal responsibility of each man for his sins; and other writers, like Isaiah and the Psalmist, beautifully describe the emotional effects of sinning, such as inner darkness, feelings of being alone and abandoned by God, self-condemnation for ingratitude to the Creator. There is a lot *about* sin, but little about self-conscious introspection: there is thus no theory of sinfulness developed, no existential evolution of insight into one's own character and its dark corners, and no struggle to transform it, and how. In fact, we might say that although there are ever more carefully calibrated categories of sin, there is no body of moral philosophy. Freud, as we shall later see, greatly admired the intellectual rigour of Moses in his creative construction of God and his handling of Israelite society (1939), but the intellect seems to have been obsessional and nosological, rather than imaginatively philosophical.

The ambiguity to which I have referred continues to run through the subtext of both Old and New Testaments. There is a double message in the Old Testament idea that though man is not naturally evil, he is inclining to evil; but where he is naturally inclined to the good, he cannot fully achieve it unless he has been chosen by God to enter into the full covenanted relation to him. Exactly the same double-bind appears more crudely throughout the history of the Christian churches, with regard to the gift of grace. Man by then was seen as naturally evil and inclined to sin, and could not be saved unless he received the gift of grace from God. But he could not earn this gift, by prayer or works, however ardently he longed for it: especially if it was faith itself which had failed him, the grossest sin at some periods. We are led to understand that grace is entirely in God's remit, and only arbitrarily does he bestow it. Before I leave the glance at Old Testament theology, I wanted to note that Yahweh himself can be, quite often, a thoroughly unpleasant, and I should have thought, by his own standards, an immoral character. The seven deadly sins were not, as such, formulated until the Middle Ages, but the God of the Old Testament could manifest rage, pride, greed, envy, jealousy and vengefulness, for which of course, he was always exonerated either because sinners had deserved it, or because his ways were inscrutable and mysterious. Perhaps not quite so mysterious from the standpoint of projective identification. Yahweh was, after all, a very considerable receptive object into whom to project.

Christianity, which was ushered in by the arrival of the person some took to be the Messiah, crystallized and detailed many aspects of sinfulness, and saw man as existing in a primary state of corruption. By doctrine this was supposed to be because the sin of Adam and Eve condemned mankind for evermore to be stained with sin, from which they could only be redeemed by the love of God for them, and his voluntary, and arbitrary, absolution. The life of Christ therefore culminated in the really fearful doctrine of the Atonement, which is a Christian Article of Faith, which means that it has to be believed, on the threat of being banished to Hell if it is not. It is believed that humanity, sinning, crucified Jesus, the incarnate Son of God; but God the Father really appears to have had a kind of master plan whereby this had to happen so that Jesus became a human sacrifice expiating – that is, atoning for – all the sins of undeserving man, if he accepts that that was what the Crucifixion and subsequent Resurrection was about. God, we have to assume – indeed, are told – was 'well pleased' with Jesus for going through with it, and graciously, on the strength of it, forgave believers their sins. Thus the ancient rites of human sacrifice, which to this day seem shocking to Christians when recorded in, for example, Mayan and Aztec culture, are the crucial lynch-pin of their own faith in salvation. However we may view the changes which have come about in the structure and function of moral systems over the last 2000 years, there is little left to the imaginative superego which could actually be said to be worse than this episode, this doctrine of human dependence upon human sacrifice for what is held out as the highest attainable spiritual goal. It occurs to me that the fear and hostility to the father, which Freud in *Totem and Taboo* (1913b) saw as rooted in ancient primal rivalries, must have in fact received an injection of intensity after the Crucifixion. In spite of his capacity for temper tantrums, the God of the Old Testament was seen as fairly reliable and benevolent, but ambivalence about his caprice and sadism in the face of sin produced greater ambivalence in his public in the Christian era.

This increased harshness is largely down to St Paul, who was responsible for much of the shaping of Christian doctrine. He was a disturbed, inspired and obsessional character who wrote the Epistles, some of which are full of beauty, and some vitriolically legalistic. The quality of sin now underwent a change; it became more inward. St Paul taught, following Jesus, that the law was not just an external set of rules, but was written in the human heart – it there co-existed uneasily with Original Sin, the natural wish and capacity of people to sin unless they attended to their conscience, informed by grace and Christian teaching. In other words, St Paul developed a sort of early structural theory; more attention was given to introspection and psychic conflict, and there is the beginning of a concept of moral development. St Paul's Epistle to the Romans is an excellent example of the struggle between sin and the superego. Sin here is usually illustrated with reference to the behaviour of the Gentiles, or the uncircumcised. The ambiguity which we are beginning to expect is manifest; for example, in one breath Paul says: 'There is no respecter of persons with God' (2:11) meaning everyone has good moral law in their hearts, and can avoid sin; and in the next: 'For when the Gentiles, who have not the law, do by nature the things contained within the law, these having not the law, are a law unto themselves' (2:14) and goes on, a little later: '. . . which show the work of the law written in their hearts, their conscience also bearing witness, and *their thoughts the meanwhile accusing, or else excusing, them*' (2:15). I have italicized this phrase as I thought these words as good a description as one may find in a sentence of the self-awareness of the conscience at work. I will end this scan of Biblical teaching with another quotation from St Paul which says indirectly something about him, as well as about the nature of sins. He is referring again to the Gentiles:

> A reprobate mind, to do those things that are not convenient; being filled with all unrighteousness, fornication, wickedness, covetousness, maliciousness, full of envy, murder, debate, deceit, malignity;

whisperers, backbiters, haters of God, despiteful, proud, boasters, inventors of evil things, disobedient to parents, without understanding, covenant-breakers, without natural affection, implacable, unmerciful . . . (1:28–3)

It is quite a relief to back away, and have a quiet think about paranoia and projective identification!

Since the production of the New Testament, in the 300 to 400 years following the death of Christ, the fundamentals of theology have not changed much. Emphasis has changed, as cultures have, and as ecclesiastical organizations grew in importance: the power of the Church, of course, is and always has been extensively dependent on the definition of sins and the coercive rules and rituals of confession, penance and absolution. The Fathers of the Church began to elaborate the psychology of morality; among them is St Augustine in the sixth century, whose influence is still marked today – though harsher and more penitential theology took over in the centuries following him. Augustine was an interesting, neurotic man, whose character has been extensively studied, including by dynamic psychologists. What matters to us in this context is that he taught that evil is not naturally the lot of humanity and that reparation and change is possible through the use of the will; in this he followed the Platonic tradition. He spoke with wisdom and the experience of having surmounted a difficult early life, unhelped by an indifferent father, and severely dominated by Monica, his controlling and invasive mother.

The fiercely penitential theology which evolved during the Middle Ages pushed moral teaching in the West towards an ever deeper preoccupation with sin, guilt, and what was called redemptive suffering, to an extent from which I think it has not even yet recovered, in spite of the reactive swings which appeared in the post-Reformation centuries. I say this partly because, for example, the theoretical basis of our penal system is several hundred years out of date, and the arcane structure of punishing in order to produce repentance and redemption, by humiliation, deprivation and incarceration ('redemptive suffering' as this used to be called), still survives.

However, massive changes in Western culture did come about with the Renaissance, and from our point of view, one of the most significant was that the ego, or self, began to emerge as a primary focus of reflection and moral philosophy. The establishment of the Protestant churches together with the rise of rationalism in European thought had as their consequence a more keenly self-conscious awareness in human beings. Existential aims included the experience of what both Wordsworth and Rousseau, quite independently, called 'the sentiment of being', and in relation to the philosopher's questions at the beginning of this paper, emphasis shifted from knowledge and rules issued by the Church, with the hope of eternal life as reward, to more immediate concerns, with the hope of peace and contentment in the here and now. Sin ceased to be a series of defined theocentric constants, and moral aims became more personalized, and matters for debate. The era of situational ethics dawned.

Increasingly, from about the early sixteenth century onwards, art, rather than the church, was expected to provide the spiritual sustenance of life. Drama, painting, architecture, sculpture, music, and, later, the novel, as well as the systems of more rational and less theological philosophers, both reflected and originated the moral concerns of the people. The seven deadly sins, or cardinal vices, and their contrasting virtues, had been codified in the Middle Ages, the definition of 'cardinal' carrying the consequence of Hell in the hereafter unless the sinner reached absolution by true repentance and the dispensation of special grace from God. The virtues (never, of course, as interesting as the vices, but essential in the armoury of the superego) were faith, hope, charity, justice, prudence, temperance and fortitude. The vices and the virtues began to appear, in the eleventh and twelfth centuries, in frescoes and sculptures, and later, iconic symbolism and allegory became popular in paintings. The appearance of the snake is a good example of the ambiguity flowing through religious doctrine, now manifesting as symbol. The snake represented evil, deceit and phallic power and lust; sometimes it stood for the poisonous effects of envy; but it was also a symbol for wisdom, prudence, fertility, moral subtlety, and healing powers. This was its meaning curled round the semi-magical staff of Aesculapius. Lust, often depicted as a goat or satyr, though sometimes as a depraved woman, is an interesting example of cultural modification in sin as it appeared in art; early on, lust and avarice were the worst of the deadly sins, and in mediaeval iconography frequently appeared as being so. But during the Renaissance, avarice faded, and the image of lust improved; not only was sensual gratification less punishable, but it actually became a vigorous and admired pursuit. Lust began to shade into love, and the depiction of sensual women, in non-religious paintings, became if anything rather idealized, often with mirrors held up to them by cupids or apes; ambiguity remains, however, for the mind of the viewer was led also towards a reflection on the place of vanity in the moral spectrum.

We might say, in a word, that after the Renaissance, sin became steadily secularized. The Church, fainter but pursuing, fell further behind the moral imperatives of what began to be called Society, with a capital S. By the middle of the nineteenth century, Nietzsche could say: 'God is dead' (1882, III. cviii); actually, in context, he was pointing out how not only did centres of religious observance still flourish, but also how incumbent it is on the individual, finding oneself alone, to transcend one's lower nature by thought, and to re-invent morality. Nineteenth-century literature, as well as art, took its spiritual burden seriously, and became more earnestly pedagogic; gradually the trend towards seeking personal moral accreditation through an appreciative absorption of art increased. Authenticity, in being and in creation, became a paramount moral criterion, and it still is today; it has almost entirely replaced a particularly English respect for 'sincerity', which used to be a strong virtue, with probity and integrity in it, but which came to have a hollower ring through greater psychological understanding of its False Self meanings. The focus of ethical concern moved further into views of human beings operating within social and political situations, and it was philosophers such as Rousseau, Hegel and Mill who were expected to fulfil the tasks of understanding and prescribing for ways in which people might live the good life – the most desirable goal, from about the seventeenth century on – in harmony and peace.

As the authority of the churches diminished, so did the fear of God and alertness to sin, and with them, inevitably, went eschatology. I am not sure that this was not the greatest loss. Eschatology is the study of last things – death, judgement, Heaven, Hell, eternity, hope. The answer to the third question, 'What may one hope for?' used to be couched in terms of a good death and a life hereafter in the presence of God. So retrospectively it is possible to see the extent to which teleology permeated the religious culture. Until the fifteenth century, the theology of Hell was awe-inspiringly strong. One has only to contemplate the journey of Dante and Vergil down through the Circles of the Inferno to realize something of the degree to which the love of God was balanced by the fear of God to a sinning believer. By now, 1990, however, a curious shift seems to have taken place in what is left of eschatology, and which is visible in the distinctly moralistic flavour of opinions about the human body. From being not only the temple of God but also the vehicle of sin, the seat of passions, it now seems to have become an object of narcissistic veneration imbued with religious fervour. One suspects that the near-conscious fantasy is that if we can only get it right, and not sin in the way we treat ourselves, death may even be avoided altogether. There is an unpleasant condemnatory edge to the whole business of theories of falling ill, whether psychically or physically, a more or less overt implication that moral fault, that is, sin, is at the root of illness; and there is a peremptory note in prophylactic prescriptions for avoiding illness, and a certain *de haut en bas* disdain often emanates from healers of diverse sorts towards patients.

Under a thin surface layer of residual morality and Christian-culture intentions, there was a considerable amount of muddle and mess and hopelessness by the end of the nineteenth century. Into this came the impact of Freud on the history of sin and the conscience. We do not need to rehearse Freud's opinions of religion, except to remind ourselves that he considered it infantile and pathological. And also that the theory of the superego, as fully developed by Freud in the 1920s (1923), is not by any means synonymous with the conscience, as it was previously understood, and indeed still is by many people. Because a great part of the superego is unconscious and is in conflict with unconscious emotional forces, Freud made it clear in *Civilization and its Discontents* (1930) that he thinks it impossible to tame, that it is inaccessible to the rational will. It has been said that psychiatry has no place for sin, but it may be a viable argument to say that Freud restored a sense of sin, or at least that a moral strength, until then dying, was restored to humanity, and in so doing he rendered a service. He saw the death instinct working ineluctably through the

superego, and exacerbating unconscious guilt. He brought some
sense of meaning to the human mind, and to the way in which
people feel, not guilty, but ill; but the self-made diagnosis is of
sin, whatever other name is attached to the aetiology, and this
guilt is the consequence, and there are psychoanalytic instruments
for treatment of this illness. This coherence is what I mean by a
service.

Freud did not exactly dismiss religion as illusion; his respect for
illusion in all sorts of other modes argues against this, besides
which, there is quite a lot of evidence that he remained fascinated
by religion and its structure and function all his life. He certainly
identified with Moses, and deeply admired his intellectual capacity
for the heights of sublime abstraction, and for his creation of law
and theocracy. In *Moses and Monotheism* (1912) he makes a very
characteristic remark, referring to himself and psychoanalysis
indirectly, which deserves to go into the balance opposite his late
extreme pessimism: 'All such advances in intellectuality have as
their consequence that the individual's self-esteem is increased, that
he is made proud – so that he feels superior to other people who
have remained under the spell of sensuality' (1939, p. 115). It may
be both a bleak and a self-revealing remark, and yet there is
something patrician in Freud's later works, and his acknowledgement of the view he had reached that ultimately the human will is
a frail weapon against the inner dialectic of Eros and death. When
I said he rendered a service, and brought some light into darkness,
I mean that Freud's pessimism can be seen, in its insistence on the
fundamental intractability of the human condition and the nature
of mind, as redefining and sustaining the tough authenticity of
human existence that formerly had been ratified only by God.
When we look back over centuries of religion at its most austere
and specific (not the sort of 'Jesus wants me for a sunbeam' stuff
that it has widely become) we see that it did go far in answering
the philosopher's three questions: 'What may I know? What ought
I to do? What can I hope for?' It attributed to each individual life
a meaning, a moral imperative and an intense subjective significance. And I think it is this element that Freud rescues. His own
vision of the human condition preserves much of the core of
toughness that ran through Greek, Roman, Jewish and Christian

traditions as they in turn responded to the harshness of human destiny.

Even as religion does, Freud accepts a mystery, the inevitability of suffering, and his deepest explanation of it is not so far removed from that offered by the doctrine of Original Sin. He is debarred by his own creation, psychoanalysis, from employing concepts like sin; but by any other name, the darker forces of the mind, all living out the life–death struggle, were the tragic elements which were those seen by the Greeks; and against their effect, he set insight, self-knowledge, and pride, a courageous self-sustaining awareness of moral imperatives to choose truth as far as we can – and these at least *do give weight to life*. Nietzsche more than anything dreaded vacuity and weightlessness, regretting, even as he proclaimed the death of God, that he feared this as the consequence; and urging individuals to try to transcend themselves, to achieve moral weight in a universe where it depends on them alone to struggle to do so. This was very congenial to Freud, who saw that weight and significance in life are grounded in its very exigence; that rich intensity of living requires the stimulus of deprivation, and a constant attempt to wrest meaning from the conflicts between our 'selves' and the powers of the superego.

Freud's views, especially as expressed in *Civilization and its Discontents* (1930), that life in civilization is largely intractable to the human will, however that will is liberated by psychoanalysis, is alien to much modern political ideology. If taken seriously, the bleak proud faith and courage which is what Freud finds himself left with cannot fail to outrage the egalitarian ideas about caringness which are the characteristic mode of moral judgement among the educated today. Paul Tillich (1949), a modern theologian, says that psychoanalysis, with its emphasis on historical–psychological determinism, confirms the tradition of Pauline and Augustinian insights into the arising of sin, the bondage of the will, acceptance of self-knowledge and possibility of transformation. He pointed out, as I mentioned before, that spirituality cannot be somehow separately enacted from psycho-social activity, by man in society, and that it is psychoanalysis which tells us most about that; but Freud's view also has Aristotelian rigour in requiring the toughly ironical position of simultaneous detachment and commitment to striving.

In the face of a lifetime's evidence that human beings are destined to suffer by their very nature from the effects of what were called sins in religious cultures, Freud could say, in *The Future of an Illusion* (1927), that suffering is mysterious, but that his God is truth, which is ultimately knowable: holding this view, the atheist has the same aims as the religious. Freud speaks there as if to the religious, and says (the following is condensed from different sections of the work):

> We desire the same things as you. *Our aim is the love of mankind and the decrease in suffering* ... but you are the more impatient, more exacting, and – why should I not say it? – more self-seeking than I and those on my side. You would have the state of bliss and that it begin directly after death; you expect the impossible from it, and you will not surrender the claims of the individual. (my italics)

As I said earlier, Freud always vigorously protested that he was not concocting a moral philosophy, had never intended to, was doing something else altogether; nevertheless there are ways of reading his works which, I think and hope you will agree, lend themselves to a series of extrapolations that, considered in conjunction, offer a coherent attempt to bring sense, weight, and meaning to the eternal factors in human life – guilt, anxiety, suffering, sin and the superego.

6

THE SILENT PATIENT

The silent patient presents special challenges to the analyst. I am not referring to patients who are quiet and reflective people, and who need spaces for thinking out what they are saying, and pondering on interpretations received, but who nevertheless, in their way, maintain a flow of communication. Silent patients are not common; I have treated only eight in thirty years. I would define the silent patient as one who speaks for approximately 10 per cent of the time, and often less. Nor is the speaking regularly spaced; there might be more sense of flow if it were. No, sometimes two or three sessions, or many more, may pass in silence. My record was one who did not speak for three and a half months, and this in spite of intermittent considered remarks from me. There is one other record which I will refer to later.

One of the main challenges is not so much to one's theorizing as to one's technique. These people stretch one's mind across a kind of decision-making process which is a magnified version of that which, on a lesser scale, faces us all the time in our work, namely, when do we speak, and what do we say? The main decision, which has to be reconsidered often and seriously in the opening stages of a silent patient's treatment, is about whether these people need, above all, that we ourselves should be silent partners. Do they urgently need space and peace? Will it be counterproductive to speak, will it feel as if the analyst is intruding, controlling, persecuting? Or is this a person who is dreadfully stuck, suffering

First published in *Psychoanalytic Dialogues: Journal of Relational Perspectives*, Volume 1, Part 3 (1991).

from profound inhibition, needing assistance and some form of guidance, unconsciously or even consciously longing for interpretative work which will loosen the constraint? Is this patient feeling abandoned, fearful or alone, unable to join with us unless we shoulder our responsibility to facilitate the movement of the clogged machinery? The kind of work one does if one diagnoses this second state may well have to be more or less guesswork; this is where some theorizing can be supportive to oneself, as also is any intuitive use of the history, taken in detail at a preliminary interview. There is still controversy, of course, about taking this sort of history; some analysts allow a preliminary interview or consultation to shape itself like an ordinary analytic session, and do little questioning or intervention. This type of interviewer may, eventually, produce a heavy interpretation, often directed at the deep unconscious, which may disturb the patient badly. This 'technique' is called 'addressing the patient's anxiety'. To my mind, it is both inept and callous, since the anxiety thus aroused cannot be worked through with the agent of its production. Others, myself included, deploy themselves actively during a consultation and garner an extensive history. I am not at all in favour of an abrupt and immediate introduction to such an unusual way of behaving as we manifest in our analytic stance. And we may learn very little about the patient. This question merits much fuller discussion and I have addressed it at length in two other papers (1987, this volume, Ch. 2; 1988). The value of the information gathered in the first interview is particularly high should the patient turn silent. I should add here that a silent patient often *cannot be predicted* right at the beginning; someone who fills the consultation, or first interview, with apparently eager and dynamic material may, when the analysis is under way, present one with a disconcerting shock, and one which taxes the analyst's skill to the utmost.

It is useful to have some theory in mind for regular contemplation, especially in conjunction with the preliminary history or with any small hints and guidelines one may have gathered subsequently. I will therefore review some of the many possible sources and developmental roots that ultimately manifest in the form of silence in the analytic situation. Some sorts of silence may be traced to the psychosexual stages of early development, although often enough we find a mixed picture in which problems ultimately traceable to very early stages are compounded by the events of later stages, especially, and most commonly, by the complicating influence of superego development. For example, silence in the presence of primitive oral pathology always carries the marks of the power of the superego and the anxiety which it can arouse. A patient who is greedy and demanding may have fears of his insatiability and its alienating effects, and this may drive him to silence. Or he may be sadistic, and afraid of his unconscious wishes to bite, devour and hurt; even, more consciously, of his known capacity for wounding verbal attack.

It is possible to have in one's mind, for scanning and assistance, a rough outline of the developmental stages, and the sorts of psychopathology which are commonly associated with them, and, always allowing for the complex interaction of developmental features, to propose some working ideas for oneself which will help to guide one's thinking. This may facilitate creative, informed attention – even, at times, inspiration.

Theoretical ideas which may constructively come to mind may be concerned with such affects as meanness, spite and grudgingness – which are not uncommon features in the silent patient. There is a type of withdrawal and retention which suggests distortions in the anal phase of development, and one may be usefully guided in the analytic work by tentatively making these theoretical connections. Meanness is sometimes disguised under the more self-acceptable concept of 'being shy', or feeling unworthy or of no importance. I am not saying that these ideas in the patient are not genuine, but it is surprising how they are never complete in themselves; the conscious convictions always conceal other characteristics which are less narcissistically agreeable to the patient. People who rather pride themselves – quaintly, to my mind – on 'being very shy', are not at all pleased to discover that they are self-absorbed, ungrateful and mean, or even spiteful and hostile.

Shame is another common proximal cause of silence; mentally reviewing one's own theory of superego development, with special attention to the formulation and maintenance of the ego-ideal, can be most useful. The analysis of shame – as opposed to guilt – can be a detailed and difficult task in the analysis of the silent patient. It is a sturbborn form of resistance. A woman whom I treated through her thirties was speechlessly ashamed, as a habitual state of mind, of the tragic eccentricity of her family history; her mother had committed suicide when the patient was four, taking the family dog with her, by jumping under a train. The father, to a great extent, abandoned the patient and her elder sister, who herself also later committed suicide while my patient was in analysis with me. This sister, though rather desperately loved by the patient, had been psychiatrically ill for many years; she strangled her cat and her budgerigars before she finally killed herself. My patient was deeply silent; we gradually unravelled a potent tangle of shame and unprocessed sorrow.

Occasionally, patients who fall silent have a great longing to please, in conflict with a deep fear of getting something wrong. This may well originate in cumulative traumata of early childhood. One encounters, very occasionally (I have treated two), examples of someone who is a liar, who knows he is a liar, who has a partial wish to speak the truth and be known, and yet, through a psychic conditioning from lying and from fear, has a double-edged problem in that he *really* does not know his truth. He may start analysis by thinking that he does, and the early months may contain much increasingly painful verbal effort to disentangle himself from this state, or – more likely – skate along over the top of it. It is when it begins to dawn on him that he has reached a state of utter confusion between lying and truth that he falls silent. This is a tough, long test of patience and skill for the analyst.

Then I had one, unique, example of a patient who came into analysis with a fixed belief that analysts speak in a sort of code, and *expect patients to do the same*. He was never silent throughout any one session, at least in the first few years, but he qualified, by my original definition, in so far as he never spoke to me for more than about 10 per cent of the time. He presented an extremely interesting problem. All his communications were quite extraordinary; it was rather like being faced with a sophisticated, intellectual word-puzzle. The whole difficulty was compounded by the fact that, although I had tried to speak back to him with the utmost simplicity, I gradually realized, from his tortuous, tangential responses, which often did not come for several days, that he was reading hidden messages into everything I said, with the result that it all turned into veiled, obscure material which was almost entirely removed from anything I had *meant*, and frequently had assumed a strong persecutory flavour. I will shortly give an example from his analysis.

Sharing a similar, but even stronger, sense of persecution, are patients who are assailed by *too much* from the unconscious. One gains the impression that under an often sociable and successful veneer, the unconscious is uncomfortably stuffed with unassimilated, unprocessed material; indeed, these patients sometimes present for treatment when the pressure from the depths becomes unbearably threatening, as if at the point where the cellar door is about to burst upon and flood the 'self' with unthinkable terrors. The presenting complaints are, understandably, confused and vague, such as: 'I just don't feel right', 'It's as if I've become overshadowed', 'I can't seem to concentrate or enjoy life as I used to.' The sociable and often charming presenter cannot accurately be termed a False Self, I think; such affect as is allowed to trickle through is genuine, and the ego development has an authentic quality. The patient may talk eagerly in analysis for several months, as the initial pressures are relieved; but then the real bulk of the cellar contents becomes unavoidable, and a kind of paralytic darkness sets in. I have written briefly about such a patient in another paper, 'Slouching towards Bethlehem . . .' (1986; this volume, Ch. 1) an account of a man who fell into a long malevolent silence, and whose analysis I only, eventually, rescued by a burst of fury. Unfortunately, that paper, as a result, has become widely known as 'the paper where Dr Coltart shouted at a patient', which to my mind, does less than justice to the rest of it! It is also an indication of how rarely analysts write about their own emotional input into their work.

One specific form of this overwhelming mass of stuff in the unconscious, leading to silence, which I encountered in one patient, was massive unprocessed sorrow. Surprisingly, this was not the woman with the suicided mother and sister, but another woman, in her early forties, who had had to become the breadwinner for her mother and younger brother and sisters at the age of sixteen, when her deeply-loved and idealized father had died very suddenly at work at the age of forty-one. She dealt with her sorrow by an extensive identification with him, in every imaginable way, until she ground to a halt, exhausted and empty, and had to wait in near silence for many months with me before we slowly prised the cellar door open, and released her mourning and her finding of her adult self. This woman, incidentally, also provides an example of a quirky aspect of our work, and that is the involuntary bestowing of a silent nickname by the analyst – I have found that when this phenomenon occurs, the nickname thrown up by the analyst's unconscious invariably carries an apt cogency about the patient's psychopathology. I went to collect this woman from the waiting-room one day, and she was sitting hunched and bowed in my low chair, crouching near the fire, and unaware when I arrived at the door. I suddenly thought of her as a little hedgehog, and 'Little Hedgehog' she is in my mind to this day.

Finally, in our theorizing about silence, we will, at some point, find ourselves thinking about resistance and what is called 'controlling the analyst'. I rather hesitate even to bring this in, let alone make much of it. This is because, in a way, it is so obvious, and can rapidly deteriorate into one of those mindless clichés that can block our attention from more subtle areas of understanding. Of course, these patients are resisting; and of course, the effect of much silence *is* to control the analyst, and this may turn out to be dynamically important in the patient's psychopathology. But if it is, and if one is going to embark on using this idea as an interpretation, one must have some way of *making it dynamic*. The kind of flat, limited statement which it can be presented as, often feels no more than accusatory to the patient, and interpretations which may be experienced as accusing should always be avoided at all costs; they lead nowhere except to further frustration and defensiveness. To my mind, this is one of the main flaws in the theory and technique which focuses from the start on very early development and its supposed fantasy life; the interpretations, especially from inexperienced or ungifted analysts, can sound like accusations, or omnipotent in their apparent clarity. To be told, for example, when one is feeling blocked and speechless and little else, that one is envious and is angrily attacking something good – *before* one has any understanding of this part of analytic territory, or is in any way conscious of the sort of thing being referred to – may only induce further resistance, unhappiness or a form of almost brainwashed subservience.

Now I want to leave the exploration of the root causes of silence and turn to technical problems presented by silent or very noncommunicative patients. First, as I said at the beginning, we have to face the fact of silence itself, often – especially in one's first experience of it – a strange and unwelcome shock. Much or all that one has faithfully taken in during one's training, and with cases under supervision, goes out of the window. We have no words from the patient, and can think of none of our own – no dreams to explore, no free association to set us out on trails, no obvious clues for detective work at all. What is this? Not what we were led to expect. Where is that chatty, desperate, seemingly open patient of the preliminary interview? Instead of searching sensitively for an opening in the patient's material in which to plant our careful interpretations, cleverly worked out to pinpoint a certain unconscious direction to that material, we are presented with almost endless openings, with practically nothing in-between! So the whole question of the timing of what we say becomes, if anything, more, not less, urgent. If the patient hasn't spoken for two days, do we open the next session? Do we say something after half-an-hour? At the end? Or not till next week? What is our countertransference telling us? Do we feel amazed, anxious, interested, peaceful or irritable? It will be appreciated – reluctantly perhaps – that I cannot give satisfactory 'answers' to the many questions that arise in the mind. Gradually, we begin to create our own ways of managing this enormous problem, and these will probably differ with each patient, though we may get out of practice, and some analysts may never even meet the problem.

This, to my mind, would be a pity and a loss. I say this not only because one's skills are taxed to the uttermost, but also because this sort of work brings its own great rewards and pleasures. I think I can safely say, now that I am nearing the end of my practice, that my own preference, above all others, is for a silent patient. We have the great privilege of time to reflect really deeply on what we are doing, and on what we eventually do say. This contrasts most agreeably with the usual hurly-burly of sessions with freely-talking patients when, if the truth is really admitted, we work on the run, largely from our unconscious and preconscious, and impose shape and meaning on the sessions afterwards at the end of the day or week, or even years later when we are writing a paper! Also, here is an opportunity to develop patience, maybe even patient endurance. The art of 'negative capability' is given a

real chance to grow. We are shown the pace of true changes, at
depth, in personalities, and this is often far slower than more
exciting day-to-day work may suggest. And above all, we have the
gratifying, if at times alarming, sense that we are truly heard in
what we say. One thing we can be sure of with a silent patient is
that both participants *listen*. Our listening, indeed our whole
attention span, becomes unbelievably sharpened. And so does that
of the silent patient. For both analyst and patient, there is time to
observe, through every available sense – hearing, sight and even
smell. In fact, I pay a lot of attention to smell; if a patient who
normally does not smell unpleasant starts sweating and smelling,
he or she is saying something as surely as if speaking. Younger
analysts often find this hard to refer to, and it never becomes easy.
But, especially if a few days pass and the phenomenon continues,
it is worth it; it does not often occur, but it is normally a mixture
of fear and aggression, and the patient *can* handle our speaking of
it, and, indeed, be grateful, and relieved.

The transference, and more especially, the countertransference,
allied with the sharpened powers of observation, become the
instruments par excellence of the work. We are given the opportunity to learn the vital distinction between doing wild analysis,
and using the countertransference, intuition, and observations to
do skilful, economic analysis to the point. Of course, one will
'guess' at times, there may be nothing else for it, but there is a
difference between partly informed guessing, and wild analysis. I
will not explore the history of the development of the use of the
countertransference, or of the transference, but I want to say here
that on this very specialized subject, the silent patient, the two
books so far produced by Christopher Bollas, *The Shadow of the
Object* (1987) and *Forces of Destiny* (1989), are no less than
inspiring.

I would like to emphasize that the best work with the silent
patient is done within the transference, by means of the finely
tuned instrument of the countertransference. One may say this is
true of all analysis; but often, here, we encounter it in its purest
form, without the mass of comment, facilitation, extra-transference
interpretation and reconstruction, which occupy the bulk of many
ordinary analytic sessions. Tiny threads of reaction and response
in the self can be examined in peace, whereas in an ordinary

analytic session they may pass unnoticed. With the silent patient, the finest details can be addressed, often leading one knows not where; yet as one works them over slowly, larger dynamic shapes appear on the horizon, until finally a comprehensive, mutative interpretation may be reached, and weeks of slow, sporadic interchange pay off.

Occasionally one may need to ask direct questions. These often feel necessary at the beginning of what may turn out to be a long silent phase, and are generalized in form – 'You seem stuck today – what are your thoughts?' or 'Is something particularly bothering you or holding you up?' or 'Is there something difficult you want to say about me or being here?' These may produce nothing, or more likely they will provide a small lead. They may be phrased, less intrusively, as tentative suggestions rather than queries, and indeed, I would recommend this in preference to the question form, which may feel pressurizing to the patient. Michael Balint used to say: 'Ask a question, and you'll get an answer. But it won't tell you much!' A special example of useful questioning occurred in the analysis of the patient who was mostly silent, but used code, to whom I referred earlier. In order to clarify the process, I found that it was increasingly necessary to ask questions which helped with the decoding: 'Are you really talking about something different?' 'Doesn't that refer to so-and-so?' or even 'What do you mean?' I gradually found the effect of this manoeuvre was to reassure the patient that I really wanted to *know*; that this wasn't some monstrous, evil word-game, and that truth could be spoken openly. However, he and I were capable of bad failures of communication, and one occurred just before a break, which carried over well into the next period of work. A brief remark I had made in the last session as a reminder about a changed session during the next term's work was (mis)understood by him to be a contemptuous and unkind allusion to the length of the holiday. Many days of silence occurred when we started work again, before he burst out accusingly about my 'cruelty' several weeks ago. I was truly dumbfounded. I thought back to that last session, including my fairly neutral reminder, which had been kindly meant. 'When? What?' I said at last, rather feebly. He tried to fill me in, with furious sarcasm. Fortunately, I knew some of his coding and his semi-psychotic states of mind well enough to be able to field this eventually in the transference at the right sort of level. But it does convey a feeling of how a mixture of silence and code can prolong extreme misunderstandings; and also of the power of the transference for the silent patient. He did a sort of personnel job in industry, and the few enigmatic references during the first couple of weeks had been to tasks arising in the course of that job, difficulties with staff. I knew he often used these as vehicles for conveying something about himself to me, but I had been completely out of touch with the fact that my remark at the end of the previous term had hit him so badly. It really taught me a lesson about not yielding to impulse at such a sensitive time as the end of a last session before a break, and also about restraining one's inclination to 'look after' people. As a child, he had suffered from excessive but completely impersonal, sometimes neglectful, care from too many people, and he responded far better now to a consistent austerity than to anything in my manner which he could construe as shallow or untrustworthy. I say 'eventually' I fielded it in the transference; my immediate reaction was almost entirely governed by my narcissism. I was taken aback, hurt and angry in about equal amounts. I think I made that sort of noise that gets written as 'Phew!' I then said he was sometimes like a submarine in the analysis which would let off occasional torpedoes and get me amidships; I added rather acidly, since he sometimes tried to play a trapping game with theory and language, that I did not intend to explore the anal symbolism of what I had just said. *Then* I started to address the transference, and we sorted it out – but it doesn't always happen at once.

Incidentally, this also presents an example of the extent to which great fears of loss and abandonment in silent patients can, if there is quite a strong psychotic element in the transference, seem to provoke precisely what is most feared. I'm not sure that this isn't in itself a fact of life – that we provoke or set up what we most fear. But I emphasize this here because it takes me back to the analyst's own silence, which occasionally may feel persecutory to the patient – and this may be extremely difficult to manage when the patient is giving one little or nothing else to go on. A key factor in the resolution of this impasse is an absence of real persecuting feelings in the analyst. One has to struggle to *learn* to be benevolent and truly patient in the silence and authentically deploy negative capability. It can't really be acted, and very few people are naturally inclined to total benevolence, but it can be learned. The manifold qualities of silence itself are a source of considerable information, but the observation of them is a two-way process; the patient is studying the analyst's silence with just as much keenness as the analyst is studying his. If the analyst is irritated, provoked, frustrated, angry, withdrawn or thinking about other things, the patient will speedily pick it up, or some distorted version of it, and one will hear about it sooner or later. This is why it is so important in learning to be silent to *practise* benevolent, neutral patience; it does come with practice. If one is truly at home with oneself, then silence will not usually feel provocative; if one is peacefully observing, one is in a far better state to pick up and recognize the patient's projections into oneself. And there will be plenty of these, and they can lead to making fairly accurate interpretations. It is thus that one of the main uses of the countertransference comes into its own.

Perhaps this is a good moment to say a little more about what I feel is the necessity for developing our own personal philosophy of life and hence of work and of treatment, if we are to work steadily in this strange job for many years; and especially with patients like these who can stretch our endurance, ingenuity and special qualities to the utmost limits. If one is fortunate enough to have a natural leaning towards silence and its manifestations, they will not tax one quite so much; but if one has not, one will be cast into the depths of self-examination and discipline, and there are certain qualities in life-attitudes which will then support one. 'There is nothing either good or bad, but thinking makes it so,' as Hamlet said; and there is no particular credit attaching to feeling comfortable with silent patients rather than not; it is no more a matter for that sort of judgement than is a preference for working with hysterics rather than obsessionals – and vice versa. But there are certain characteristics of our philosophy which need constant attention if we are to develop them into strong, flexible, and reliable features on which we can depend when we do *not* have conscious time or space for attention to them. These include patience, the capacity to tolerate not knowing, benevolent neutrality and a kind of sustained close interest, all of which I have referred to already. But there are larger encompassing containers for these, which I think of as the living matrix for all we are and do. I have written about them from different perspectives, and in different papers, already. One is faith, which is really what 'Slouching towards Bethlehem' (1986; this volume, Ch. 1) is about; faith in our training, in the extraordinary process which we help to create – psychoanalysis, and in ourselves as, 'avoiding memory and desire' (Bion, 1970, p. 34), we sit out the mysterious process day by day. The other, which I touched on in 'On the tightrope' (this volume, Ch. 7), and wrote about more fully in 'What does it mean: "Love is not enough"?' (this volume, Ch. 8), is love. I am speaking of love here not in any careless, sentimental, or erotic way. I am not talking about 'liking' our patients. Indeed, if love, in the deep sustaining mode which I am meaning, is operating quietly, as the living infrastructure of our life-philosophy, and therefore of our philosophy of work, it is perfectly possible to dislike, or even hate, a patient for necessary periods of time during analysis, secure in the faith that this is a temporary problem, due either to projections, the patient's pathology, or our own countertransference, and that it can be survived creatively, having yielded valuable information. Liking people is anyway subject to fluctuations in a way that love is not. A deep and thorough professional attitude which may best be described as being *with* patients, *on their side* in the search for truth and health, does not necessarily entail an obligation, moral or otherwise, to like them and certainly not to 'take their side' in a prejudiced way; it is one of the strongest therapeutic factors in psychoanalysis that our whole style and attitude makes the patient feel, rightly, *important* to us over a long period, and this is fundamentally different from partisanship. Vicissitudes of this feeling are there for analysts to work on within themselves, and are helpful pointers rather than insuperable obstacles. I imagine, anyway, that we all mostly have the repeated experience of coming to like, certainly to care for, and probably, if we are deeply open to ourselves, and unafraid, to *love*, each patient as the analysis unfolds. I intensely disliked the code-man for a long time, and eventually had a huge row with him before I finally came to loving him. I hesitated to employ this emotive and frequently misunderstood word for many years until such time as it was borne in on me compellingly that it *was* the word I wanted – for the main informing ingredient of this vital matrix of our philosophy of doing analysis, and most especially with patients who test one in certain extreme ways, as silent patients most surely do.

I have referred to the importance of economy in making interpretations. A little goes a very long way with silent patients. Often they can take in no more than they can give, maybe less. Efforts should be made not only to be as accurate as possible, but to be as simple as possible. I will not stress the importance of leaving out any sort of language which smacks of theorizing or the intellectual, because this would hold for all analyses. But in the virtual absence of communications, simple interpretations about weekends, holidays, the last session, have strength and impact. Interpretations which may often develop a kind of banal quality of cliché when made many times during the course of an ordinary talking analysis, for example, 'I think you may be rather dreading the break' take on a new and luminous quality when they fall into a pool of silence, especially if the atmosphere seems anxious or apprehensive. When I referred earlier to fine detail in the transference–countertransference work, I did not mean wordiness. The analyst should avoid the temptation to speak too much, as if for the relief of hearing a voice, even if it is only his own. Most things that we think of to say, even quite complicated things, can be pruned, and one of the privileges of work with a silent patient is that we have the space and time to develop our own style at its most economical, pruned of superfluous verbiage.

Some people advocate the use of comments on body language as a way of breaking through the barriers. I think this can be very useful, but I would advise extreme caution. With luck, one may have had an early opportunity to get to know one's patient fairly well before a silent phase occurs, and then carefully-honed interpretations of body language may be valuable. But it is worse than useless to say to a patient who, for example, already suffers from severe self-consciousness, 'You seem very angular and tense in your movements today.' Or to an erythrophobic patient, 'I noticed you blushed when I spoke yesterday.' The effect will be counterproductive; the patient may even not come for the next session.

This brings me directly to a few thoughts on eccentric forms of silence. One of these is absence; after all, a patient who voluntarily stays away is for that time a silent patient. A patient of mine whose father had spent most of the war in hiding in an enemy country while he and his mother were safely over here, stayed away from the analysis at a crucial stage for nearly three months. Using intuition, combined with what I already knew, I did not try to recall or contact him. I sent him a bill every four weeks and he paid it. When he returned, we were able to work out the hitherto unprocessed miseries of his own guilt at being safe – and of his identification with his (temporarily) 'lost', hidden father. The first task for the analyst when the patient returns is to listen attentively for the meaning of the absence, and tackle it before all else. A mute acceptance by the analyst of any clear piece of acting-out is technically wrong. The patient will be waiting for that piece of analysis, even if only fearfully, with a fantasy of punishment or the analyst's hurt feelings; and to omit it is felt by the patient to be a let-down, or confirmation of a fear.

Another manifestation of silence is sleep. I would not suggest that a patient be woken up, except at the end of a session, nor at that point, I think, should the analyst comment on it. We must respect our patients' needs, even if the primary need is for defence, and eventually, analysis of the phenomenon will be permitted to occur. My most dramatic sleeping patient was the woman who was silent in the early part of her analysis through shame and sorrow over what she regarded as her unbearably eccentric and tragic family history. We did four years' work on that, and she became in many ways a talking patient, and a bit better from her lifelong depression. Then she suddenly fell asleep, and she slept without speaking for seven months! This is the record I referred to early in this paper. It sounds like one of those long trance states described by Oliver Sacks in his extraordinary book *Awakenings* (1973). And as far as her sessions with me were concerned, that is exactly what it was like. I assumed, rightly as it turned out later, that she had continued to go to work and lead her life otherwise during those months – in which, of course, two breaks, the Easter and the summer ones, intervened. Eventually, she awakened, an immeasurably changed person. From having been severely depressed, flattened in affect, slow in speech even when not silent, she now prattled – no other word would be quite so accurate – gaily and endlessly about the details of her life; her whole life, including the good bits of the past, which I had never heard about before. We came to the conclusion that she was living out something she had never had or done; it was 'as if' she was coming in from school, or the playground, and chattering about her life to her mother. This continued for nearly a year, during which we also worked deeply into what had been the meaning of her sleep phase, how it had contained exorcism of the internalized dead mother, as well as trust and regression to preverbal feeding and caring. Then, with a strong sense of something attempted, something done, she quite soon ended her analysis, and from then on lived a reasonably happy and normal life. She keeps in touch by means of the occasional letter. She and I came to understand that the sleeping was an essential period of recuperation, healing and renewal. She had, by the time it appeared, exhausted for the moment her capacity to make use of ordinary analysis which she had used fruitfully for a couple of years after emerging from the shame-silence. I would say overall that this was one of the most successful analytic treatments that has occurred in my practice, and yet it was, for long stretches of time, one of the most unorthodox. This leads me to realize, in this context and perhaps for the first time, that as a matter of fact, all my silent patients did well in the end. I am not sure what this means and it will probably repay further study.

A very brief word on humour. It is characteristic of the silent patient, and can be explored most valuably: I have written and spoken elsewhere (this volume, Ch. 7) of some of the dangers inherent in the use of humour by the analyst, especially the use of heavy irony, which is open to misunderstanding; or telling jokes, which is always a recipe for disaster. But not to appreciate and respond to humour in a patient is, I think, churlish and affected: even when used defensively or aggressively, which is often, it can, if really funny, be appreciated audibly as well as analysed. Many very silent patients are skilful in their use of irony, double meanings, and seeing the wrily funny side of things: a humorous remark by a patient which can be responded to in kind by the analyst may cover a lot of ground, and have more impact than the most careful, fully serious, longer interpretation. With close attention to not colluding in defences to the exclusion of work, humour can be a useful and enjoyable mode of exchange. I will not give any examples, as in my experience nothing falls flatter or sounds deadlier than an old, reported 'funny' passage in analysis.

There is one thing more I want to say about the silent patient, the most salient and perhaps surprising feature of the whole phenomenon. Maybe I have indicated it already – I hope so. It is that these patients are never boring. I am not even quite sure why not. But I know from my experience with my eight silent patients that they do not send me to sleep, invite my attention to wander, nor bore me. Perhaps the hidden reason for this lies in one of the best comments that was ever made about such people – by an analyst called Arlow, in a paper in 1961. He said 'The magnificence of silence . . . is its very ambiguity' (p. 51).

7

On the tightrope: therapeutic and non-therapeutic factors in psychoanalysis

I was asked to be one of the speakers at a symposium, organized by the British Psycho-Analytical Society, on therapeutic and non-therapeutic factors in psychoanalysis. I welcomed the opportunity to put together some thoughts about the exercise of our 'impossible profession'. It occurred to me that one might compare the daily work of an analyst to that of a tightrope walker. The tightrope itself is the years-long stretch of sessions, in which we try to do, in partnership with our patients, something which has been called impossible and is by any standards unusual. Of course, the analogy fails in the sense that we do actually walk to the very end of the tightrope, wherever that may be. But what are the factors which contribute to the balancing act? The all-embracing subtitle provides us with an opportunity to examine some of them in detail.

If one is on a tightrope and it is not far from the ground, and so there is not far to fall, then it may not matter; sooner or later, and quite often, fall one will. By falling to one side of the analytic tightrope, one may do something therapeutic, and by falling to the other, non-therapeutic. The metaphor can be developed to the point of exaggeration, so that, for example, falling off the tightrope one way may be experienced as abrasive and assaulting to one's patients, and falling off it the other way may be experienced as frightening or dislocating to oneself – though perhaps not too bad at all for the patient. It is a source of great surprise to the young analyst – and never becomes a matter for complacency – that, more

This is an amended version of a paper first given at a day conference of the British Psycho-Analytical Society, in 1987.

frequently than not, a clumsy, ill-timed interpretation, or something that may seem like a worryingly awkward technical error, is later reported back to one as having been helpful, enlightening, or a rich source of further reflection. Such an event is not only a relief, but also a healthy reminder of just how little one knows much of the time. The constant aim is to stay on the tightrope, and maybe a psychoanalyst's early years have to be spent in never-flagging attempts to refine and perfect one's balancing acts. The metaphor itself wobbles as one searches for a definition of 'positive' therapeutic factors; it begins to look as if it is the complex act of *staying on the rope*, however achieved, the act of movement while balancing, that is positive, whatever the constituents of the 'therapeutic factors' involved.

If there is anything that can accurately be considered to be the one aid the tightrope walker always carries – the pole – it has to be interpretation. There is little new or original to be written about interpretation, from any angle; nor, truthfully, about its subordinates – comment, confrontation, explanation, 'preparation' – these are all the groundwork done in the build-up to interpretations. But interpretation has silent partners, too, which need repeated acts of attention from us, not only as we work, but also at the beginnings and endings of the working day. Silent, unnoticed, as they often are, they are, or can be in their quiet way, consistently positive therapeutic factors. They are the features which become so much part of our daily life and work with patients that direct observation and reference to them may only rarely be made during the course of analyses: they include consistency of the setting, provision for quietness, attention to punctuality, exactness about money, and an alert awareness to any changes which may occur in any of these. This last point includes listening for oblique references to such changes, from the patient, or, if none is heard, alluding to the changes ourselves, if we have spotted them, because extremely detailed noticing by patients goes on, even if some of it is unconscious or suppressed. I have written more fully elsewhere (1990; this volume, Ch. 12) on factors such as these, both in relation to our patients and, at deeper levels which touch on our whole philosophy of life, to ourselves as analysts.

Although so much has long since been said, it is impossible to avoid completely the subject of interpretation, its theory and

technique. It is vast and daunting. For three quarters of a century
now, this one subject – our balancing pole on the tightrope – has
provided scope for discussion, definition, disputes, denigrations,
demonstrations and development. Controversy flows back and
forth. In the end it is individual analysts who use their own
analysis, their training and themselves to realize the truth of the
ever-recurring phenomenon that one becomes what suits one best,
and what gives one the deepest sense of self-forgetful confidence.
The temptation here to discover and subdivide and discuss a
number of selected ideas within the field is great. When, why, how
and what to interpret is the balancing act of our daily lives. Some
theorists would see us struggling to make a transference interpretation at all costs – perhaps at the cost of falling off the rope into
the pit of ignoring historical meaning; this is a real danger,
especially to the inexperienced. We may fall into an inclination to
exaggerate the intense influence of the analyst, to the exclusion of
all other object-relationships in the patient's life. Some theorists,
on the other hand, stress continued reference to the past, with
many laborious reconstructions; with this technique there is a
danger of ignoring the potential illumination of the here-and-now
impact, or of making the patient feel misunderstood and neglected
in the present. Persistent avoidance of the immediate message of
the living transference is an anti-therapeutic factor, a fall from the
tightrope; but sustained ignorance of the developmental, chronological nuances which give meaning to a patient's life is the opposite
danger. Patients have a great need to have their intimate personal
history heard, known and used. We owe an everlasting debt to
Strachey for his unforgettable statement on the mutative interpretation; this was in his paper in the *International Journal of Psycho-
Analysis* of 1934, in which he is now almost exclusively remembered for saying that only the transference interpretation effects
mutation; we owe him gratitude for its positive teaching. But there
is a price to be paid for his clarifying, and his forceful advocacy;
the price is that he evokes a kind of anxiety in many people, while
they are learning their own balancing act, by misleading us with
what Blum called his 'sweeping charismatic absolutism' (1983,
p. 594). *Pure transference analysis is an idealized fiction*, and it was
the *core* of truth in Strachey's remark, which has become idealized,
that has fostered the dangerous notion that it can be realizable. It

is often forgotten that towards the end of that classic paper, Strachey was *also* writing:

> If I may take an analogy from trench warfare, the acceptance of the transference interpretation corresponds to the capture of a key position, while the extra-transference interpretations correspond to the general advance . . . An oscillation of this kind between transference and extra-transference interpretations will represent the normal course of events in an analysis. (p. 158)

One of the only things I want to add to this brief consideration of the act of interpreting is an absolute necessity: that one should have reached it with conviction oneself. This holds for our constant scrutiny and attempts to understand the countertransference, as well. If the countertransference is scrupulously observed and there is a serious wish and intention to build an interpretation based on information derived from it, then it must be done with great care, for the sake of authenticity; not too theoretical, not forced, not overemotional (though the subjective experience we are having may be deeply felt), but reflectively authentic. To keep the countertransference as 'pure' as possible, as Betty Joseph has expressed it, is part of our daily self-study.

In this connection, we may consider further a particular aspect of therapy which is to do with our technique. This has to be organically linked to our theories, but it is, of course, also an expression of our character, our ways of thinking and our personal style. There is a paradox here -- a subject I delve into more deeply in 'What does it mean: "Love is not enough"?' (this volume, Ch. 8). On the one hand it is essential to study and learn and develop a *general* technique, with attention to timing, tact, dosage, selection of language, and level of interpretation; on the other hand, there is the ever-present phenomenon that every patient is unique, and any generalized statement about how to do what, when, where and why, must always be subject to modifications in the light of the patient's uniqueness and our unique developing relationship to him and his personality. This is at the heart of clinical skill as opposed to clinical cleverness; the latter is nothing of the sort if it produces a piece of intellectual brilliance but fails to communicate with the patient in a mode which can be understood. The art of the positive therapeutic approach is to watch and learn and *follow* and adjust technique to meet the needs of each individual. How do we create the 'right atmosphere' for the process of good-enough analysis? This is not an easily answerable question; one arranges the setting, and keeps it quiet and constant, but the atmosphere of the analysis is the joint creation of the patient and the analyst, and between this unique pair it grows and 'happens'. In fact, if I were to settle for which of the pair in the therapeutic dyad has more influence than the other on the whole way-of-being of an analysis, I would say it is the patient. Throughout his two excellent books, *The Shadow of the Object* (1987), and *Forces of Destiny* (1989), Christopher Bollas describes this process of creation from many viewpoints. In any given treatment, the methods operating in the patient as he 'uses' his analyst inevitably ordain to a great extent the whole of the analyst's response, however personalized his own most deeply characterological style may be.

However, one of our own contributions to this creation, which we can never avoid, stretches from the beginning to the end of our professional lives and changes with ourselves alone; we have no choice about being on this aspect of the tightrope, and learning to walk it every day. I refer to where we are in our lives – in other words, our age – both chronological and as trained analysts: there are positive and negative therapeutic characteristics at all ages. Sometimes I notice that students feel, or this gets projected into them, that to be young is a horrible handicap, which with luck will be grown out of; but one of the positive factors about being young in analytic years is enthusiasm. Freshness to the whole thing is another. There is often a strong devotion to the task, a flexible readiness to learn and to explore, and eagerness to *practise* and listen with an open mind, as yet not too clouded by theory, views and opinions. Such qualities contribute towards successful treatments; they compensate for anxieties, inexperience, and excessive respect for elders, the sort of idealizing transferences which float about in Institutes.

Sometimes, now, when I look back over the early years of building up a practice, when one gratefully accepted whatever came one's way, and just got stuck in, I shudder and wonder at some of the gross psychopathology that revealed itself on our proud, young couches. Or at times, of course, *off* them, as we sat through session after session of violent acting-out, with the patient storming,

crying, crouching, throwing things, in one case cutting herself –
either in one's room, or God knew where. Across my mind's eye,
there lurches such a procession – the woman who brought a long
kitchen knife, and sat in the chair opposite me, twirling it and
humming a careless little tune; this same woman, maddened with
anger because I 'tricked' her into handing over the knife, leaping
out of the chair and with one great sweep of her arm, hurling
everything on my mantelpiece off it on to the floor and all over me
– a carriage clock, two silver vases filled with water and freesias, a
little box which sprang open and poured out pins, brooches and
kerbigrips; an ivory carved netsuke, several postcards, and a cut-
glass scent jar. She stood over me triumphantly as I sat and dripped
among the ruins. 'There!' she spat out. 'You *minded*, didn't you? I
can see you blushing . . .' Then there was the woman of seventy-
three who had to end every session by crawling to the end of the
couch and diving head first off it to the floor; she called it 'being
born again'. She never listened to a word I said; this diving activity
was what she came for. And the extremely sadomasochistic doctor
with severe, life-threatening ulcerative colitis, who could start to
bleed from his rectum if I said something he didn't like, on one
occasion so profusely that he trembled and screamed in the lavatory
while I telephoned for the ambulance – and then visited him in
hospital daily for four weeks. And the senior 'alternative' therapist
(though that epithet had not yet arrived on the scene), who prowled
like an angry panther up and down, up and down, but if I spoke,
darted behind a chair and crouched there, making whimpering
animal cries, but glancing out from time to time to give me sharp,
baleful glares . . .

Yes, in youth one tackles tough cases, out of ignorance: I might
be terminally baffled or fed up *now*, but then – no. Baffled, yes,
but then that was part of the ignorance. I had worked in mental
hospitals, and I began to think that this was not so very different.
And since fools rush in where angels fear to tread, the foolish,
strictly dynamic interpretations one rushed in with must have done
something; it was almost as if chutzpah was the healing factor, or
what I earlier called our zeal, our fresh enthusiasm. All these
patients, with the exception of the exsanguinating doctor, did well,
after months or years of Uproar, as Beachcomber would have
called it. Early on, when one accepted severely disturbed people

out of ignorance and innocence and gratitude, I was given the
opportunity to learn how very often the deep causes of improvement in a patient's wellbeing are (and still often so remain) a
mystery.

Life goes on, and early zeal and fresh cathexis of the task in hand
are gradually replaced by increasing knowledge and confidence;
anxieties are slowly worked through, one learns some technical
skills, and there grows a developing sense of strength and security.
There is a saying that by the time you're fifty, you've got the face
you deserve; by now, I think too that by the time you're fifty,
you've got the analytic skill and style you deserve. Thus one set of
positive therapeutic factors is slowly, almost imperceptibly,
replaced by another: but in the latter, one is endangered by falls
from the tightrope in new directions. One may fall from clarity
and flexibility in one's thought processes, into more rigid positions.
It cannot be denied that arthritic changes slowly come about in
thought processes; the familiar awareness, which we are all
shrewdly perspicacious about *in other people*, of becoming more
dogmatic, more unavailable for mind-changing, slower, more con-
servative with a small c ('further to the right' is the political phrase
for it), brings real problems for us all. One of the greatest is that
this onset of rheumatic mental stiffness is harder to spot in
ourselves, and trying to work on it is a constant requirement, for
fear of self-scotomization, so fatally easy in the most experienced
analysts.

Leading on from this, I would like to refer to a comment which
a member of the audience made at the time when I first gave this
paper. He said that some people near him in the audience had
thought that, during the discussion, I 'hadn't talked enough' in
response to some of the questions and criticisms. This comment
revealed a paradoxical link with the foregoing survey of some of
the dangerous changes that may take place in us, imperceptibly, as
we grow older; for many people, these must include talking too
much. There is a distinct tendency, in ageing, perhaps especially in
women – am I wrong here? I hope so, but I fear not – to become
steadily more verbose. It is by no means restricted to analysts,
indeed it happens in almost every social stratum one encounters. It
is something to do with becoming less shy, less socially insecure,
more self-confident over all, and these are desirable things; but it

is also to do with becoming more dogmatic in one's view and one's thinking. If one does observe it in one's own self-scanning it is a feature that one should guard most scrupulously against. It may tend towards pomposity, which can turn into a dreadful sort of windbag effect; liking the sound of one's own voice, being very sure one is right, developing a conviction of authority to pontificate and impose one's views not only on the young, but on anyone at all who is listening. All this can be – is – not only deeply boring but also counter-therapeutic. A long-winded, heavy, slightly mud-dled interpretation, which may cover too much ground, lacks impact *in direct ratio* to its length and weight. In doing our psychoanalytic therapy there are a few – not many – Golden Rules: 'When in doubt, say nothing', and 'Prune where you can' are two which are always worth remembering. Winnicott used to teach 'Never deal with more than one thing in an interpretation'; this simple-sounding maxim is extraordinarily hard to achieve. If one catches oneself saying 'On the one hand . . . and on the other . . .', one needs to rein oneself in, however great the temptation to clarify with the patient a number of things in which one may just have perceived coherence; the patient is most unlikely to take in more than one thing, and even that may be made more difficult if confused with one or several others.

Patients are charitable, on the whole, and they get used to us and our personal styles and idiosyncrasies. The transference is often, itself, a scotoma for them: but often it is not, and they can be reflecting mirrors to their analysts as they nudge and criticize, and it is of positive value, to them and to us, that we heed them.

Contemplation of the subtle interactions of the transference and the countertransference leads on to 'mistakes'; a 'mistake', in content, or understanding, or direction of an interpretation, is not necessarily non-therapeutic. By what means and to what extent one *acknowledges* mistakes is worth a lot of consideration; there is another tightrope here. To fall off one way is to fail to refer to the error straight away if perceived, or anyway later; letting patients struggle on alone, without the required correction, and therefore under a remediable misapprehension not of their own making, compounds the mistake. Falling off the other way into a maelstrom of guilt (at the recognition that one has done something wrong) is a sign of unresolved anxiety in the analyst, besides being a dead end and a waste of energy. It blocks clear thinking, and may well inhibit the analyst from an unselfconscious look at exactly how the patient is responding and what can and should be made of that. There is nothing to be said for analytical sackcloth and ashes, which may in fact only strengthen a tendency to a sadistic response in the patient; or an insecure patient will become more uneasy still in the presence of an analyst who will be perceived to be unduly anxious and self-abasing. Acknowledgement of a crude mistake, the simplest example being over times or bills, is very likely, if skilfully and courteously handled, to become a positive therapeutic factor. Once an analyst has made this acknowledgement, indicating that not only does one not feel one ought to be omniscient but also that one can bear not being so, a mistake may be a fertile source of reminiscence and free association in the patient. Over the years, I have come to think that it is in itself a mistake to attach exaggerated power to *any one thing* that we say or do; from this overestimation can arise constricting and anxious fears, especially in the young analyst, about being 'destructive' to a patient or a treatment. This kind of anxiety is an error of judgement which may in itself be non-therapeutic, in that it may prevent one, for example, from hearing or seeing the way in which a mistake can be reclaimed, or from noticing potentially positive features arising from the event. These may include relief in the patient. Patients are in an exposed and dependent position; subtle ways in which they retain any power are not easily accessible to them; it is not our job to overemphasize their dependence or to strip them of realistic power, and it may well be that a recognition by them that the analyst can be wrong, or stupid, or know less than they do about various things, including themselves, may lead to beneficial results. On this matter of not attaching too much importance to any one thing one may say, it is instructive to meet patients *after* treatment – they often come back for one or two sessions, or to 'report'; and they often say 'I've never forgotten when you said . . .' and then go on to quote something one either does not remember or, more amazingly, something which at the time one thought was rather feeble, or more likely, not to the point, or even a mistake.

The event just described may, in a simple and straightforward way, even cause some quiet amusement in both patient and analyst, but the whole subject of amusement, and humour, and laughing, is not simple at all. On the contrary, it is very complex, and, within the metaphor of the tightrope, can be the cause of severe loss of balance, and maybe sharp and painful falls. I would like to concur here with a comment in a paper by Dr R. Baker in a *Bulletin* (1987) (the *Bulletin* is a sort of house magazine of the British Psycho-Analytical Society) concerning the hopeless ineptitude of ever 'telling a joke' to a patient: it may well take some considerable working through. To do it once is a salutary lesson; even as one embarks on it, a horrid sixth sense says that it is not going to be as funny as it might be at a party, or over dinner; one lumbers on to the punchline; either the patient rather tolerantly, or compliantly, laughs *or* there ensues the sort of reverberating silence that is not in any way pleasing to one's narcissism. One may find oneself immediately embarking on a further elaboration of *why* one made this now deeply tedious joke in the first place, and how it is supposed to relate to the patient; or one may sink back, covered in mortification, while the patient with weary aggression changes the subject, or, quite rightly, starts to criticize or express, at the very least, justifiable annoyance or, even worse, caps the joke with one of his own, and the imbroglio deepens. Occasionally, a patient who has the gift for telling a really funny story will recount a joke; it may be very amusing, and it would be inappropriate and rude to stifle laughter; nearly always it is extremely illuminating and one may then proceed to analyse it. For ourselves, to use humour to *make* a little joke (which is very different from telling one) at an exact psychological moment, can be an effective and succinct form of interpretation. A 'joke' in this sense can be one line or even one word – perhaps in a particular tone of voice which will be significant to the patient; or perhaps to underline a shared memory. But a word of warning is needed here, in terms of technique, and especially of timing; it is not a good idea to make a 'joke', as just described, or sound humorous or ironic, until a patient has been in treatment for quite a long time, and analyst and patient know each other pretty well; it can be heard in a persecutory or belittling way, and early in treatment is no time to risk this. Also, at any phase of the treatment one's aim and intention will be to perceive very accurately the current mood of patients, and not introduce a jarring 'humorous' note if they are cast down or depressed, or deeply reflective or very regressed.

It will have become apparent to my readers by now that I do not think that the tightrope, the daily balancing act, disappears, or is replaced by broad, firm, sunlit uplands as one grows older; on the contrary, though anxiety decreases and unselfconscious confidence in one's technique grows, new difficulties concomitant with the ageing process appear. But if, having practised for thirty years, one does not have *some* sorts of depths on which one relies with conviction, and which may be used as reserves of strength and inspiration and from which one can speak, with experience, then I think equally one would deserve criticism for impoverishment. A difficult area to tackle in this connection but one which I do not feel inclined to omit, is that of the philosophy which we develop about our life, ourselves and our work. Our own analyses helped, we hope, to stabilize our own psychic structure, and continuing development of our own internalized analytic function – for our own self-study – is a vital ingredient of the job. But alongside this many of us also incline to develop a conscious, active philosophy of life, deriving perhaps from some other field of study; for example, an ego-syntonic version of a religion, cultivated as an interest, a support or a sublimation, and organized in such a way that it becomes a philosophy of work as well as life. Whatever its origin, it helps us to continue to grow and not stagnate both emotionally and psychologically, and is a valuable instrument for managing ourselves in the taxing work we have chosen. It will assist in resolving anxieties in ourselves, and thus removing hindrances to self-disciplined creativity. I might make particular mention of the value of learning how to harness our aggression skilfully in the service of clinical work. Securely based in good theory, this in itself is a strongly positive factor. To learn to be tough and direct in analysis is important, and may take quite a long time. I can only say that patients always welcome it and experience it with relief. A sharply observant patient who is tuned in to his analyst with his 'third ear' just as surely as the analyst is to him, will probably know very well if one is flannelling a bit, and trying to be less sharp than one feels; equally if one is genuinely concerned for his wellbeing, the patient will recognize it, however tough one is in the work. And one cannot be authentically tough, even hard if required, unless one is free of anxiety, and truly unafraid in oneself, at great depth. To be consistently loving in one's behaviour takes much practice, and an essential ingredient is to be unafraid. To speak about it in direct language is truly difficult. There is a very real potential for loss of balance on the tightrope; criticisms of sloppiness, evasion of theoretical issues, and sentimentality may arise and may be well-founded. Overtones of religiosity – as opposed to thought rooted in experience of a genuine philosophical or religious tradition – rightly stand as anathema to psychoanalysts; to some they are exaggeratedly distasteful, especially to analysts whose own cultural condition is profoundly secular, and this is part of the difficulty of the balancing act on this particular tightrope. The concept of love, not by any means always arising from religious convictions, as the informing energy of various professional practices, including our own, has in fact nothing sentimental, careless or erotic about it. Indeed, since anxiety about a feeble technique, or a shallow, inauthentic quality, is aroused by this sort of language, it might be as well to remind ourselves that both in Greek philosophy and early religious thought the concept of agape is used to describe a strongly-felt, but non-sensual love, in contrast to that of eros. Agape was originally the term used for the religious feast which was shared by loving friends, hence Holy Communion. It could also mean a ceremonial form of celebration between two or more people; this view of it is valuable to us. As Bollas has described in *Forces of Destiny* (1989), celebration between analyst and patient over a piece of significant work achieved can be a genuine and integral part of an analysis, and can consolidate an already positive piece of work.

Our continued involvement in the psychic suffering of others, our drive to maintain this involvement with a view to making people 'feel better', must, it seems to me, of necessity have a whole conceptual, philosophical, framework round it. We need to work continuously on building, strengthening and deepening such a philosophy, which some reflection reveals as a philosophy of life itself, *for* ourselves, with, for us, its very special dimension relating to our work. Many people become more aware of the need for this as they grow older, when they have more space and peace of mind to contemplate it after the primary construction of their years of detailed work on theory and technique. We need to ask ourselves often why we do *this* work, where do our sustained urges to repair and heal come from, and not lose touch with the meaning of this for *us*. It is primarily for our own benefit that we make this enquiry of ourselves, but the direct result which we can rest on in our working life is that this life is deepened and strengthened by the enquiry. Our own personal religious or philosophical views should not, in my opinion, be directly referred to in communication with patients, with only very rare exceptions. But if we ourselves find we need a reliable philosophy of life, which we may reflect and act upon – which is thinkable, in other words – it can only prove to be a refreshing source of renewable energy. We must all face the tasks of ageing and of our death, and if we deny the enhancing support of studying our lives and their meanings for us, it is likely that we will create emptier analyses. A kind of automaticity is a danger here, as we rely on routines, safe ways we have trodden many times before, which, conjoined with the possibilities of rigidification which I touched on earlier, may lead to a kind of despair, a very late development of a *false self* in ourselves as analysts. An analogy which comes to mind is that of the priest who loses his faith, and is trapped in the only rituals and words he knows how to perform and utter, while experiencing a darkness in his soul. To begin earlier on in our own lives to develop a philosophical attitude to them and to our choices (and by this I do *not* mean that our own views will be a suitable prescription for anybody else) will ensure that as age becomes real and death approaches as a sure event for us, our philosophical musculature is ready and working, enabling us to embrace these events in ways that are positive for ourselves and therefore for us in our working life. For comprehensive reliability our personal philosophy should, in my view, be independent of any psychoanalytical *Weltanschauung*. I have referred in greater detail to this whole subject in a paper entitled 'What does it mean: "Love is not enough"?' (this volume, Ch. 8).

I must hope that the reader has not been misled here into thinking that I have been exploring an almost totally different subject, but one which crops up in discussion from time to time – rather than in the literature. This is the one about whether *liking* one's patients is a positive therapeutic factor: it is deliberate that this subject was preceded by the last paragraph, on the concept of love, because I see *that* as more fundamental to the positive therapeutic process. Liking people is anyway subject to fluctuations in a way that love is not. A deep and thorough professional attitude which may best be described as being *with* our patients in their search for truth and health, does not necessarily entail an obligation, moral or otherwise, to like them and certainly not to 'take sides' in a prejudiced way; it is one of the strongest therapeutic factors in psychoanalysis that our whole style and attitude make the patient feel, rightly, *important* to us over a long period and this is fundamentally different from a kind of partisanship. Vicissitudes of this feeling in ourselves are there for our own self-analysis as we proceed, and are inevitable. One might go so far as to say that they are what the countertransference is *about*. And I imagine that we mostly have the repeated experience of coming to like, certainly to care for, each patient as the analysis unfolds. Again however this must be distinguished from an off-balance failure in perspective, when we may fall into the delusion that all our geese are swans; special favouritism, getting caught in idealizations, even becoming over-preoccupied with a particular patient, all say something about a temporary impairment in our own judgement and detachment. An interesting variant of this matter is that being thoroughly dislikable can be a major symptom of a rewarding form of psychopathology to treat, and I am not of the opinion that a prospective patient should be turned down at first interview on these grounds alone, though the countertransference work may be tough and slow. I will now describe an example.

Many years ago, a man in his late fifties was sent to me by a colleague who had been running a therapeutic group for several years. The group was a consolidated one, and had worked steadily on as a group all that time. This man was a member of it. I cannot remember now how or why he got into group therapy in the first place; I rather think some definite symptoms had presented and had cleared up. He was referred to me for the possibility of analysis on the rather unusual grounds that nobody liked him. He was proposing to leave the group, as he did not like any of them, either. A lot had been worked on, including this very matter, but usually only in rather disguised ways, for example, he was very often the selected bad object, or the excluded one, in the group work. I am not sure that the way my colleague put it to me had ever quite been put to this man in such bald terms – indeed, as a sort of diagnosis, which is what it was. I found this not only unusual, but

challenging and after a preliminary interview, I took this man into
analysis. I soon saw exactly what my colleague and his group had
meant. He had an air of almost insufferable, humourless self-
righteousness about him, and yet that in itself was only an
approximate formulation. There was an indefinable *something*
which was unattractive and dislikeable, a slightly whingeing quality, a kind of subtle self-pity. This was unattractively meshed with
a demanding insensitivity. Everything he said was a self-orientated
statement, which immediately put one's back up, but also made
one think of things which might indeed provoke such an attitude.
He was clearly not an agreeable member of a group. It slowly
transpired in analysis that this man had, almost consciously,
adopted a scapegoat role in his childhood; he had identified, at an
early age, with an attitude of his parents and siblings which was
for certain complex reasons, completely understandable, but deeply
excluding. Very rapidly, and very young, he assembled a defensive
armour whereby he achieved a number of things – he identified
with the aggressors, he became defiant and gloried in his role – like
Richard Crouchback, he was himself, alone; he showed, and came
to believe, that he Didn't Care and of course, he set up a constantly
self-fulfilling prophecy. I was already very interested in the ways
in which children, and later adults, try to give meaning to themselves and their lives, often at the cost of great suffering, as if this
sense of meaning is of the highest importance for survival and
sanity; from this I began to deduce that it *is* of the highest
importance, since the resulting personality is often disturbed and
even unloveable, and yet it makes a kind of deep existential sense
to the patient. In the case of this particular man, it was as if he had
perceived and said to himself: 'Well, people seem to treat me as if I
am bad and not loveable, so perhaps they are right; perhaps I am
not loveable or at least if I behave as if I am not, they will love me
for being brave and spotting the truth.' It was an intricate and long
analysis but when we really got hold of this central idea, it slowly
became possible to unravel the long tangled skein of his life. He
quite simply, and in many different ways, got better. He became
likeable, and then somewhat loveable. This is not simply the
prejudiced view of the analyst who is pleased with her own
handiwork; he married and became a happier and more generous
person with his wife, his new young children, and his friends. He

had had the 'will to work' at his analysis and a kind of hope which sustained us through many a tough and painful passage.

While I am on this subject, I would like to go to its furthest extreme and make a point about something we work towards in analysis with people who *hate* – especially one or other or both of their parents, who may indeed truly have been hateful, and hurt and damaged the patient. Slowly, as the patient emerges from chronic pain and damage, he may come to be able to analyse for himself the damaging parent and may come to see that he or she, in their ways, were young and hopeful once, before they became injured and hateful. They may come to see that he or she was, or could have been, likeable. The patient may well come to forgive the parent, or at least to replace hate with tolerance and a kind of love.

We have come a long way from the excited enthusiasm of our first faltering steps on the tightrope of our daily life as analysts. If I am asked now to select one comprehensive feature as the most constantly and positvely therapeutic, what would be my choice? Without doubt, the quality of sustained, unflagging *attention*. The slow development of this kind of attention reminds us of how paradoxical the analytical attributes need to be; our attention should be both detached and involved, both scanning and focused; if possible it should be, as Bion suggested, free from memory and desire (1970, p. 34). At first encounter, people sometimes have difficulty with Bion's idea; but it is an idea which is relative, firstly to our overall goals in treatment, and secondly to time. To speak succinctly, our only goal in analysis should be that the patient's disturbed unhappiness and symptomatology should be reduced. During every session, we clear our conscious minds of his and our own memories; thus we free all our psychic and emotional energies for attending to his here-and-now; blended with a strong curiosity and an unexploitative wish to reduce his suffering, attention forms the constant matrix of a positive therapeutic attitude to our work.

8

WHAT DOES IT MEAN: 'LOVE IS NOT ENOUGH'?

As many people will recognize, the statement in my title is taken from an early book of Bruno Bettelheim's (1950). However, in that book he was writing about a very special project, close to his heart – the school for deeply disturbed children, especially refugees, that he set up and ran, with hand-picked staff. The school continues, and did not die with him. I thought it would be valuable to extend that title far beyond the boundaries to which he restricted himself, and to wonder whether our whole technique and philosophy of work might not be its appropriate context.

There is an angle from which it is possible to study all psycho-analytic papers whatever their subject matter; this is the angle which explores the implicit morality of psychoanalysis as a system. It is interesting to allow this viewpoint to predominate in one's mind for a while, and then to read a number of different papers by different people addressing different subjects. One has to make a conscious decision to retain the viewpoint while reading, since it is not normally anywhere near the surface of our minds, and we are unlikely to appreciate papers which keep nudging us to remind us about it, when their subject matter is elsewhere. This small project consistently reveals a strongly moral infrastructure which informs both the theory and practice of our *Impossible Profession*: indeed, it is part of what makes it impossible. I am here using the subtitle of a readable book by Janet Malcolm (1981), which had the unusual

The paper was given at a day conference of THERIP (The Higher Education Network for Research and Information in Psychoanalysis) in London in 1990, and subsequently several times in the USA.

distinction of being serialized in the *New Yorker*, though the phrase was first used by Freud himself (1937a, p. 248).

Neville Symington, a member of the British Psycho-Analytical Society who has now, to our loss, emigrated to Australia, often writes about psychoanalysis and religion. He brings to analysis a long and intimate experience of Roman Catholicism. He recently published a short article in the *Bulletin of the British Psycho-Analytical Society*, called 'Virtue and mental health' (Feb. 1990), which I am sure he will develop further. He talks about fundamental moral choices that we make, partly in the unconscious, and how such choices influence the very atmosphere we create. This is his last short paragraph:

> To create a good atmosphere is to be virtuous. Its source lies in an openness and love towards people. To create a bad atmosphere is vicious. The former is concurrent with mental health; the latter with mental illness. In the desire for mental health there is concealed a desire to be virtuous. It is not possible to be mentally healthy but morally vicious.

Perhaps a very simple way of putting these teachings, and what Symington is saying, in a nutshell, is 'Try to be good and you will probably be happy.' Of course people have been telling us that ever since we were small! The problem is to make it fresh. I would also like, for our purposes, to reverse the shape of one of Symington's sentences, thus: 'In the aim to be virtuous lies the outcome – mental health', and I hope there may be some agreement if, from this, I infer that we may equate 'mental health' with happiness, and peace of mind. I would then add a more specific view, but I think there is a sequence of logic here: 'We need to seek virtue, for ourselves and others, if we are genuinely committed to promoting mental health.' This could stand as a synoptic statement about the morality inherent in the practice of psycho-analysis as a therapeutic method.

The current state of Western social values suggests – though the notion may be oversimplified – that a moral muddle has developed in the twentieth century, whereby an idea of 'happiness' is believed, at a preconscious level, to be linked with material success. Many prejudices flourish, especially amongst young people who have not thought out their ideas, and older people who have reached the time in life when unconscious envy and criticism of the young often become a staple of conversation. But time and thought can be wasted giving one's prejudices an airing, and indeed in a paper called 'On the tightrope' (this volume, Ch. 7), I address the dangers that beset us in our particular profession, as we get older, of complacency, arthritis in the thinking, and dwelling on the ghastly faults of others (that is, prejudice). But I do observe that one of the main constituents of what I am calling a moral muddle is the confusion between loving, and being in love. Psychoanalysis, which has done so much to shape the psychological thinking of the twentieth century, has curiously little to say about this confusion, and there is little or no literature about it, let alone a coherent theory. Or at least, not in the direct sense.

However, one of the few exceptions which prove this rule was a paper in the *Journal of the American Psychoanalytic Association* in 1988 by Martin Bergman, who has addressed the subject directly and who moreover usefully brings together the few scattered traces – over many years – of other analysts' thinking about it. This is the paper I referred to at the beginning. As so often, we find that Freud had some ideas on the matter, slipped into papers on other subjects almost in passing, and, again as so often, there is a quality to these which is startlingly predictive of later work, viewed from this end of the century. Bergman's article is called 'Freud's three theories of love in the light of later developments': in it he has culled from many people's writings, and abstracted the resultant crop of apparently random findings. Not without irony, Freud claimed that when psychoanalysis touches on the subject of love, its touch must be clumsy by comparison with that of the poets, and he approached the topic reluctantly himself. Bergman says that 'Freud contributed more to the understanding of love than anyone else after Plato' (p. 653) and further adds that he, Bergman, wishes 'to disprove a widely held opinion, both outside and within psychoanalysis, that Freud, who changed so fundamentally our understanding of sexuality, had little or nothing to say about love' (*ibid.*). This error arose, he says, from the fact that Freud had 'never unified his thinking on love along the lines of dream theory or the theory of sexuality' (*ibid.*). The Greeks, who reflected deeply on love, would never have made the error of confusing falling in love with the capacity to maintain prolonged loving fidelity. But as early as the seventeenth century, the emphasis shifted, and the maintenance of a love tie, of which a long and happy marriage is the prime example, began to be confused with the distinctly different phenomenon of falling in love. Bergman reminds us – and thus isolated, it becomes rather astonishing – that it was as early as 1905 that Freud, in the *Three Essays on the Theory of Sexuality*, adumbrated what was built into solid theory only fifty years or so later when he said: 'A child sucking at his mother's breast has become the prototype of every relation of love. The finding of an object is in fact a refinding of it' (p. 222). Here we have the kernel of Kleinian and object-relations theory in a sentence! Freud's first theory could thus be called 'the genetic'. The second, 'the narcissistic', may be understood from the 1914 paper 'On narcissism' (1914a): it relates particularly to the conditions for falling in love. The third is best called 'the nucleus of the object-related theory', and it originates in a series of difficult passages in 'Instincts and their vicissitudes' (1915). The obscurity of this paper was probably responsible for the widespread belief that Freud confused love with sex. It does seem as if some confusion, at this very creative, energetic stage of his own development, *was* there; Freud was still struggling for clarity. 'Love,' he said, as if for the moment baffled, cannot be 'some kind of special component instinct of sexuality'. Rather, he thought, it was 'the expression of the *whole* sexual current of feeling; of the relation of the total ego to its object' (p. 133). He concluded, for the time, then, that love could only be said to exist 'after there has been a synthesis of all the component instincts of sexuality under the primacy of the genitals' (p. 138). He would, of course, have had fresh in his memory the very recent paper 'On narcissism' and was now wrestling with a much bigger, or rather, more complex idea, namely, what is love and how can it last? All these nuclear theories of Freud's were modified, and expanded, by subsequent developments, but none has lost its validity.

One could say that Freud was, at one important level, confronting a problem of definition; this is still often true when we try to communicate with each other today. A renewed glance at my title – 'What does it mean: "Love is not enough"?' – leads one to think: 'Well, it depends what is meant by love . . .', and it does; definitions are not just dictionary games. Psychoanalysis may be defined as a moral activity; certainly, the great series of papers which Freud produced in the early and middle 1920s, when the superego first appeared in his theory as the internal agent of judgement, point directly to this. But Freud always felt peculiarly vulnerable to the many accusations of immorality levelled at him, and in one of the outstanding papers of that series, *The Ego and the Id* (1923), almost as if provoked beyond his normal endurance, he wrote the passage which I have quoted at length above (p. 49), and which includes the following:

> So long as we had to concern ourselves with the study of what is repressed in mental life, there was no need for us to share in any agitated apprehension as to the whereabouts of the higher side of man. But now that we have embarked on the analysis of the ego we can give an answer to all those whose moral sense has been shocked and who have complained that there must surely be a higher nature in man: 'Very true,' we can say, 'and here we have that higher nature, in this ego ideal or super-ego, the representative of our relation to our parents. When we were little children we knew these higher natures, we admired them and feared them; and later we took them into ourselves.' . . . What has belonged to the lowest part of the mental life of each of us is changed, through the formation of the ideal, into what is highest in the human mind by our scale of values. (pp. 35–6)

I love this passage, in Freud's unique and most personal style, in which he trusts to clarity to express emphasis.

But with the term 'moral', I am really referring to some clearer *inherent* quality in our philosophy of theory and practice, not just to the structural theory itself; something more like what Symington would call its 'atmosphere'. I think being an analytical therapist has a vocational quality. There is likely to be some, perhaps rather uneasy, agreement with this idea, though it is rare to encounter an analyst who actually believes in God, or practises a theistic religion, and the word 'vocation' has become linked to religion. Perhaps Christopher Bollas's phrase in his book, *Forces of Destiny* (1989), about 'living out one's true destiny' has more appeal. Whatever we call it, many therapists commit themselves, having already undergone a long emotional apprenticeship, their analysis, on top of previous professional qualifications, to trying to improve the mental health of other people (and therefore, by Symington's definition, increase their potential for virtue). We need to ask ourselves what is required of us, all day and every day, by the

patients who constitute the largest part of our working life. Over
and above a long training, a quiet setting, and attention to practical
details, there are a number of other requirements tacitly made of
us.

We may raise a signpost here by posing two questions. What do
our patients require of us? What do we require of ourselves? There
may be a broad answer to each, and we need to inspect different
levels of consciousness in ourselves to find them. Those of us who
are doctors are required to *forget* a great deal of our training, and,
to a considerable extent, abandon youthful ambitions; ambition is
not well served in a psychoanalytic practice. It is required of us
that we endure, understand and help to change some extremes of
emotion and fantasy in our patients; that we do not use the
transference or the countertransference destructively, but only to
create greater insight between the patient and ourselves; that we do
not exploit his or her dependence on us, emotionally, intellectually,
sexually or financially; that we assess when and how to draw the
treatment to an appropriate close, and that we facilitate the patient's
leaving of us as completely as possible. When I spoke of different
levels of consciousness, I meant that most of these requirements
are not conscious to the patient. *We* have to remain aware of them,
and fulfil them, throughout his or her time with us. There is no
true dividing line, of course, between these requirements and those
that are entirely private to ourselves, which I will come to in a
moment. They fuse and interconnect in every session. In this
context, we also have to reflect seriously on the many people from
all walks of life who carry about with them a stereotype of an
analyst – who is lazy, greedy, selfish, cut off from the things of the
real world, uncaring about true suffering, and who probably goes
to bed with his or her patients. There is a parallel stereotype of an
analytic patient, too – female, middle-aged, well-off, bored and
sexually frustrated. It is no good our just dismissing these with a
superior little laugh; they are widespread and powerful, and we
may well be the only example of the ghastly caricature of ourselves
whom the patient ever experiences. On us as individuals lies the
burden of changing these images in the public's mind.

The maintenance of our own moral or ethical systems – I think
the terms may be used interchangeably – requires the application
of our willed attention. The machinery will start to creak, and then

to rust, unless we attend to keeping the wheels oiled. We need to nurture the strength to maintain patience, and patients, in a benevolent way. We have to foster the capacity to direct single-minded attention to what is happening while at the very same time allowing the inner flow of free-associative thoughts and images; we must maintain a detachment rooted in thorough self-knowledge, so that we experience and examine the countertransference and our own feelings, again at one and the same time as we scrutinize the transference. Both these last skills involve a sort of trick, a highly desirable trick of the mind, which it takes a lot of practice to develop until it is really fluent, and instantly accessible when working. To achieve it, there has to evolve an intended and invaluable *psychic split*. It represents one of the many paradoxes in psychoanalysis. Examples of others which necessitate doing two things at once in the mind are: sharply focusing, and scanning; complex involvement in feelings, and cool observation of them; close attention to the patient, and close attention to ourselves; distinguishing our own true feelings from subtle projections into us; communicating insight clearly, yet not imposing it; drawing constantly on resources of knowledge, yet being ready to know nothing for long periods; willing the best for our patients and ourselves, yet abandoning memory and desire; a kind of tolerant steadiness which holds us while we make innumerable, minute moral decisions, yet steering clear of being judgemental. Alongside and around these paradoxical features, I think a sense of humour is vital, and real toughness, and enjoyment; and the ability to value our private lives, and take rest and refreshment from them. And, as I wrote about in 'Slouching towards Bethlehem . . .' (1986; this volume, Ch. 1), the matrix of all these things is faith; faith in ourselves, and in this strange process which daily we create with our patients, faith with a small f, not a large F which might imply a kind of credulous attitude towards a theory or a doctrine, but a faith in our daily-increasing experience that, between the analytical couple, things *happen*.

The demands of morality, or what I think Symington is calling virtue, permeate the whole theory of interpretation. Another question now presents itself: what is interpretation for? It is to make the unconscious conscious, to bring about the state in which where id was, there ego shall be; by now, these definitions have

developed the ring of cliché. We can also say that it is to relieve
psychic pain, to restore peace of mind, to strengthen the capacity
for concern, and for contentment. I do not think it is too emphatic
to say that to try to help people to be *relatively* happier, is a self-
evidently moral goal of psychoanalysis. A great deal of interpretative work, one way or another, is directed towards slowly relieving
the pains inflicted by the archaic powers of the superego. Repression, denial, splitting, projection, displacement, amnesias all occur
in the psychic system out of fear. Fear either of direct disapproval
for transgressing the moral laws of our world, which includes our
superego; or of our potential for harm, which may, in turn, evoke
disapproval, rejection, punishment and then symptoms. Fear fuels
all anxiety, and all neurotic anxiety arises in the shadow of the fear
of the tyrant superego. The book of Proverbs says 'The fear of the
Lord is the beginning of wisdom' (9:10); fear of the superego *may*
be the beginning of wisdom, but more often it is the beginning of
neurosis. Analysis teaches implicitly what the Old Testament King,
Solomon, was really talking about – that is, respect. We do have to
learn – and sometimes relearn, through analytic treatment – to
respect the superego, but in the right spirit, and when its excesses
and harsh edges have been softened.

As I assembled above some of the qualities we need to nurture,
I thought that many have, at first glance, a somewhat impersonal
feel to them, but they are not nurtured just for our own narcissistic
pleasure, as if they were worldly goods. We are not likely to think
gloatingly to ourselves, 'Oh, I am an extremely non-judgemental
person!' There is a smell of complacency, and of triumph, as in a
competition, about this thought. A brief consideration of it gives
the game away – it is an extremely judgemental thought, a
superiority over a hierarchy of named or nameless Others who
have, by implication, been found to be less moral than us. We are
on a tricky tightrope here. To be equally conscious of *some* of our
virtues as of some of our vices is, from time to time, necessary; this
in itself is something the British, especially, are conditioned to
consider vaguely immoral. But at the same time, if we are to be
aware of exercizing our willed energy to try to develop something,
it is essential that we are, at some level, clear about what that
something *is*. The qualities of patience, endurance, humour, kind-
ness and courage are, when we examine them, essentially object-

related, and it is this which belies the impersonal first impression. Even the detachment which is the container of our sharp emotional focus is developed as a means to an object-related end.

Can all these qualities be subsumed under the name of love? Is this justifiable? And does it matter? I think my answer is yes, to all three questions. Love is a transcendental *idea*; human beings long for it, seek it, and many achieve it in all sorts of ways. It gives meaning to life. It is not a static condition, or rather it tends to wither and fade if it becomes static. Loss, or lack, of it brings about depression, alienation, feelings of emptiness, and False-Self manifestations – 'being brave', 'keeping cheerful', and so on . . .

All the psychoanalytic thinkers who have written seriously about love seem to reach a two-part conclusion, whatever their approach. One is that it is an integrative state, which has worked through many stages before attainment. Balint was too restricted when he spoke of the theory of genital love; he gives the impression that his ideas were larger than his theory allowed for, a quart of experience trying to fit into a pint-pot of theory. Also, he was the first analyst to define the capacity to love in negative terms: it is not oral greed, not anally possessive, not genitally inhibited, not desirous of humiliating or hurting, not ashamed, not guilty. He reminds me of St Paul, in the famous chapter of his First Epistle to the Corinthians: 'Love suffereth long, and is kind; love envieth not: love vaunteth not itself, is not puffed up; doth not behave itself unseemly, seeketh not her own, is not easily provoked, thinketh no evil, rejoiceth not in iniquity . . . Love never faileth . . .' (13:4–8). Balint eventually felt the need to go beyond the limitations of the genital theory, which he came to see was still an immature stage. A full capacity to love, he decided, *may* contain, in some small degree, all the developmental constituents which at first he felt should have gone – oral greed, anal possessiveness and so on – but they are 'natural' he said, and real loving has to be learned – which I think is what I am meaning by the use of willed attention, namely, that this kind of loving can be learned. He concluded that there is, in true love, sensitivity, choice, generosity, the ability to be open to a certain sort of identification, and tenderness. And all these qualities are necessary to a creative technique.

In 'On the tightrope' (this volume, Ch. 7), I discussed the need for analysts to develop a philosophy of life which stretches them,

and which they find congenial, which would include the kinds of
ego-ideals which are not so much there to be reached, but which
act as incentives for unceasing attention. I am not convinced that
psychoanalysis itself offers such a philosophical structure. There
are many analysts and therapists who, without having particularly
thought it out, vaguely assume that it does, or simply that its
enormous demands are quite enough to be going on with. There
are also many, however, with what may be called a religious
temperament but without a religious faith to fulfil it, who either
try to organize their psychoanalytical knowledge to meet the need,
or who search around for a philosophy or religion which meshes
creatively at many points with psychoanalysis. This I found
Buddhism did for me.

The very use of the word 'love' in psychoanalysis is often felt to
be dangerous, or open to misconstruction. I mentioned earlier that
all the writers who refer to love come to a double conclusion; the
first part is the integrating effect, the second is that love – I am
tempted to say 'in the last analysis' – evades pinning down. There
is ultimately a failure of definition in our theoretical terms – a
mystery. Love is ultimately indefinable by the language of psychological theory. Human beings *are* essentially mysterious; however
long we have sat with patients, they escape our final comprehension. Psychosomatic symptoms, for example, bring this home to us
very clearly. Even if we manage to cure them, the truth is we are
not sure how we did it, and striking the same symbolic interpretation which succeeded the first time, may have no effect if we use it
again later, in the event of symptom recurrence.

Here I want to draw once more a distinction I have touched on
before, in other papers – between loving and liking. It is not
necesary to like a person – at least, not in the first instance, or in
their initial presentation – in order to practise love; this sounds
rather cold-blooded, and I do not mean to imply that we should
tighten our jaws and get down to it in the same way that we might
practise scales on the piano. And yet there is a similarity, except
that scales can be stopped after twenty minutes, and forgotten for
a week. I am talking about something which really has to go on –
for ever – and we might more properly use the metaphor of *flexing
our muscles*. We need to keep our philosophical musculature in
good trim, so that faced with an unpleasant patch of work, or a

thoroughly dislikable person in a consultation, we can draw upon readily available resources, and work towards the penetrative, transcendent effect which such an attitude will bring about. I think that good psychoanalytic work is fed at its roots by the capacity to love, which is 'ingredient x' in the integrative outcome of the gruelling tasks which face us. I would like to emphasize here that I am speaking of a true transcendence, in the sense that love may well be the *matrix* of a piece of work, short or long, but that love is not necessarily – by any means – always the prevailing affective experience in the analyst. On the contrary, when I refer to the matrix, I mean that it is the only trustworthy container in which we may have to *feel* hatred, rage or contempt for varying periods of time. These are occasions when the countertransference comes into its own as our most sensitive instrument. Bollas, in his two books, *The Shadow of the Object* (1987) and *Forces of Destiny* (1989), has written so sympathetically, to my mind, of the uses of the countertransference, that I would only urge you here to read his original views.

Two much earlier papers came to mind when I was reflecting on this subject: the first was 'The effort to drive the other person crazy', published by Harold Searles in 1959, and the second, 'Hate in the counter-transference' by Donald Winnicott, at the almost unbelievably early date of 1947. These papers share the enchanting quality of giving one a deep sense of relief about very difficult, ugly feelings that one has experienced while working as an analyst; and also a sort of permission, not only to have such feelings, but to use them as a source of insight, information and strength. In the very middle of his paper, dealing mainly with vicious and vengeful impulses in the patient which not only get confusingly projected, but also stir up similar terrible feelings from the therapist's own depths, Searles suddenly says:

> The fostering of the other person's intrapersonal and interpersonal integration and self-realisation is a part of the loving relatedness defined by the philosopher–theologian, Martin Buber. Buber refers to this as 'making the other person present', and adds: 'The help that human beings give each other in becoming a self leads the life between them to its height . . .' To put it in other words, it seems to me that the essence of loving relatedness entails a responding to the wholeness of the other person, including responding to a *larger*

person in him than he is himself aware of being, to help restore that
wholeness. I speak of psychotherapy here, but I mean, in some
degree, to all people. (1959, pp. 269–70)

This encapsulates succinctly and better than I can what I am calling
the moral infrastructure of our job.

I once experienced a long crescendo of hate in the countertransference, which taught me a great deal – in the end. But it was hard
to endure, and to continue to work on the mass of angry,
contemptuous and horrible feelings which grew in me over a
period of months. It came in the sixth year of a full, classical but
extremely tortuous analysis. By that I mean that I found the actual
day-to-day work of trying to understand and interpret consistently
more taxing than I think I have in any analysis ever – and by then
I had been doing this work for many hours a day for many years.
This man, in his fifties, came from a family streaked with intermittent psychosis through several generations. He was intelligent and
hard-working, separated from his wife, with whom he had had
four grown-up children; he came to analysis because he was afraid
that, under a talented social manner, a dark void, which he had
been faintly aware of for years, was getting larger. He was a
secretive, schizoid character, not exactly a False Self, but quite
happy for people to be somewhat baffled by him, and feel he was
not easy to know. Fortunately, from some early preverbal experience with someone, whom we later deduced may have been a
comfortably good Nannie, he had in him, ultimately, a deep and
strong well-spring of capacity for loving. This had been extensively
buried, both by conscious and unconscious manoeuvres, and had
become choked with rocky boulders, arising from many neglected
and deprived experiences throughout childhood; but it was not
lost forever, and it was not simply a primitive yearning to *be* loved
and cared for. It was a genuine source of love, of a transforming
kind, and as the stones and weeds were painfully cleared away
from the conduits, it began to become ever-more accessible, and
enjoyable to the patient.

Moreover, his stated, and conscious, attitude to his analysis was
one of keen, hard-working commitment. He was, indeed, difficult
to know, and his communications, for years, were often disjointed
and mystifying. For two years, I was allowed to be aware that he

was not telling me something important, the fleeting impression occasionally being that this was at the request of somebody else, and that he was in growing conflict over it when with me. He never learned anything approaching free association, and indeed would often halt in the middle of a sentence and leave me tantalized, wondering what it had been about. He suffered from severe tension when with me, and often cried quietly for a few minutes, occasionally springing up suddenly and departing as if some intolerable pressure impelled him. I also sometimes detected a kind of scornfulness in a slight change of tone in his well-modulated and unrevealing voice.

Given little material on which to exercise what I might think of as ordinary interpretative skill, I soon realized that a mixture of intuition and countertransference was to be my main source of information. I have rarely encountered such tenacious resistances, in a context which I nevertheless always, throughout all those early years, judged to be almost desperately motivated to *work* in the analysis. It sounds completely paradoxical, and it was. He added to the difficulties by speaking frequently in a sort of code, since I discovered, years later, that he in turn believed me to be not only a thought-reader but also encoding what I said. This compounded the enigma, since, however clearly and simply I tried to phrase what I said, I always had to be on the look-out for something quite other which he would have decided I *meant*. There were thus at least four levels of spoken communication between us, before even beginning to reflect on the non-verbal – three of them his, if not four, because his paranoid decoding of my simplest sentences left me unsure as to whether he heard, or rather, understood, what I actually said.

After about two years I had put together as many hints and clues as I could, and I confronted him with the large and emotion-laden segment of his life which I deduced was the Secret. This caused shock and intense distress for a while, but since the trail had been clear enough for me to get it approximately right, he soon experienced considerable relief. Few of the other resistances diminished, however, and I continued, as I had all along, to try to analyse his *way* of relating to me rather than the fragmentary content of what he managed to say. Thus slowly I evolved a kind of theory as to what the analysis was about. I may say it took me just over two and a half years to conceptualize even the outline of this theory, but it was remarkable what the effect of clarifying my own thinking was. I have read a little about this phenomenon, I cannot remember where, again written by Neville Symington; the quite odd but undeniable fact that a clear, insightful change in intellectual conceptualizing by the analyst about a patient can convey a sense of relief and movement into the treatment without any spoken reference to its occurrence. It sounds almost mystical, but it certainly happens.

The simple step forward that I took was to reread *The Basic Fault* by Michael Balint (1968), and reflect on the idea that the patient belonged in the basic fault category, and that he was in a version of what Balint describes as a malignant regression. As if by magic, the work between us became more fluent and I noticed that the patient began, for the first time, to trust me. Some years later he confirmed this, almost to the day. His view was that he had not known why it came about, but he began, quite suddenly, to feel safer and more hopeful about coming, after over two years of tormented conflict. Trust and hope do not figure in a malignant regression, so the next event in the sequence, ironically enough, was that I began to shift my theory again! In spite of the improvement in his psychic state the style of communication continued much as before, but from then on, I was able to construct more in the way of ideas; these were little more than bits of handrail to help us on our way, but this is nevertheless one of the tasks of the analyst, to keep a sort of working space round the dyad by the aid of small pieces of theory which gradually evolve into understanding.

The deathly secret had, of course, been about a relationship, which had perverse and difficult ingredients. It took me nearly another three years to realize fully that the unconscious wish this patient brought into analysis was to *take revenge*, in a very particular way, once and for all, on the near-psychotic mother of his lonely childhood. Although it was, to begin with, largely split off from his conscious awareness, he was still symbiotically merged with this mother, by now dead, but very much alive as a superego tyrant. His particular method of taking revenge was to obtain omnipotent control over someone, who then became, first of all, his victim, and secondly, the recipient of his most terrible feelings, which were not only projected into the victim – who had to be bound to him by some strong libidinal force – but which were then also enacted by this victim, with the patient as their target. The patient thus arranged that he both tortured his victim, *and* was punished for doing so. The gradual overall effect of this long-drawn-out manoeuvre was to drive the other person crazy: the patient's partner, that is. Although I did slowly begin to understand this, there was no possibility that *I* would escape, since in order to come to know it in the most exact detail, I had to experience my version of it.

Towards the end of our fifth year of work, I noticed that I often felt a brief flash of annoyance, or something like contempt, directed mentally either at the patient, or more often at his secret partner. The latter was so enmeshed in the fusional state that he – the patient – would often pass on to me critical and sarcastic remarks that had been made about me by his hapless partner, instantly dissociating himself from their content but making the partner his mouthpiece. Fortunately, though I did not understand its full import, I did see through this, and had started interpreting the projection and dissociation long before the volcano blew up. This explosion happened, however, when my countertransference eventually became too unwieldy to contain and observe fully, and for several weeks the atmosphere between us was one of growling hostility; I endeavoured to keep some hold on this by verbalizing the violent negative content of what I recognized as alien to *my own* states of feeling and which was being powerfully projected into me both by the patient and, via the patient, by his partner. Much later, when it was all over and fully understood, we came to know this as 'the diabolical manoeuvre'.

The patient had always been very afraid of overt anger, and had used the subtle, critical forces of disdain as its only vehicle with me. However, one day the volcanic rumblings erupted into a white-hot row between us, when we were both screaming at each other out of all our pent-up rage and frustration. You may well think this is inelegant behaviour for an analyst, and you may be right. I can only say that even in the intense involvement with the moment I remained aware of precisely where we were, and I kept a sharp eye on what was happening – hence the enormous value of the sort of psychological trick of sustaining the working split in the analytic ego that I described earlier. I also felt delighted, because I knew in my bones that none of this was irretrievable, and would yield up many precious secrets about his unconscious world when we had settled down again. And indeed it did. I do not recommend it as a piece of technique; or at least, not until you have practised for many years; and I realize that using it here may only add to the reputation for occasional outbursts, which I began to get when I described a similar incident in 'Slouching towards Bethlehem . . .' (1986; this volume, Ch. 1)! What I do recommend is that the practice of analysis, if it is to *work*, must come from within one's most authentic self. If perpetual attention is directed towards the sorts of features I have considered in this paper, then the analyst's ego is resilient and ready for anything, and such alarms and excursions as I here describe may be the unforgettable way-stations on the road to health for the patient.

Moving towards my conclusion, I must add that I have heard of the concept of 'operating professionally out of strong reparative drives as a sustaining positive therapeutic factor', and this may be a more generally acceptable way of phrasing it, but I think it leaves much to be desired, and can itself be subsumed under the broader construct of the practice of the capacity to love. We need to nurture this overriding idea, I believe, because just as the world seems bleaker and emptier without a person, or people, to love – and, if we are fortunate, to be loved by, though I think that this is less important – so the pursuit of doing psychoanalysis may go the same way if the active deployment of our own personal philosophy suffers from neglect. There is a danger of despair setting in, and the work to which we brought such zeal in our early years may fade into automatic routines, and a reliance on tricks of technique which we learned the hard way through experience. A warning signal of this danger may be a dwindling sense of the lively curiosity which is such a necessary ingredient of our work. We do need to protect ourselves as we get older against a kind of rigidifying which can creep up on us like a thief in the night, and steal away our creative spontaneity. When this creative spontaneity is operating intuitively in high gear, it generates much of our best work, which may at times feel so satisfying and yet so ephemeral.

It was not for nothing that I said earlier, at the very beginning of my more detailed list of requirements, that we have to abandon ambition. In a very particular way this is especially true for analysts, because of what I have just said about the ephemeral quality. When our only instruments are ourselves, and our main desire for our patients is that they should be able to go away from us, happier than when they came, it may be easily imagined that our best, most creative work is directly known only to one other person – the patient – and to ourselves. An analyst called Michael Parsons wrote an unpublished paper on this, called 'The dove that vanishes'. He used the metaphor of the doves which Noah sent out from the Ark to search for land. One dove brought back an olive branch, so it must have found a tree. But the surest message that a dove had found good solid land was that it never came back. So it is with our therapeutic successes. No-one can ever truly make a judgement about another analyst's personal work with a patient. Lots of people *do*, in fact, and every time we write a paper, of course, we are vulnerable to such judgements, which have no other data to rely on. But we never really know about a colleague's direct creative work, at its best or worst, which by definition takes place alone with a patient. This inevitably contributes to the gossip and the bizarre power-struggles within analytic societies, and the overinvestment of committee work, and teaching, with significance – as if activity on a committee ever reflected anything but a faint distorted image of the analyst in his chair. I cannot think of any job, other than that of the secluded religious, which has so little in the way of end products for the world to see and judge. The faith in ourselves, and in our work, which this needs is the kit-bag we are required to carry, and in it assemble these tools of our trade about which I have spoken.

Unless this whole extraordinary and recurring phenomenon, which constitutes our working life, can be called the work of the capacity to love, then I would agree that love is not enough. On the other hand, if you consider that I have justified my argument, I might – at risk of being misunderstood – even dare to say: then 'All You Need is Love'.

9

Manners makyth man: true or false?

It occurred to me that it would be possible to carry out a collective test of modern manners when giving a paper to an audience; I decided not to, but it could be instructive. One of the significant factors that would affect the test result is that it could be defined as a middle-class audience; I think I'm safe with this generalization, although it is the sort of sweeping statement that immediately engenders resistance, so that I can imagine a number of reservations or qualifications might rapidly arise in a number of minds. But the generalization is not trying to deny facts about social history; its point is that *that* audience would have chosen to be present at the sort of paper I give, and wherever they started from, or whatever blood ran in their veins, I think that defines them as undertaking an activity with a middle-class status. My test would be to tell a joke. My bet would be that they would feel bound to oblige me with anything ranging from a polite smile to a burst of laughter. Underlying this would be their wish to enjoy the occasion; they have probably made an effort to be there – it might be a Saturday afternoon, after all, or a Friday evening; they have no particular animosity towards me, and somewhere, probably preconsciously, they would be aware that if they pleased me by laughing at my joke, however feeble or badly-told, they would also be preparing their inner ground to be more pleased *by* me. To appreciate me and my attempt to amuse them would evoke a warmer, more receptive feeling in them. And, the logic goes, I would be aware of that, and enjoy it, and our mutual appreciation would be height-

First given at a meeting of the Squiggle Foundation in November 1990.

ened and reinforced: even if they had felt like sighing or groaning at my joke, that would soon be forgotten, or outweighed by the emotional logic of the dominant process; and this process falls into the general category which can be labelled Good Manners.

A piece of serendipity occurred as I was about to embark on this paper. I came across an anonymous old book on etiquette, full title *Complete Etiquette for Ladies and Gentlemen: a Guide to the Observances of Good Society*. Curiously, I could find no reference to dates, but internal evidence suggests that it first appeared in the late Victorian era and has been updated occasionally, with rather awkward insertions on such things as air travel. Even that example locates itself many years ago, since it not only instructs ladies how to dispose of their hats and gloves, but it also advises that one should arrive at the airport 'at least quarter of an hour' before departure time! Overall, it is remarkably comprehensive, attending in minute detail to every conceivable social situation, from small bridge parties to entertaining Royalty; but the really interesting feature of this handbook is that, without ever quite acknowledging that this is what it is doing, it distinguishes between the sort of behaviour which is quite clearly a stylized, artificial product of obedience to fashionable demands of its time, and the other sort – the sort of manners I am more concerned with here, which substantially express the moral and emotional character of individual human beings as they interact with one another.

It is tempting to select from amongst the great numbers of real gems, as they make diverting quotations, but I will confine myself to one; this one not only addresses the undeniable power of early conditioning, but also reflects the archaic, rather idealized and unreal tone of the whole book:

> The finest attribute of a lady is habitual courtesy, not only to her nearest and dearest, but to everyone who crosses her path. The nursery of good manners is the home, the keynote of which is provided and maintained by the mother: if she be of a sweet and sunny disposition, practising constant self-control, keeping back the hasty word of fault-finding, even when she is ill or worried, her children will unconsciously emulate her. On the other hand, if she is wont to come down to breakfast [I love this – 'come down to breakfast' indeed – presumably already prepared for the family by an eager, humble staff of servants!] with a frown on her face, or a grumble on her lips, and a tendency to repress the innocent fun of

children, she is not acting as a lady and should be well aware of the
fact.

By now, we begin to see that manners are significant, subtle and
multifaceted. The only real difficulty presented by a study of the
subject is to decide what to leave out. Even definitions are instantly
restrictive, useful only as springboards, especially as, on this
subject, the immediate response to a definition – in the same way
as to being told that one is middle class – is a 'Yes, but . . .' For
example, the *Shorter Oxford English Dictionary* (1933; that's the
huge two-volume one which always makes me wonder what the
Longer one is like) has seventeen definitions. Of these, at random,
I select: 'Customary mode of acting or behaviour or habitual
practice.' Yes, but consider the massive change from a definition
dated 1694: 'A distinguished or fashionable air, polite behaviour in
social intercourse', to one in 1794: 'A person's habitual conduct, in
its moral aspect, the representation of his moral character as
embodied in his sentiment and behaviour.'

Already we approach the query in my title. The comedies of
manners in the seventeenth and early eighteenth centuries presented fashionable social behaviour, which, leaning as it did
towards the ridiculous, the grossly affected and the foppish, was
accepted as an artifact; the witty, shallow caricatures in these plays
of people who were essentially self-regarding, were crafted to
amuse and mock, not to express inner depths of personality.
Earnestness and moral sobriety were actively avoided, and it was
in the elegantly constructed artificiality that success of the whole
production lay. The same held true later of the plays of Oscar
Wilde. The question that arises in the mind of the viewer (supposing that we suspend belief, and imagine a Millamant or a Lady
Sneerwell to be real people), is whether the great conscious effort
that must have been brought to bear on the creation of such a
persona would have influenced that character to such a degree that
the whole self became as fragile and crystalline and amoral as the
face presented in society. A little reflection convinces me that it
probably would have; although the plays present caricatures, they
were undoubtedly based on human types whose behaviour in
fashionable society was quite similar. Although it is hard to be
precise, I think it has long been tacitly assumed that the outer self

is a faithful reflection of the inner, and from this we might deduce that extremely detailed attention paid predominantly to the construction of the *outer*, would, conversely, be reflected in the inner self.

In social exchange today, we do seem to take it more or less for granted that as a person behaves, so he or she is. After all, we can only come to know a very small number of people really well, intimately, in our lives, and thus for most of the time, their social behaviour – or manners – is all we have to go on. One notices, at least in Britain, and also in the United States, that in any gathering of people unknown to each other, an early, frequent question is: 'What do you do?' More often than not, it may be observed that the questioner does not exactly know what to do with the answer when it is provided. A blank look, or a pause, is followed by a hasty assembling of some manners, and an often uncomprehending, or at least, inadequate response is mustered. 'Oh, how interesting, you must tell me all about it sometime' is one example, said in such a way as to imply the opposite. By the time one reaches my age as a psychoanalyst, one can make a reliable short list of the predictable responses, and it is an enjoyable silent game to try to guess which one any individual will produce at any particular time. One is: 'Oh, how absolutely fascinating, you must get told the most amazing things.' Another, and one I have learned to dread, is: 'Oh, then you'll be interested in either (a) what happened to me when I had my nervous breakdown, or (b) this simply extraordinary dream I had last night.' The first carries the promise of boredom, but the second is the more to be dreaded, as the new acquaintance then goes on to recount a startlingly transparent dream in which, with an uncanny insight unlike any that ever visits one in the consulting room, one may perceive violence, severe anxiety, murderous wishes, marital discord, and sexual perversions of the most recondite variety. 'There,' says the speaker triumphantly, 'now what do you make of that? Tell me all about myself.' Although I am sometimes tempted, there is no doubt that a truthful response to this eager, innocent request would rapidly produce an alienation effect of some magnitude. The ingenuity of one's own good manners is taxed in such situations, and it is as well to have a few brief phrases stacked away in one's repertoire for use in similar emergencies. It is both dangerous and – if I may say so without sounding unduly didactic – unprofessional, ever to make anything approaching an interpretation. A response I have found useful is: 'That certainly is a magnificent dream. I wonder if you've ever thought of writing your dreams down in a Dream Book? They make for such interesting reading when you have a whole series.' This has the virtue of not being dishonest, because I do mean it, and is immeasurably better than, for example: 'Goodness, how awful! I think you ought to get into analysis as soon as possible.'

A not infrequent but, to my mind, surprisingly impolite response to my own admission of being a psychoanalyst, is: 'It must be lovely just to sit and get paid to listen to people talking about themselves', and there are a few other rude versions, for example: 'Oh, I thought all that was old hat now', or: 'But of course you don't actually believe in that stuff, do you?' This end of the response-spectrum has long since taught me that even in sophisticated society where manners overall are seen to be desirable, courteous and mature, there are certain subjects which seem to act solely as *agents provocateurs*, and psychoanalysis is one of them. It can provoke a primitive, assaultive response, and normally wellmannered people can behave in the most remarkable way, producing comments of unparalleled rudeness as if there were a sort of tacit common licence to do so. These very same people would be shocked and horrified to hear one addressing one's doctor or vicar or butcher or lawyer or grocer in similar vein. I have not yet quite understood this phenomenon. It may arise from fear, as occasionally people show genuine anxiety, and make reference to the not uncommon myth that we have x-ray eyes, and are, at that very moment, seeing through the outer armour, and deep into their souls.

To return to the point I am making about the frequency of the question 'What do you do?' among strangers, I think that the way the information, once given, tends to trickle into the sand underlines the probability that *it is the wrong question*. This is not to say that I think there is a 'right' one which fails to get asked; it does not get asked because it cannot be thought or framed or said. Is it not much more likely that what people are trying to begin to find out about each other is not 'What do you do?' but 'What are you like?' It is only by observing and interacting with people for a while that we can begin to answer this one, as what they are, and what they are like, expresses itself in their ways of being – their manners.

Recently, I asked a number of people what they thought manners were. Some tried to define them; quite a few answered more in terms of what they are for, and how they operate. Most did both, and it became clearer that the two are virtually inseparable. Interestingly, all of them took for granted the view that manners are the outward manifestation of a moral code, however elementary, in human behaviour; and most made some reference to their conviction that one can fairly easily see through false charm or insincerity. The definitions of manners included a sensitivity to the wishes and needs of others, considerateness, respect, tact, putting another person at ease, meeting obligations, and being truthful as far as possible without being hurtful. Ways of controlling other people came to seem important as we discussed it, as well as keeping control over uglier and more primitive parts of the self. As to what manners are for: they are to give freedom and space to the minds and feelings of the self and others; they combine with purposeful activity to keep civilization alive and flourishing; they oil the wheels of social intercourse; they make life easier and perhaps a bit happier for everyone; they control chaos. An experienced and, by now, somewhat cynical old GP said: 'Human nature is basically nasty; by inclination we are greedy, aggressive and selfish; we have to be taught to be nice, not to snatch and grab, to notice that other people are there and they might have needs, too – manners are what get banged into children to do as they would be done by.'

This last phrase, of course, reminded us of *The Water Babies* (1863) by Charles Kingsley, the nineteenth-century morality tale for children, which is still a classic. You will recall that Tom, the little chimney-sweep, falls into the water, where he has adventures and meets all sorts of characters, who virtually cleanse him and teach him manners, so that he is a fit companion for Ellie, a rather posh little girl who has also fallen into the water. The two most memorable characters are the magic fairies, who look just like old women, but one is apparently nicer than the other – she is Mrs Doasyouwouldbedoneby while the uglier, crosser one is Mrs Bedonebyasyoudid – although, of course, this being a proper

Morality Play, Tom learns her value in the end, when she becomes, mysteriously, indistinguishable from the nicer one!

I thought that there was a comprehensive overview of manners collected in my soundings, and only wanted to add to them an oblique and Delphic gloss coming from Freud himself. In *The Ego and the Id* in 1923, he gave his first full presentation of his new structural theory and concentrated on the development of the superego; he said that not only is man more immoral than he believes, but he is also *far more moral than he knows* (my italics). On the whole, psychoanalysis would probably agree with the GP that human nature is basically nasty, although, as is implied in Freud's comment, it would allow more credit to the unconscious ego and its efforts, which, after all, included the creation of the judging moral agency, the superego.

There is no doubt that early conditioning by the family environment has an enormous part to play in shaping the essential ingredients of what become the child's manners. It is from this fountainhead that some quite comic stereotypes arise, which, like many of the jokes played by life and fate, are seen to be also sad and serious when closely investigated. There are a number of national stereotypes in most Western cultures, and their existence, lurking in the preconscious of many people, can quite powerfully influence one's expectations and even one's direct experience, of meeting strangers. The preservation of these fantasy figures in people's minds, especially in relation to foreigners, is not, of course, diminished by the fact that every so often one *does* encounter classical examples of such caricatures, who seem to have been given a handbook of the required features at an impressionable age, and obeyed it faithfully. Very occasionally, they may present themselves for analysis, usually complaining of depression or a sense of deadness, or having lost their way or their energy. If they can take it, the treatment really consists of a slow and often painful undoing of a deep conditioning to certain types of manners, which can harden into character armour and act as almost impenetrable defences.

Such a one is the stereotypical middle-class Englishman, the product of an emotionally immature and repressive family who often worked for long periods abroad, necessitating, they believed, that their child be sent home to board at a public school. A number of repetitive rationalizations accompanies this enforced separation, which often continues right through the school holidays when the child stays with an aunt or a grandmother or even with total strangers. One of these rationalizations is that the experience will 'make a man of him', teach him to stand on his own two feet, and another is that, whatever else, he will be taught good manners. Indeed, these children quite soon manifest a precocious pseudo-independence, and a way of being with others which may well pass for good manners, but which is, in truth, an often heroic, quiet attempt to master misery and despair, and submit to the apparently inevitable with as good a grace as can be mustered. The young man who emerges from these ten or twelve years is severely emotionally limited, with repression and continued suppression both playing their part, since showing anything which could be labelled 'emotion' is under strong taboo. Although some emotions do continue to be felt, they are rarely shared or shown, the language of feelings is scarcely learned, and the psychophysical muscles of expression atrophy and wither away. Hence the familiar description of the 'stiff upper lip'.

Alongside this severe crippling, the stereotype Englishman is encouraged to be brave, uncomplaining, dutiful, truthful, kind to animals and able to laugh, a sense of humour being one of his most prized possessions. He himself, and many of his associates, do not notice that the laugh often has a rather hollow, mechanical quality. Close attention to the humour and laughter reveals, also, that like his manners in general, it is not only rather frighteningly empty, but is stuck at a developmental level which is predominantly anal in character, and may be the only surviving channel for his lost anger and hostility. An extreme prudishness about all actual bodily functions accompanies a humour in which the most genuine laughter is provoked by excretory noises and schoolboyishly 'rude' jokes. His personal sexuality is handicapped through ignorance, inexperience of women, and fear, and may well be stuck at a perverse or homosexual stage; it does not allow for easy laughter at sexual jokes. His fantasy life and imagination suffer from the overall crippling, the exception being if this imagination can be partially channelled into organization; whatever one's political views of history, no one ever denied that the British Empire was well organized. Indeed, with the decline of the Empire it is possible

that this type also is disappearing, since the safety net of Empire-
building preserved it intact. What was called leadership was a
treasured quality, and extensively deployed in the Empire, where
large numbers of people who seemed to be even more ignorant
than himself had to be subjugated and told what to do. Sophistication, subtlety, self-knowledge, irony and the capacity for intimacy were not prominent in his make-up, and this probably
facilitated withstanding the strangeness and loneliness of much
of his life. The character himself, if asked point blank, would
admit, leaving aside his inbuilt modesty for a moment, that his
manners were probably impeccable, reliable, and helped also to
sustain him.

What can he mean? Are we talking about true or false here? This
is the grey area of overlap; we may think, in the words of William
Cowper (1782):

> Manner is all in all, whate'er is writ,
> The substitute for genius, sense and wit. (lines 542–3)

Yet because stereotypes evoke humour, it is easy to judge them
harshly. This man is, after all, *living a life*, he has made of his
painful early experiences what he can, he is real to himself in so far
as he can think in those terms, even if he is not sure what people
actually mean when they speak of 'the self', or feelings, or
happiness. He would not steal from you, let you down, break his
word, or fail in small conventional attentions in conventional
situations that he understands. If a percentage of good manners is
knowing what to do with one's body in public, he would pass that
test. He would do his best to oil the social machinery. At one level
of definition, he is truly well mannered.

On the other hand, we soon begin to discover that we are limited
to that level. He neither controls others nor inspires them. One
can sense a shrinking and a shrivelling in his presence. He does not
stimulate the imagination, does not touch one's deeper feelings –
except perhaps, as Aristotle said tragedy should, of pity and horror
– does not evoke one's own humour, laughter or wit. His social
conduct certainly comes nowhere near Dr Johnson's comment
(Boswell, 1791, p. 188) on Lord Chesterfield's *Letters to his Son*
(1774) 'They teach the morals of a whore, and the manners of a
dancing master'! He quite probably is boring, and it is not

courteous for his companion or listener to show boredom, so he
may set up a struggle in another person. The deep unchangingness
of his manners and his moral code has a frustrating quality about
it, one senses that he is so identified with his conditioning that it is
like a skin, even more than a camouflage. His lack of subtlety
would never let him aspire to the succinct definition which my
grandmother, a Victorian snob, was fond of quoting, that a
gentleman is never rude except on purpose. One fears that all
unwittingly, his very self would be a spanner in the works of
marriage, if it were not for the fact that until fairly recently, enough
women had undergone a sufficiently similar conditioning to provide him with a choice of a suitable wife.

The people whose manners we genuinely admire and enjoy are
those who, without it being obvious, skilfully enhance our sense
of significance and worth. All contact, whether conversational or
silent, is accompanied by an atmosphere of warmth and generosity;
this promotes trust and openness. As it is said, they bring out the
best in us. Although we may not often think about it, we might
confidently anticipate that the original root and stem of considerate
manners was positive. These are people, quite simply, who have
introjected at least one loving and trustworthy parental object.
They are not afraid. If, on the other hand, an individual has
unconscious needs and fears which have constructed reaction-
formations rather than unselfconscious, genuine ways of being,
there is some noticeably different quality about the behaviour; it
may be impossible to locate or describe with any degree of
precision what this difference is, but it may be an almost indefinable sense of falsity, of forcing. There is something uneasy about
being on the receiving end of this type of manners – they are not
spontaneously and intuitively flexible, not tailored exactly to the
minute facets of their object. It occurs to me only now that one of
the ways of beginning to think about this difference may be
connected with the difference between the narcissistic and the truly
object-related character.

Opening this up brings two further trains of thought in its wake.
One is about continuous development and the capacity for change
and adaptation. There is a quality in the narcissistic character which
conveys an impression of stasis, a kind of underlying fixed frozen-
ness, long since dislocated from the organs of attention and the

associated use of the conscious will. Constant close attention to
the Other includes as part of its purpose a readiness for responsive
change, not necessarily at depth where the sources of moral energy
remain reliably constant, but in numerous small ways which allow
for more sophisticated adaptations; this is regularly encountered in
an individual whose object-relating capacity is securely established.
Those of us who have analyzed narcissistic character disorder over
a long period know, from direct experience, not only that we may
not even be sure that that *is* what we are doing for many months,
so effective are the layers of disguise; but also that there is a deep
resistance to change, a dense unyielding quality in the structures of
the inner self. There is an actual dread of change, as if the petrified
rituals and systems may simply be unable to accommodate, or, if
the effort is made, they will break or fail. I think it is the outer,
masked reflection of this dread which can give to another person,
on a social level, an obscure sense of unease, almost of facelessness.
One is in touch with a manneristic constant, not a pliant behaviour
designed to perceive the Other as an individual, to be respected
and followed. Hence the experience of being rather unpleasantly
controlled, a bit depersonalized, which can and does occur in the
recipient.

Examples come to mind: the person who is, for narcissistic
reasons, dedicated to 'unselfish' sacrifice in the service of others,
frequently makes available, perhaps in a subtle but certainly in a
controlling way, services that do not quite fit with what is needed
at that moment. Help is difficult both to give and to receive at the
best of times; if it is proffered in a manner which is unimaginative
or over-forceful, it can become an imposition. There is nothing
quite like getting someone slightly, and rather obviously, in your
debt for arousing an underlying antagonism towards them in you
– or towards you in them. A small social event which I notice
occurs with quite amazing frequency is the attempt, apparently
offered in a friendly way, to coerce another person to stop doing
something he or she is doing – and is accustomed to doing – but
who may be enjoying a transient grumble about it, and do it
another way, that is, the way offered by the giver. This, I am sorry
to say, is a phenomenon which occurs more often among women,
perhaps because they operate with certain currencies of social
interchange more than men do; one notices that the listener ceases

to listen to the casual account which may be only superficial, a minor complaint, a 'letting-off steam', and is instead preparing the offer, which is given with great force and insistence. The speaker is urged to go to this dentist, or that shop, or another holiday resort altogether – the list is virtually endless; in fact the only regularly exempt piece of property, which is never offered in this controlling way, is the listener's therapist, no doubt for complex reasons; a little reflection on why this should be so might throw some light on the whole phenomenon!

I said just now that two trains of thought had arisen out of comparing and contrasting narcissistic and object-related manners. The second is to do with old age. Increasing opportunities to observe the elderly, and, particularly for my purposes here, the dementing, suggest that a lifetime of genuinely sensitive and considerate good manners, rooted in the kind of moral character which goes on trying to practise a robust and unsentimental love for fellow humans, is more enduring than the narcissistic kind. In the latter, when more often than not a secret mirror held up to the self has been the primary focus, and the gratification of narcissistic needs the strongest motivation, the manners, though 'impeccable', are the habitual facade of barriers against inner change, and more rapid disintegration may ensue. The structure, though it may have served its purpose, is more brittle. These are the people who, faced with the painful, boring and often humiliating changes of old age, manifest little endurance or fortitude and become querulous and fractious, until the young steer clear of them, and their carers are driven to rage, unhappiness, and intense death wishes. The sense of loss and devastation all round is terrible. And it is very unlike the atmosphere surrounding characters who may manifest a kind of simplicity, serenity and sweetness with what is left of their minds, and who retain love, care and gratitude as if in reward for a lifetime of having genuinely given these things. If these observations have led to a valid distinction here, then what a warning to ourselves is carried in it! Is it ever too late to start?

No, it is probably never too late to try to change, which brings me directly to the consulting room, where one of the features of our faith in the process which we help to create there is our faith that there is always hope. I want to consider the question of manners in our practice as analysts and therapists. I have met with the idea that manners are not part of practice, but I find this difficult to take in, not really being able to imagine how they would be shelved, or taken off for the day as if they were not part of our working uniform. I hope by now I have said enough in this paper, both directly and indirectly, to indicate that if manners are the continuous, minutely detailed expression of our characteristic selves in our whole ways of being – in the world and therefore in society – then it follows that they are simply *there* in our encounters with our patients – they cannot fail to be. If someone were to insist that manners play no part in professional technique and ways of being with individual patients, then I would have to say that either this is incomprehensible to me, or that perhaps what is being referred to is a thin layer of obligatory charm, a polite facade, which can indeed be taken off, and probably should be, in our working lives. Or, of course, if I were feeling argumentative, that it is rubbish.

Whether we like it or not, we are certainly obliged to scrutinize in some depth the personal working style which we all develop, which says as much about us as does the most elaborate formal occasion. Our manners permeate our technique at every conceivable point, every choice we make over what and when and why and how we speak. And not only speak, though we are the current guardians of a long, long tradition of treatment, counselling, and healing in which speech is the predominant instrument. There are many aspects of our working life, which might be called apparent trivia, to which our attention must be continually redirected, which may become second nature to us, and may never be particularly noticed by the patient. Quite apart from the need to attend to our own state of optimum health, both mental and physical, and the maintenance of peace, warmth, cleanliness, punctuality, and freedom from intrusion in our working milieu, the tensions and demands of our professional lives may involve us in quite elaborate tasks, and yet they are not options, but essentials. I wrote about this at much greater length in a paper called 'Attention' (1990; this volume, Ch. 12), in which I explored the meaning and uses of this much neglected subject, which is nevertheless constantly in use, by us; the fact is that it becomes so natural, this absolutely solid foundation of our working technique, that it has dropped from view in our thinking and is most of the time simply taken for granted, as if it were a necessary 'given' informing all we do. *It is not.* The capacity to be attentive in all its essential modes is a highly disciplined and hard-earned skill. We need to pay constant attention *to* attention, its uses, its value, and our power to sharpen it up and refine it.

There are special sorts of details of our working style which are more obviously connected with manners, although I don't think any of the things to which I have referred in the previous paragraphs fall outside that category. An example of the more specialized kind is handshaking, about which there is a surprising number of different opinions, veering from one end of the spectrum where analysts never, under any circumstances, shake hands with patients, to the other end where there was Michael Balint. I introduce him here, in this rather bald statement, because he exemplified an extreme position so clearly and so consistently. He shook hands at the beginning and end of every session, a demonstration, at least in part, of how strongly one's early national culture – in his case, Hungarian – can imprint habits on to one's behaviour. In Britain, learning of this practice usually provokes quite strong reactions, including in myself; my main objection to it is an idea that it could interfere with the flow of the process, especially in an acutely negative phase, rather as if having to reassure one's analyst at the end of every session, especially an angry, hostile one, that one still loves him.

In conclusion, these thoughts about the contrast between Balint and a more 'English' type of analytical technique in the matter of handshaking lead me to a subject I touched on before in a paper called 'What does it mean: "Love is not enough"?' (this volume, Ch. 8); the subject of the many engaging paradoxes which are found in psychoanalysis. Examples of these include the necessity for close involvement alongside a genuine detachment; the capacity to focus attentively on any current material, while at the same time remaining open to all free associations, memories and feelings experienced in the countertransference; the need for constant decision-making about what we are hearing and are going to say, together with restraint in the formation of subjectively critical moral judgements; the importance of knowing, remembering and storing away an enormous quantity of information, as well as striving to remain free from memory and desire, as Bion described it (1970, p. 41);

our handling and development of all these could, from various angles, be seen to arise from, or at the very least be influenced by, our moral and emotional character and hence our manners. But for our purposes, I would like to underline one of the most difficult technical paradoxes of them all – the need for consistent scanning and judging, not only of what the other person says, but of what *we* are about to say, and are saying; and with this scanning, the need for rapid continuous thinking, which may be only half-conscious; the need for repeated moral and technical decision-making; *and yet*, if it is to convey truth, and more importantly, authenticity, in our style of speech we must also master intuitive, unlaboured *spontaneity*. This is an extremely demanding and complex requirement. I think its skilful development is the main reason why it takes another ten years after qualification as an analyst really to become an analyst. It depends, for success, exactly as do really good manners, on another paradox – the combination of unselfconscious self-forgetfulness with deep self-confidence.

A distinguished literary critic, Lionel Trilling, wrote a readable book in the early 1970s called *Sincerity and Authenticity* (1972), in which he describes and examines the rise and fall of sincerity as a moral criterion in society from the fifteenth to the nineteenth centuries, and explores how and why it declined and came to be replaced by authenticity as a more stringent criterion. Both in France and England the concept, or rather the attribute, of sincerity came to be more and more suspect, but there is still a kind of moral strength attached to the notion of authenticity, and Trilling makes the point that authenticity is a more strenuous moral experience than sincerity. Although I suspect that authenticity itself is beginning to develop quotation marks around it, in the sense that its true meaning is becoming contaminated by fashionable overuse, especially in the world of art, I am not sure what is going to replace it, and it will have to stand as an ideal for us to aim for in our self-expression through our working manners. The basis of it, deep in ourselves, must, I think, be founded on a personal philosophical study of what we consider to be the good and the true for ourselves, and how these are incorporated and can best be practised in our chosen vocation. Then perhaps, as we try to summarize how manners and personal style operate at their level of maximum skill

and authenticity in our lives and work, we cannot improve upon
Polonius' advice to Laertes, in a long speech which is all about the
deepest meaning of manners, and which ends:

> Th s above all: to thine own self be true,
> And it must follow, as the night the day,
> Thou canst not then be false to any man. (*Hamlet*, I. iii. 78)

10

THE ANALYSIS OF AN ELDERLY PATIENT

Freud was not optimistic about analysis with older patients, partly because of what he thought of as the mass of mental material to be dealt with, and also because of the rigidity of the character and the defences that comes with old age; though one has to add that strangely it seems as if he may have left one important older person out of this viewpoint, namely, himself. Of recent years, older patients have been treated more often by psychoanalysis, and accounts of them have appeared in the literature during the last twenty years. I have found that as I myself age, my interest in treating older patients has also grown steadily, and there is a quality to the work which in the last few years I have found increasingly appealing, and which has guided my choice in selecting new people with whom to work. This quality has much to do with a kind of now-or-never feeling which the patient brings into the analysis. There is a single-minded, often clear, sense of need, an intensity of devotion to the work, a skill in recognizing shorthand opportunities, and a reduction in shame and embarrassment (as if to say 'Oh, I haven't got time for all that') which is very attractive. The patient under discussion, however, was one of my first, and at the point when the analysis started, I could not be said even to have entered upon early old age. He taught me a lot which I have found valuable since then, as the number of older patients in my practice has risen.

I hope to refer, sometimes obliquely, but with an underlying

First published in the *International Journal of Psycho-Analysis*, Volume 72, Part 2 (1991).

sense of direction, to three themes in particular: first, the dynamic and convincing quality of constructions when they can be accurately pinpointed, and based on the transference; second, specific features which, in my view, are peculiar to the older patient; and third, the necessity of, and reasons for, accepting what with younger patients might be seen as limited gains.

THE STORY

Once upon a time, about seventy-five years ago now, a first child, a son, was born to a middle-class couple living in the North of England. The husband was thirty-eight, and the wife was thirty-four, so they were not in the first flush of youth. The wife was not in some ways a very womanly woman, and the husband, though a decent genial fellow, was not a very manly man. I think that the wife, during the Great War, when she married, maybe thought that if she did not do so then, she might not do so at all, and she wanted to. She married an Army officer who survived the war unharmed, but who was, of course, away for the greater part of the young boy's first four years. It seems that the wife had respected and feared her own Victorian father, that she liked her husband well enough, but rather despised him, especially as *his* father was a cheery drunken ne'er-do-well, and that she fell passionately in love with her firstborn son. I think that their early union was intense, and that she, as well as he, had ambivalent feelings when she became pregnant again within the year, and her second son was born when the first was eighteen months old. She was a lady of strong principle as well as strong personality, and I am sure she made every endeavour to show love to the boys equally, and to instil in them a strong morality; but the first son was her chosen love, and in some deep ground of her being she never truly let him go.

The little boy, too, was strong and spirited. His innate disposition was one of fierce emotions, an 'extreme' temperament. Capable of wholehearted delight, I inferred, in his primary secluded year with his mother, it became clear in the transference, as I will later show, that a murderous rage towards her and the new baby, which has been partly preserved in family legend, was not simply a construction. Nor was it by any means entirely repressed – then. But his ego became rapidly sophisticated; and his superego development, in keeping with the weighty ethical traditions of his mother's family, and fuelled by his own reserves of aggression, was powerful and harsh. For the year or so during which he hated his mother and his brother, I think he suffered a period of depressive gloom, and history strongly suggests that ferocious anal-retentive warfare was waged: this was again later borne out by the quality of some of the transference. Certain family anecdotes foretell his character structure: for example, when he was aged three, an aunt offered to share an egg with him. He announced unequivocally that if he could not have a whole egg, he wasn't having any egg at all, and he made a vigorous attempt to run away from home, taking a toy suitcase with his teddy and his toothbrush in it. He also has a vivid screen-memory from the age of four and a half; he was standing in a wood, watching his mother who was watching his brother who was playing on a tree trunk. He said to his mother, 'You love John more than me.' She looked at him silently for a moment, and then said quietly and fiercely, 'No I do *not* – but he is smaller than you.' He could still tell this memory with poignantly intense affect.

Shortly after this, and coinciding closely with the return home of father, a decisive turn in his emotional kaleidoscope occurred, in which certain configurations were rearranged, and in analysis it came to seem to us as if one of the underlying patterns thereafter remained the locked-in, dominant and – it is essential to add – repressed key motif of his life. I will briefly describe this in synoptic form, in which approximately five years of analysis is condensed into a paragraph which represents the accumulated construction in all its complexity.

The love for his mother, arising from delight in his first year, was nevertheless later compounded by, first, fear of engulfment, and then, oedipally, by severe castration anxiety, and the resulting ambivalence was intolerable; he was impelled to negotiate a solution, so he split and rearranged his feelings and his objects. He refocused much of the libidinal attachment to his mother on to his little brother; this indirectly pleased his mother, insofar as he became devoted to John; and, consequent upon this displacement from his mother, he also relieved some (but by no means all) of his oedipal fear of his father. He never really separated from his mother, but he withdrew from her on his emotionally conscious surface, and he also omnipotently identified with her role towards his brother: thus he preserved his capacity to love, and the infantile narcissistic idealization – of his mother – in the personal bond with the brother, who became his most deeply loved object-choice. He remained thereafter fixated to this solution, which produced the necessary inner peace at the time. The pre-oedipal, homosexual and narcissistic unconscious meanings of, and conflicts surrounding, this object choice were each so weighty and so finely balanced that, with their pulls and counter-pulls, they anchored him forever to a central psychic structure which was like a great fragile rock. When we eventually became convinced that he had fallen in love with his brother and *stayed* there, it was as if it were a surprise, an amazement, and yet at the same time carried the simple conviction of something deeply known to him nearly all his life.

The intensive, detailed work with this patient gave me an enjoyable clear picture of how the dynamic quality of sequential periods of life resemble a series of plays, with existing characters taking on new roles as the scenarios shift, and development takes place. Joyce McDougall's book, *Theatres of the Mind* (1986), supplied a valuable metaphor for my thinking about this patient, appearing as it did some years after the end of his analysis. The sense of evolving conviction, which has to be equally shared and strong in both analyst and patient and which compares well with that of a well-produced play, was very much a feature of the analysis, particularly surrounding the work which is compressed in the foregoing paragraph. I will have more to say about this towards the end of the paper.

From then on, he had a good-enough childhood. He was clever, with a special emphasis on that oft-recurring mixture of mathematics and music; he was also good at sport, and throughout his life sport has continued to sponge up a lot of his energy. In these ways he identified with, and made friends with, his father, and his latency period was generally quite jolly. His puberty was complicated only by the fact that by the time he was twelve he played practically everything, including the piano, *better* than his father. He somehow managed to compartmentalize sport to his advantage, but his piano-playing became irrevocably sexualized and hence, for him, contaminated by anxiety, although by a mixture of talent and aggression he managed to maintain it intermittently. But it had undergone severe vicissitudes, and when he started his analysis, he had not played for several years, though often longing to: he had a truly phobic reaction to the piano.

He did well at school, and left at sixteen to go straight into the world of finance. All through his schooldays he did most things with his brother, though he made good friends as well. I would like to stress at this point, in order to address a query that may well be arising in the reader's mind, that he had never been conscious of homosexual inclination or anxiety. His brother, to complete his personal appearance in my story, clearly flourished in the loving matrix provided for him, and had a satisfactory and normal life. He became eminent in his chosen field. He also was able to marry happily, and had several grown-up children. The patient came back to see me for some sessions several years after the end of the analysis, when his brother was killed in an accident: I read about this untimely death in the papers, and was already expecting the appearance of the patient.

When the war came, the patient was commissioned into the Army and had what is known as a 'good war', adventurous, brave, and enjoyable. He emerged as a major with a high decoration. During the war he was in a big, exotic, Middle-Eastern city. Here he had the first, and only, sexual affair of his life with a wealthy and glamorous courtesan – or so I was led to believe. The patient was not a liar. This city figured in his dreams as a sexual place. He did not love this woman, and he had a brief, terrified conviction thereafter that she had given him VD, which she had not.

He then went on to one of the European enemy countries with the Allied Forces, and there he formed a romantic, idealizing and non-sexual attachment to a local girl. The war ended and he came home, fully intending, so he *thought*, to return immediately and bring her home and marry her. He told his parents this, and they both evinced strong disapproval – a foreigner, of a race who had been a recent enemy, and a Catholic! Significantly, in spite of the strength and purity of his love for her, as he remembers it, he put up no opposition to them. He withdrew from home, parents, and consciously from all thoughts about the girl, whom he never contacted again. Parts of her country often appeared in dreams as

erotic – rather than sexualized – places, though she never herself
figured in them.

He took up his career again in the world of finance, and became
extremely successful and rich. He became a 'clubbable' man with a
host of friends, many of them married couples. He was a big, tall,
personable character, always expensively dressed in casual or City
style. In society, he displayed, I imagine, a beguiling mixture of
cheerful friendliness and reserve, always ready with an excellently
recounted story or joke against himself, yet rarely doing what is
known as 'giving himself away'. He never fell in love again and
was always conscious of unease, amounting at times to distinct
anxiety, when alone with women. In his early forties, he 'inadvertently', as he put it, got entangled with the wife of a friend who
had to go abroad for a while, and this woman fell in love with him.
At that very time his father died. These two events became
psychically condensed and he went into a panic and then became
depressed, after extricating himself with clumsy vigour from the
woman, and failing to mourn his father of whom he had been
deeply fond. I think his oedipal guilt flooded him, and the whole
thing had to go into repression, but left him burdened and
withdrawn, and he had been unable to transcend it alone.

At that point, he embarked on several years of weekly psychotherapy which relieved his depression. It struck me when I first
heard his story that his seeking out, first, analytical psychotherapy,
and second, full analysis, was a measure of his independence and
singularity. He lived and moved in a milieu which was almost
entirely ignorant of the impact of psychoanalysis on the culture of
the twentieth century. The very unlikelihood of the steps he took
to seek help was a guarantee of privacy. He kept in touch with that
therapist on a moderately social basis when the therapy finished,
since the therapist was someone who permitted a small measure of
socializing following a successful treatment, and it was to him that
he spoke at last, with great diffidence. He had become increasingly
prone, again – and this time, without any obvious precipitating
cause – to longer and longer episodes of severe depression. He
finally told his first therapist that he thought it would not be long
before he committed suicide. He was perfectly serious about this,
and as he is devoid of hysterical features in his self-expression, his

therapist took him perfectly seriously and referred him to me for
analysis.

A THERAPEUTIC CHALLENGE

The patient was fifteen years older than myself. I experienced my
agreeing to undertake his analysis as an engaging challenge. I think
there were two aspects to this feeling. One was that this eminently
successful – in a worldly sense – man was telling me that the whole
complex structure, which had taken him nearly half a century to
build, was breaking down; things were falling apart, the centre was
not holding. (This allusion to Yeats' poem, 'The Second Coming',
arises naturally here because I described a clinical vignette from
this man's analysis in an earlier paper in which I explored a long
metaphor from that poem (1986; this volume, Ch. 1). The patient
was in deadly earnest when he austerely referred to the imminent
possibility of death by suicide unless we could make some sense of
what was happening to him and in so doing, relieve his suffering. I
felt that, although we might not win, we had, at this point, nothing
to lose.

The second ingredient of the challenge was, of course, his age.
There is a profound difference between analysing anyone who is
either the same age as, or younger than, oneself, and analysing an
older patient who is, experientially, deep into territory which is, as
yet, totally unknown to the analyst. However different the basic
psychopathology, the common human experience of ageing itself
brings continual shifts and changes, and this feature, I am sure
older readers will agree, becomes more marked, more noticeable
and more complex, the further on one goes. I sensed that part of
the challenge here would be to a specially sensitive deployment of
that blend of identification, imagination and intuition which is
called empathy.

The referral to a woman analyst was correct. I was soon in no
doubt that the fact that I was a woman evoked an extraordinarily
intense transference more speedily and more wholly than would
have occurred with a male analyst. In *this* patient, at *this* particular
point in his life's journey, the rich and constant source of information provided by the transference, which often manifested both

erotic and psychotic features, was exactly the instrument required to do the work which was, by then, desperately crying out to be done. Indeed, I would say that this man deepened my knowledge of three things in particular – one was the detailed use of the transference and the countertransference; the second was the capacity to sit it out day after day opposite a patient in psychotic regression, since he always absolutely refused to lie down on the couch, and during parts of his analysis he was in this state; and the third was to respect the syllable 'um', which I will come to in a moment.

There was, very slowly, a remarkable amount of verbal communication from this deeply secretive man, but at the price of great effort. From the beginning, he wasted no time on superficialities; he knew he was desperate, and, having had some analytical therapy, he knew what he must do, though much of the time he could not do it. Nevertheless, he somehow enabled me, almost from the start, to understand *some* of the communication from the unconscious *most* of the time. Indeed, often I found that my insight had become sharp and clear and I was eager to feed it back while he was still trying slowly and painfully to articulate something. This is what I mean about the syllable 'um'. I learned, the hard way – and I think it is sometimes harder for us with a face-to-face patient – never to speak when he had *apparently* finished a sentence or paragraph, if he had at that point, however quietly, added 'um' on to the end of it. If I spoke into the silence preceded by 'um' it would always be too soon; I would have spoiled something, taken something away, imposed my way of seeing something that he was gradually reaching for himself. It was with this man that I conceived the use of the metaphor of the Rough Beast slowly coming up to the light, which I subsequently used in the paper 'Slouching towards Bethlehem . . .' (1986; this volume, Ch. 1). Through the door opened by this subtle manoeuvre, that is, his use of 'um' not only in mid-communication, but, as I slowly realized, as a transference signal, I really came to know how he had never separated out from his mother, and how easy it was, through his projective identification of her, for me to threaten him with engulfment or annihilation. We were at the deepest level of being, so fused with each other that a tentative 'um' from him was his only possible attempt to signal something that, accurately translated meant: 'Hold on, shut up, don't interrupt me, let me finish, stand back, *get off me.*'

He had a romantic honeymoon phase at the beginning of analysis, lasting several months and carrying him through the first long summer break. He started analysis early in the year, and until about September was enchanted with me, with life, with his renewed love of piano-playing. He felt, he said, 'reborn'. It was from the experience of these months that I derived most of my thoughts about his first year of life. In fact, in a remarkable, condensed way, he truly did relive his early life in exact sequential order in the analysis.

By this I mean, more specifically, that in a way which was both extraordinary and impressive, and which greatly facilitated the creation of constructions, he showed me, through the changing windows of the transference, his psychological and affective drama from the beginning: the difference was that he could now think and speak – sometimes! – and there was an interpreter. For example, the significant use of the words 'I feel reborn': it was a true message. After the ecstatic early months – for he regressed almost instantly to the earliest phase of life – he lived through this changing developmental drama, as described in the very compressed paragraph above (pp. 146–7), in the exact order of its original happening, and with ample clues as to its inner meanings. It was my protracted experience of the inevitability of his psychic logic, as in a play, which continually informed the shared conviction to which I also referred.

Although it was a good thing for him to be relieved of the suicidal depression and to form a therapeutic alliance, I recognized, in fact, a sustained level of hypomania, and wondered what it meant and what was to come. Towards the end of this phase, and without any idea of what he might be giving away about himself (as he much later realized, to his profound horror!), he brought to a session one day what we subsequently always referred to as the 'pork-chop fantasy'. I did not realize at the time how rare an event this was to prove to be. Although he developed an expressive talent for dreaming during the analysis, he was always in some degree protected from shame and anxiety by the slight distance from conscious responsibility which is permitted by dreams, and because of this he could allow them to be explored and interpreted. But exposure of *conscious* fantasy very rarely occurred; I had little access, beyond sadistically tantalizing hints, to what I nevertheless know to have been a vivid conscious fantasy life. This is a man who sometimes said that, for all his problems, he could never be bored with an imagination like his! And, as with all other silent patients I have treated – for he became that for a period later on – he never bored me. I have written about this rather surprising phenomenon elsewhere (1991; this volume, Ch. 6). I suppose it is something to do with the curiosity which is a necessary component in an analyst's make-up; one always has the feeling that there is more – of great significance – to find out and know, and that at any moment it will appear. The 'pork-chop fantasy' contains a nuclear statement about his psychopathology and we returned to it over and over again, like a seminal dream, and since he wrote it down and it has a title I present it to you in its entirety as he presented it to me. In his lapidary language every word and metaphor is deep with potential meaning.

Fantasy whilst eating a pork-chop to the accompaniment of Rubinstein playing Chopin

I suddenly get angry with Nina – she thinks she has my behaviour under control but this angers me, and I suddenly go berserk and attack her – to strangle her perhaps, or rape her. She puts up a tremendous struggle although I can see she is very frightened and has bitten off more than she can chew. I know I will win and she hasn't a hope. There is a sort of ecstasy about it on both our parts in spite of fear and pain. I pass out. When I come to, I wonder if I have killed her, but she smiles, and we are reconciled, and the police ring the bell to come to the rescue, but she says everything is all right and asks them to go away and not pursue the matter. The next patient comes but runs away and leaves us. I realize that Nina is very brave and is taking a big risk with a patient like me but is also *worthy of me*. (his italics)

This is the end of the fantasy.

He would not associate to the fantasy at the time. Beyond commenting upon the importance of the reconciliation, I did not say any more at the time either. I have been criticized, in presenting earlier versions of this paper, for not getting down to it and wringing more out of it straight away. I can only say that with this patient, I know that would have been a counterproductive waste. I felt intuitively that it would have been inept to express my astonishment at the sudden eruption into the transference of an elaborate perversion, complete in every detail, including the symbolic appearance of the powerful superego and the stress on his narcissistic evaluation of my worth. Contemplating the fantasy, I felt like stout Cortez as he 'stared at the Pacific' (Keats, 1816, line 12) when he discovered it. I also had a rapid, parody thought about Voltaire's comment on God; that is to say, faced with a fantasy of these rich and detailed proportions from such a reticent man, I felt that if Freud had not existed, it would have been necessary to invent him.

THE AGE OF DARKNESS

Shortly after this, and *exactly* eighteen months after the start of the analysis (and it will be recalled that he was eighteen months old when his brother was born), his whole way of being suddenly changed; I was faced for the first time with an entirely different person, whom I was to come to know only too well, and who gave me some of the hardest times I have ever had with a patient in analysis. I will not enumerate the occasions of the arrival of this person (at first there were alternating, ever-shorter, periods of his previous self there) but only condense them by saying that gradually I came to recognize the deep, powerful material that was being offered to me, and – very gradually – I came to know how to use it.

At the time of the change, his very appearance in the waiting room was different. I can best describe it as shifty. He would come in and sit heavily and disjointedly down in the chair and avoid my eyes, apart from a few darting glances which usually convinced him, I later discovered, that I was looking scornful, cold or ugly. Never a rapid starter or an easily free-associative talker, the change in these sessions – which often continued uninterruptedly day after day, for weeks at a time – made his other self seem garrulous and confiding by contrast. At first I slowly tried out my repertoire for engaging with a silent patient; to no avail. He occasionally grunted, but even that soon stopped. His posture, expression, and, more

than anything, the extraordinarily powerful atmosphere he generated, radiated black, hateful, withdrawn depression, sometimes
permeated with acute anxiety and sometimes with a kind of electric
fury. Eventually in these sessions he might, and often did, fall
asleep. At the end of the hour I would, as usual, get to my feet,
whereupon he would instantly waken and lurch heavily from the
room, darting an evil, secretive glance at me as he went. After three
weeks of the first round of this, I composed a construction – that
he was reliving with me what it had been like when the joyful
omnipotent days of his babyhood were interrupted by the arrival
of his brother, who then became a permanent resident. Here I was,
in part, drawing on one of the features of the 'pork-chop fantasy',
namely that 'The next patient comes but runs away', which I
interpreted as what, in the very first months of his brother's life,
he wished the brother had done. The effect, as many analytic
events with this man proved to be, was quite dramatic. He sat up
and blinked into focus and out of psychosis; we then discovered
(he had not, of course, been aware of this at the time) that the
'pork-chop fantasy' had arisen and been written down on the day
after his brother's birthday! Such occasional findings are the small,
golden rewards of our impossible profession.

However, the periods of black, psychotic regression continued
to erupt into the analysis, and each time I was initially as startled
as any intimate of Dr Jekyll must have been at confronting the
sudden takeover of Mr Hyde. Each time, the intervening work had
been so fruitful and so engaging, and such real progress had been
made, that I was repeatedly unprepared for the sudden and
qualitative extremity of the change; but each time we ultimately
learnt more from these events and their meanings. I, after all, at
least had plenty of time to think during these silent periods; and
the countertransference became a valuable instrument of radar in
the darkness. Sometimes, by projection, he made me temporarily
have his despair, not just empathize with it; sometimes I became
violently aware of the murderous wish to destroy me and the
analysis; the sense of being made useless and excluded was a fairly
constant accompaniment; on a couple of occasions I experienced
over a period of days a slow crescendo of anger which I ultimately,
and with some calculation, albeit also with spontaneity – such
paradoxical states of mind are, I find, perfectly possible in the

analyst in a condition of attention (1990; this volume, Ch. 12) –
then allowed to explode into a few furious sentences about what
he was *doing* to me and thus to the analysis – again with dramatic
effects. I think that repression and suppression of anger had been a
moral imperative in this patient's family, all round, and the
explosion from me was proof of not being dead, damaged, forget-
ful, withdrawn, attending to somebody else, or uncaring. I was
aware that during my two or three major explosions I could be
said to be 'acting in' a variation of the 'pork-chop fantasy', and
later he and I discussed this, including the intensely relieving, and
almost orgasmic, effect on him. He would emerge alert, cheerful
and communicative, and for a while everything would be as merry
as a marriage-bell; I use the phrase advisedly, for he had a very
transparent dream shortly after one of these resolutions of our
impasses, in which he revealed his secret plan that the end of the
analysis would lead to our marriage; this, of course, would be the
apotheosis of the 'pork-chop fantasy', as we discussed at considerable length.

I will give one more dramatic example of the 'black hole'
phenomenon. In the third year of the analysis he had to have an
operation; he had a slowly developing oesophageal pouch which
was making it more and more difficult for him to swallow and he
would sometimes choke distressingly while eating. I need hardly
say that things did not go smoothly. The operation was a success,
but the patient damn near died. In the immediate post-operative
period, a clip slipped off an artery and he bled into his lungs and
almost drowned in his own blood. He was in an intensive-care unit
for three weeks but made a good recovery, as he was very fit. He
returned to the analysis, gave me a cheerful, sane and undramatic
account of what had happened, and dived straight into a black
silence. He growled out one remark on the second day of the
silence that time: 'You got me into this bloody mess – you bloody
well get me out.' We ultimately constructed that he had presented,
not only an operation for tonsils and adenoids when he was three,
but also, in a primary-process reversal or an example of mad
symmetry, that it had been as if *I* had left *him* in order to go into
hospital to have his baby brother, and that *I* had nearly died as a
result of his violent bloody attacks on me.

This massive construction, which, of course, contained a considerable amount of hitherto chronically unconscious meaning, had to be revisited by us in the analysis many times over the next few years; we stitched it slowly together with the understandings which I have compressed into the earlier paragraph about the rearrangement of the configurations in his emotional kaleidoscope following the birth of his brother (pp. 146–7), a rearrangement which we could now date more accurately as having conclusively occurred in his third year, when he had had the tonsillectomy. At the risk of sounding too elementary here, I would like to say that the psychic ability to master, at great depth, such extended interpretation as was demanded by this material, only comes slowly to any patient, and, I think, more slowly to an elderly patient. This patient was in analysis five days a week for nine years, and I do not consider it a reductionist simplification to say that the opening sentence of that paragraph describes the whole work of the analysis.

Following his operation, I cannot say that analytic life visibly settled down or became less prone to momentous destabilization from the Mr Hyde phases. But gradually, as our faith in the psychoanalytic process allows us to predict, the effect of functioning insight began to sink in, and produce change and improvement. We weathered the fact of his retirement, which – fortunately, I think – occurred during his time in analysis. He had dreaded it, with a deep and horrid dread, and was agreeably surprised to find that ongoing analysis of his dark fears had lightened the pathway: during this time, he came to feel more appreciative of his father, through increased understanding of almost totally unconscious identification with him; we also explored in detail his fears of death, which had become condensed in his mind with the prospect of retirement. (I wonder if this is not the case for many people?) It was part of the challenge of the work with this patient that I was made to investigate my own latent thoughts and fantasies about eschatology in order to work as fully as possible into his.

It was in the sixth year of the analysis, when he had finally become convinced about the joyful opportunities of retirement, the delights of expanded time (as opposed to his previous terror of shrinking time), and the consistent renewal of his pleasure in piano-playing, now disentangled from over-sexualization, that he began to demonstrate that the end of the analysis was thinkable. The regressed, hateful lapses disappeared, as did the bouts of ecstatic, hypomanic energy, whose quality had been unreliable. These were greatly eased by constant reworking of his alternating adoration and hate of me in the transference. His vivid dreaming continued to be a rich source of information. It was a dream about a bus, which the patient had boarded having alighted from a train, coming into a terminus, which signalled the approaching end of the analysis. I, or rather a composite figure who stood for me and with whom we were by then familiar from many other dreams, had stayed on the train, and had continued my journey alone. Thus he had gracefully yielded his long-held hope and fantasy that I would marry him as the only fitting conclusion to our joint venture.

He terminated the analysis after nine years, by which time he was nearly seventy. He became rather depressed a few months later, and asked to come and see me. He said in a letter that it was, however, nothing like it used to be, because of what he called 'a change of inner grounding'. He added that he understood that this was compatible with becoming depressed at times; he thought he could be helped by a few sessions, which he was. Thenceforward, for several years, he maintained a cheerful equanimity, but requested a session at approximately six-monthly intervals, during which we plunged straight into deep layers of analytic work. When his brother was killed in an accident about five years after termination, he came for about fifteen sessions, which seemed also to bring the overall work to completion. My impression was that, as he worked with real courage through the meaning to him of the life and death of his dearly loved brother, he became able to decathect me more fully. He emerged from that period more alone, but safer and stronger. He continued to send me a Christmas card, signed only with his full name – no news or comments. This was perfectly in keeping with his need for control and privacy, and I expected no more.

When all is said and done: some thoughts on the work

Two papers in the *International Journal of Psycho-Analysis* (1980) came to mind while reflecting on this patient, and have been useful. They were by Harold Blum and Eric Brenman, who were both considering the subject of 'The value of reconstruction in adult analysis'. Blum writes:

> The analysis of conflict derivatives could only be effectively accomplished in the here and now of the transference. The transference was a form of remembering, a living revival of the past in the analytic situation. The transference replaced what was forgotten and was itself a remobilised, though still disguised, return of the repressed. (p. 40)

Blum also reminds us that Freud referred, in his paper 'Constructions in analysis', (1937b) to '. . . an assured conviction of the truth of the construction which achieves the same therapeutic result as recaptured memory' (p. 266). In Brenman's paper I noted, particularly in relation to this patient, the examination of the transference phenomenon of 'The sadomasochistic fixation of clinging and hating with a corresponding relentless superego' (p. 57). Brenman goes on to describe: 'The bringing alive of past creative interactions and integrating these with creative constructions in the analysis and giving up past grievances of negative relationships . . .' (*ibid.*). This process he calls 'the analytic work and life work' (*ibid.*).

It is interesting to note that both Freud and Brenman employ this term 'construction', without distinguishing it from 'reconstruction'. I hope I am not splitting hairs when I say that there appears to me to be a clear distinction, in that 'reconstruction' suggests the exact reproducing of a lost memory, a piece of the past, whereas 'construction' gives adequate and respectful weight to the way in which every event in life is *new*, even in analysis, and that what the transference enables us to see and build is a strong skeletal structure (of recovery, and re-experience, true messages from the hinterlands of the past) clothed in new flesh, the direct, unique, personal experience of the analyst in the present. Brenman would not, I think, disagree with this distinctive definition. Christopher Bollas' two books, *The Shadow of the Object* (1987) and *Forces of Destiny* (1989), shed light on the *uniqueness* of the analytical experience of the present; he gives full attention to the primary and essential use of the transference and countertransference in the creation of constructions, but I think his great contribution to psychoanalysis in this last decade lies in a shift of

emphasis, with extensive use of clinical material to support his
ideas, so that full and appropriate weight is given to the ways in
which analytic experiences are also uniquely themselves, new, in
the here and now.

Of dominant interest in this analysis was the meaning of the
black silences: slowly elucidated, it became clear that they were
deeply overdetermined. They contained, depending on the transference context, varying combinations of the following elements:

1   fear of castration, or of being taken over and engulfed, by
the powerful woman;
2   a violent, punishing attack on me for being that woman;
3   a negative therapeutic reaction, whose main ingredients were
defiant obstinacy and envy;
4   linked with this last was a great fear of giving up the
entrenched pathological position. This is a form of resistance
which we very frequently encounter in psychoanalysis. It's a
'Better the devil you know than the devil you don't' attitude. It
has a last-ditch quality about it, and is often one of the hardest
and last of resistances to dissolve analytically.
5   A withdrawal to a secret fantasy world, more conscious than
he ever let on to me, where he could reign in solipsistic
splendour, and control everyone and everything:
6   suicidal despair:
7   anal–sadistic retentiveness:
8   a vital, reliving recovery of lost affect, true re-experience, or
new experience for the conscious self, showing what it was really
like down there, and the emotional darkness of the underground
river of his affective life.

These eight features figured prominently in much of the day-to-
day work of his analysis: not so much during a silent phase, when
the hallmark was no communication between us, but in the periods
of more tranquil retrospective exploring for which we sooner or
later found opportunity. A construction by me which triggered
emergence from a black hole always centred, more or less starkly
and boldly, on one or other of these points. As I have indicated
previously, an interpretative effort in this particular context was not
by any means always offered by me in the austere and benevolently
neutral manner which we hold as our working ideal. On more than

one occasion, I was pushed by introjected and/or subjective frustration, despair or fury into a display of affect which could at least be said to be consistent with the content of what I was interpreting. I am wholeheartedly prepared to stand by this behaviour as by now I believe with some authority that we can do no harm to a patient by showing authentic affect, within the limits of scrupulous self-observation. I am talking about being, not doing, perhaps I should emphasize. I am not arguing for emotionally directed action – such as touching, caressing, hitting, walking out – but for truth in our emotional being with a patient.

PARTICULAR PROBLEMS WITH OLDER PATIENTS WITH SPECIFIC REFERENCE TO LIMITED GAINS

For some years into the analysis, the patient, quite understandably, entertained the hope (wish) that the analysis might rid him of his inhibitions to the extent that even at this late stage he might achieve a satisfying sexual relationship with a woman, which he had never had. The work on what this meant was both facilitated and complicated by the strongly erotic aspects of the transference. As I have said, the simple (?) fantasy of marrying me was a dominant part of it, which served at times to conceal from him how much he also hated and feared me. It gradually became apparent to him that not only was this outcome an illusion, but that enlarging the idea to include managing sexual love with *any* woman was extremely unlikely. He was, and continued to be, 'a confirmed bachelor', and as he examined his life style in detail, he saw that there was much about it that was secure and ego-syntonic, and which depended on aloneness, and which he was simply not prepared even to contemplate giving up. Moreover, it seemed possible to me, and finally to him, that his deepest anxieties about sex, women and intimacy, though by the end extensively worked through, might re-awaken if he attempted to set up a close and continuing relationship with a woman. I am sure it is possible, especially in younger patients, for such full working-through of deep anxieties to take place that a patient is inoculated against them forever; this was certainly believed in the early years of this century, though I do not see it as an article of faith among many analysts today. I think the likelihood is greatly reduced in direct ratio to the increase in age of the patient. Anyway, I would not have trusted it with this patient, and by the end, neither would he.

What I am saying, therefore, is that in terms of his real, everyday life style, we had to settle for limited gains. There is a 'stickiness' about libidinal attachments in the later part of life, even as Freud said there was in certain character-types (Freud, 1916). The capacity to love takes longer to arouse, and once awoken, is less likely to be malleable. Anxieties which have been dealt with by competent psychic defence systems for over half a century cannot be expected to steal away and silently vanish forever. They can be considerably reduced, and furthermore, defences can be made more flexible and strengthened. This part of the analytic work may well need more detailed attention than will be the case in younger patients.

It should be borne in mind, also, that however extensive and effective our constructions had been about this man's sexuality, his presenting *symptom* was suicidal depression, and the impossibility, as it seemed to him, of enjoying – even *having* – the rest of his life at all. And this, I did and do believe, had gone; he had been successfully inoculated against it. However limited some of the gains may have been, this one was not; and I thought then, and think now, that to relieve severe depression is very near the top of any list of needs and hopes that is brought to analysis.

The patient had established a greater confidence with women socially, and was therefore drawing upon less energy for defence than previously, in the highly sociable milieu in which he moved. This improvement was rooted in a reduction in his paranoid vulnerability to psychotic distortion – a symptom which can be greatly helped in the elderly. We could, in fact, date this reduction precisely from a point at which, on emerging from a black hole, which itself had followed a mild overture to him by a woman during an analytic break, he was able to say with a deep and convincing simplicity: 'Yes, I see that all my life I have felt as if all women were my mother.' Another of the unsung rewards of our work is a moment like this – when something one has said, in various ways, a hundred times to a patient, comes back to us, quietly, with conviction, as if fresh-minted.

For interest, I will add that a curious phenomenon in this man's analysis was that until its seventh year, his mother was actually alive, alert and – in that rather grim way which does, I notice, happen in very old people – more 'like herself' than ever. My patient's very tense lifelong relationship with her improved as the analysis went on (and I drew a lot of the banked-up underlying fires on to myself in the transference); they had some friendly and forgiving meetings. It was when she died that he took the opportunity to mourn his father fully, as well as her; for all her mythic power of monstrous fascination and horror, she had been a woman of parts, with some sterling, admirable and witty characteristics – quite a Person, as they say. Even more importantly, the patient, now in his mid-sixties, began to face the prospect of his own death realistically and to mourn some of the lost opportunities of his life. These, I think, are two of the major special tasks in the analytic work with an elderly patient, and he faced them with seriousness and yet a kind of zest, such as had characterized the real achievements of his life.

I have said that he came back for sessions for some years following termination, and this I want to enlarge upon, finally, since I think it represented one of the ultimate problems in the analysis of an older person. This may be particularly the case when there has been a very intense analytic experience, after severe depressive breakdown. The transference is enriched by deep and long-pent-up emotion; but it is much more difficult to achieve a full and satisfactory termination, although this in itself is a concept that probably many of us come to question as we get older. With this patient, as with some other older ones I have treated, the amount of residual cathexis of the analyst absorbs more space and emotion than it might in a younger person who, amongst other things, is still more likely to go out and find new objects. In this particular patient's life, the extent of the years of deep emotional isolation made it very difficult to achieve the fuller degree of transference resolution which might normally be more available. However, he handled the double loss of his brother and myself with the dignity and courage one would have expected of him, and, apart from the intensive work we used to do in his occasional sessions, he went on his way more happily, but, as before, alone.

11

THE PRACTICE OF PSYCHOANALYSIS AND BUDDHISM

There is a long study yet to be written comparing and contrasting the practice of psychoanalysis and the practice of Buddhism. This is not it. This is a sketch for a more detailed exploration which I hope to make at some point in the future. Psychoanalysis and Buddhism are in many ways profoundly different, and indeed belong to different orders or categories, and yet on a simple, practical and philosophical level, they have much in common.

The evolution towards Buddhism in my thinking, as with a number of people I have met, goes back to Christianity. I was a practising Christian until a year or so before I went into analysis; so it was not the demon Freud who undermined my faith, it was a natural development. As it is said, 'I lost my faith', almost from one day to the next. I have come to think that this is rather an odd phrase because in a very real, but altered sense, *faith* was precisely the quality I retained, that is, faith in the ultimate and present value of the long, slow, often frustrating daily practice of both Buddhism and psychoanalysis. What I lost was belief in the existence of a personal, or any form of conceivable, God, and it has never returned. I missed this and the Christian practice a lot, and was in the wilderness for a long time, searching around for another path; and thus gradually moved towards and finally into Buddhism, in the Theravada tradition, about twenty year ago. The Theravada practice, as with all the main schools of Buddhism, centres on daily formal sitting meditation.

This is an amended version of a paper published in *The Middle Way*, the journal of the Buddhist Society, in 1985, under the title 'Freud and Buddhism'.

There has never been, from the earliest days, any sense of conflict about combining the practice of Buddhism with that of full-time psychoanalysis. Of course there are differences, which I will move on to now, and it is important to know what they are, and to maintain certain distinctions clearly in one's mind. But there are many more extensive and subtle ways in which they flow in and out of each other, and are mutually reinforcing and clarifying. A short summary of the main features of Buddhist teaching will be described, and a view of how they can be seen to contain the essentials of psychoanalysis, as I understand it.

It is a truth universally acknowledged that the work of Freud is the root and stem of all development in psychological thinking in the twentieth century, however diverse and under whatever titles. Bloom, writing in 1986, said that Freud's 'conceptions . . . have begun to merge with our culture, and indeed now form the only Western mythology that contemporary intellectuals have in common' (p. 26). To my mind it is a waste of time to use it up by niggling away at criticism of ideas which, like them or not, have their place in our history, and which have often served as springboards for further thought and theorizing. It also misses a larger point which is very relevant to this paper, namely, that anyone who is engaged in the wide field of psychotherapy, whatever their 'school' or 'training', is essentially interested in human nature, and keen to effect what reparation of ills they can with the tools available, and by now they are more or less agreed on two enormous main factors: first, that there is an area of the mind that is unconscious, and second, that human behaviour has *meaning* and can be understood psychologically, and that this is in itself therapeutic.

Let us consider some important differences. Dynamic psychotherapy is non-religious; it has evolved in the West from centuries of philosophic thought going back to the establishment of Cartesian rationalism. If there is one central question at the heart of the Western systems, out of which Freud himself grew, it is 'Who am I?' Christianity has, by its basic doctrines, helped to perpetuate the cult of the individual, and we are deeply conditioned in the West to the necessity of establishing a strong and stable ego-identity; psychotherapy is geared to this end, and, though it may in effect have many other by-products, its aim is thus limited, unlike the

aims of the Eastern spiritual tradition; theoretically psychotherapy
can be said to have goals. With the rooted assumption prevailing in
the West that a strong and resilient self can live in this world in a
state of more or less happy adjustment, Freud's great contribution
was that an increase in self-knowledge, in the context of a faithful
adherence to truth, can liberate the human spirit, his view as
expressed in a wonderful late paper, 'Analysis terminable and
interminable' (1937a). His famous dictum, 'Where Id was, there
shall Ego be' expressed the goal – psychoanalysis is the means to
it. In the Western view of psycho-structure, the ego is the mediator
between the unruly passions and fantasies of man, and the external
world, and the more self-knowledge leads to satisfactory internal
adjustment between the two, the more successful the outcome of
analytic psychotherapy is considered to be. I repeat, therefore, that
psychotherapy is essentially a means to an end, and not an end in
itself. Freud himself persistently maintained that he was *not*
constructing a philosophy of life, that his investigation into the
nature of the unconscious in relation to our whole sense of self was
not intended to be an ethical system, and that his intention was,
first and last, that human suffering could be healed or diminished
by the growth of self-awareness. Attempts to bend his theory into
a long-term philosophy of living, or world-view, whether this is
seen to be morally positive or, as has so often been the case, amoral
or even immoral, are a misinterpretation of his own thought on the
matter. Psychotherapy in our tradition encourages deep reflection;
this is quite different from the technique of meditation. By his
phrase 'liberation of the spirit', Freud did not mean the same thing
as is meant by 'liberation' as an Eastern religious goal; he meant
freedom from neurotic symptoms, inhibitions and anxiety. He
never, in fact, used the word 'identity' in the sense it has taken on
in the post-Freudian era, but his intention was to strengthen our
sense of individual identity. I would like here to quote a succinct
passage from an essay called 'Psychiatry and the sacred' by Jacob
Needleman; this essay appears in an excellent book of contributions from people who know something of the practice of both
sorts of discipline, variations on the two we are now considering.
The book is called *On the Way to Self-Knowledge*. Needleman
says:

In the great traditions (referring to the Eastern spiritual ones) the term self-knowledge has an extraordinary meaning. It is neither the acquisition of information about oneself, nor a deeply felt insight, nor moments of recognition against the ground of psychological theory. It is the principal means by which the evolving portion of mind can be nourished by an energy that is as real, or more so, as the energy delivered to the physical organism by the food we eat. Thus it is not a question of acquiring strength, independence, self-esteem, and security, 'meaningful relationships', or any of the other goods upon which the western social order is based and which have been identified as the components of psychological health. It is solely a matter of digesting deep impressions of myself as I actually *am* from moment to moment, a disconnected, helpless collection of impulses and reactions, a being of disharmonised mind, feelings and instinct. (Needleman and Lewis, p. 18)

The temptation to go on quoting from this essay is considerable, but I think that passage says clearly something about differences, and something which even a little reflection will show to be quite mysterious to our Western minds.

Before proceeding to similarities, or overlap, I would like to say something about what might be called 'meditation and muddles'. I refer to the ways in which the practice of meditation, the heart of the Buddhist tradition, can be misunderstood or misused by us in the West, and for our purposes here I refer most specifically to those of us who work in the field of therapy. Many practitioners will be familiar with the kinds of things I mean. Roughly speaking, however much we might disguise the stark nature of the fact from ourselves, I think it is true to say that people start on both these paths – therapy and meditation – with the wish for increased comfort and peace of mind; muddles can occur when aims are lost sight of, when there is inadequate teaching at the very beginning; and there is a danger peculiar to the West which I think cannot be overemphasized. For a Westerner to proceed healthily on the spiritual path which may lead to self-transcendence, and loss of 'the fortress of I', there needs must *exist already* a stable, strong sense of personal identity, albeit not necessarily a happy one. If this is lacking, then psychotherapeutic help may be needed to repair and stabilize the ego first before embarking seriously on a meditation practice. Eastern teachings either take for granted that a person already has a healthy structure or they define this differently in a totally different culture. This kind of assumption is dangerous in the West. If a person has not developed the ability to make at least some strong and wholesome personal relationships, or is ignorant of, or unable to express, his or her feelings, or is plagued by anxieties, then psychotherapy may well be the first treatment of choice before turning to meditation. Psychotherapy helps people to understand themselves in ways that are essentially pragmatic. I quote from John Welwood in *Awakening the Heart*: 'To attempt to skip over this area of our development in favour of some spiritual bliss beyond is *asking for trouble*' (1985, p. 82; my italics). And Robin Skynner, in an essay 'Psycho-therapy and spiritual traditions' adds (and here I paraphrase for brevity's sake): Some people following sacred traditions do indeed change a lot, and problems which might have taken them to a psychotherapist fade away imperceptibly; but they may inadvertently take from the spiritual movement that which actually keeps the ego strong; or some may, as a result of going into a spiritual system, become more closed, narrow and intolerant. This group is the most intractable of all, for the knowledge derived from a religious tradition has been put to the service of perceptual advances, of complacency, of narcissistic self-satisfaction, of comfort and security (Needleman and Lewis, pp. 220–21). A note of clear warning is issued by many authors in these books, of which I select John Welwood again for one final thought – that: 'the psychologizing of Eastern contemplative disciplines could rob those disciplines of their spiritual substance. It could pervert them into a Western mental-health gimmick, and thereby prevent them from introducing the sharply *alternative* vision of life they are capable of bringing us.' To this I would only add here that one sees too often that such a spiritual practice in the West may be used as an escape from growth; spiritual growth may for a while be commensurate with psychological growth, the latter here being the road to self-mastery through knowledge, towards a more flexible, healthier adjustment to the world in which we find ourselves living out our existence; pyschotherapy does *not* aim at 'self-transcendence', and there may be a sad confusion of concepts when, say, detachment leads to a kind of neurotic spiritual inflation, or a certain depth of awareness leads to a mistaken and crudely omnipotent notion that one is nearing enlightenment, or even has 'it'.

Unfortunately, but, I suppose, predictably a number of narcissistic personalities have flourished in the culture of the last thirty years, who manifest undoubted skills in crowd control, group-analytic techniques, hypnotic manipulation, and a cold, greedy love of power, who are reverentially followed by many unhappy people seeking comfort. They are capable of working a heavily-controlled audience up to a point of exaltation during the course of a weekend, people who then reel out into the world, brain-washed to an alarming degree, and exuding a dreadful kind of smug vacuity, which they mistake for IT or instant enlightenment. These modern gurus are deeply irresponsible, but inaccessible to control themselves.

Psychological adjustment is not liberation. The path of spiritual growth cuts off at an angle to that of psychological growth, and to confuse the two may be to get stuck unawares, or with a sense of disillusionment. The intense disillusionment and bitter emptiness which follow upon the loss of the exalted experience just described are sad to see, and there is no doubt that for many of these gullible people, their last state is worse than their first. Why, even if they have not been hypnotically organized to a false state of manic exaltation (which *always* fades and leaves only desolation), do so many people drop away from a practice of meditation? Either because they begin to break down under its influence, having misjudged its power and really do then need psychological help; or more commonly because it genuinely does strengthen them, makes them more comfortable, reduces their anxiety, and then they are satisfied that they have reached a point which, properly speaking, is only a point on the same road which would have been followed by the pragmatic secular psychotherapist, and is nothing to do with a spiritual search.

I will now attempt to show how the practices of Buddhism and psychoanalysis interconnect and work, each to potentiate the other, by outlining the simple skeletal structure of Buddhist teaching as I understand it in the Theravada tradition, and then trying to see how well it relates to our analytic understanding and intentions.

The Buddha taught what are called the Four Noble Truths. These are:

1 That suffering exists;
2 That suffering can be understood to arise (have a cause);

3 That suffering can be understood to cease (the cause can be removed);
4 That there is a reliable path leading to the cessation of suffering.

The arising and ceasing of suffering is based on the law of Dependent Origination, or what we would more familiarly call 'cause and effect'. The Buddha taught that there are three inescapable signs of being, meaning truths about human existence; these are that all beings suffer, that all beings and states are impermanent, and that all things ultimately are without self. In Pali these are *dukkha*, *anicca*, and *anatta*. *Dukkha*, though translated usually as 'suffering', is a very compound word, referring also to disease, discomfort, anxiety, disappointment, longing; in fact all shades and variations of psychic and physical states that are imperfect and discontented. I need hardly add here that it is the third, *anatta*, that boggles the Western mind, and absolutely, and only, belongs to the path where spiritual understanding has already left the path of psychological understanding: it is totally alien to the European philosophical cast of mind, as I hope I have already fully shown. We will not concern ourselves with it further, though I may add here that to reach a deep realization of its truth is one of the most liberating experiences there can be. It is not easily approached by intellectual ratiocination, though logical thought about all concepts was always encouraged by the Buddha, provided it does not exclude meditative contemplation. For about twelve years of daily meditation practice within the Theravada tradition, I had no idea what *anatta* 'meant', and it *is* particularly hard for those of us whose life-work is dedicated to exploring and strengthening the ego. I had simply left *anatta* alone. Then about twelve years ago, it suddenly dawned on me that it made absolute, inescapable, perfect sense, and I could not, from that moment on, imagine quite what it had been like not to have 'real-ized' it. It was, continues to be, a liberation of the spirit to do so. It also opens the door to the appreciation of a great cosmic joke about our work, which I might now express as something like 'Of *course* one has to know one's Ego is strong and understood before there is a chance of seeing that it doesn't exist.' As I have said elsewhere ('What does it mean: "Love is not enough"?'; this volume, Ch. 8) our work is full of paradoxes, and this is the most radical and delightful of them all. But for the purposes of this paper, we may now leave *anatta* alone again; it belongs to the realm to which I referred earlier, in which spiritual practice is simply of a different order of things to psychological practice, and there is nothing to be gained by forcing unfruitful connections.

The 'path' referred to in the Fourth Noble Truth is called the Eightfold Noble Path, and I will spell it out: right view, right thinking; right speech, right action, right livelihood; and right effort, right concentration, and right wisdom. You will see that I have presented the path in three little groups of linked features, one of two, and two of three. Of course it is really a tightly knit circle – the first group of two, view and thought, is of necessity dependent upon a serious investment in developing the last group, effort, concentration and wisdom. Equally, the middle group, speech, action and livelihood, cannot exist in isolation without the others, and so on. It is this Path which the Buddha also called The Middle Way. The Middle Way is not some dreary, safe, lowest common denominator; it is hard to define, but roughly it refers to a subtle, attentive, continuous striving after refined distillations of what is *good* in all the hundreds of various extremes in all dimensions of life.

At a meeting of Buddhists in our tradition we take what are called the Five Precepts. These do not say anything like 'Thou shalt not'; they say 'I will *endeavour to refrain* from destroying life, stealing, lying, sexual misconduct and taking substances which alter the state of consciousness' (my italics). The Buddha also taught the Eight *kleshas*, or hindrances, to development; these are hatred, greed, ignorance, lust, pride, envy, sloth and doubt. And this is the sum total of the basic teaching, except for the most important activity – the heart of the teaching, round which the understanding, and working on all the foregoing, centres – of meditation, both as a formal practice and as a continuing attitude and way of being, where it is more appropriately called mindfulness.

Now for the link-ups with psychoanalysis. First with The Four Noble Truths – I think we would certainly be in agreement that our work is about suffering; indeed, the very word 'patient' – which I notice some people have a sort of aversion to, using other words like 'client' – is an honourable old word, and comes from

the Latin root *patio*, I suffer. We have to believe, to move on to
the second and third Noble Truths, that mental suffering has a
cause and that it is capable, by the seeking out of the cause, of
being brought to cessation, or we would not do what we do. We
therefore operate on the principle of Dependent Origination, and,
without too much mind-bending, but with a simple attention to
the inner meanings of the features of the Eightfold Noble Path, I
think we can see that not only our own professional standards but
our hopes and aims for our patients are embedded in it. We only
need a little imagination and free association around the old
language that is used. For example, another way of considering
'wrong view' and 'wrong thought' is that they present themselves
to us as psychological symptoms – a psychotic or neurotic view of
life, of the self, and of others, which we believe to be capable of
improvement, even full healing, by insight and change, in the
direction of what the Eightfold Path calls 'right view' and 'right
thought', that is, views and thoughts unclouded by fear, anxiety or
delusion. To move on to the last three features of the Path, we
know that in our profession the patient has to do a great deal of
the work involved; brilliantly accurate interpretation is no good if
it falls on stony ground. Unless there is a growing openness on the
part of both patient and therapist, each to the other, and a
willingness by both to make *efforts* in an atmosphere of trust, no
treatment occurs. Concentration on the matter in hand in every
single session would be taken almost as a necessary given. 'Right
speech, right action and right livelihood' are not bald and static
prescriptions; none of the parts of the Eightfold Noble Path is
regarded as an absolute except in the highest spiritual practice; for
our purposes here, they are relative. People come to us with many
variations of wrong speech, wrong action, and wrong or inhibited
ways of living; we see thought block, excessive shyness, verbal
inadequacy; much disturbed behaviour, often accompanied by
aggression, guilt and shame; feelings of powerlessness, meaning-
lessness and futility in living; energy blocks, and neurotic preoccupations which grossly interfere with effective action or peaceful
life; and almost always, everywhere, anxiety, spoiling any or all of
the ingredients of the Eightfold Noble Path. 'Right wisdom' may
sound a tall order, even as a relative goal, but a moment's thought
will enable us to translate the concept to something simpler,

humbler, desirable, and often, as a result of therapy, attainable. It can hardly be said to be wise to be hampered by neurosis, especially if earnestly and consciously one longs for change; but change may not be attainable without the concentrated efforts of the therapeutic partnership in an atmosphere of mindful striving towards just 'getting better'.

Although the Eight Hindrances at first have the rather ominous biblical ring of the seven deadly sins, we can on reflection see that they are only archaic names for the various kinds of psychological dis-ease which turn people in our direction. Indeed, the Tavistock Public Lectures for 1990 took the seven deadly sins as their subject matter, and seven psychoanalysts studied them, one by one, from a psychodynamic point of view. Referring back to our list, a few translated examples of the hindrances will serve – destructive tendencies in whatever sphere; contamination of the potential for love by envy, pride or greed; the paralysing effect of doubt in such states as obsessional neurosis and, underlying them all, what is called 'ignorance', which for dynamic purposes I would most closely translate as the power of the unconscious; and always our main efforts are directed to loosening and reducing that power through psychological work and insight.

Finally, a few words about the use of meditation, as central to the Buddhist practice, and therefore, for a psychoanalyst, to his or her working life. Because really what the whole of this paper is about is a ludicrous falsity in any notion that for part of each day, one is a sort of practising Buddhist and for another part, a sort of practising analyst, and for the bits in between a sort of nothing. Here it is relevant to emphasize the powerful inherent meaning of the very word 'practise'. It is all practice, and all the practice can only be today and here and now. Certainly the formal practice of sitting meditation with concentration on the meditation object is an important part of the day. In the Theravada tradition the object is either the breath (in *samatha* meditation), or the stream of arising and ceasing thoughts and feelings, or self-observation (which is *vipassana*). One of its richest fruits can be a deepening of a quality which is essential for the good-enough practice of psychoanalysis; I refer to something for which there is no one exact word, but it has to do with patience, with waiting, with 'negative capability' which, inseparably linked with the continued exercise of bare attention, create the deepest atmosphere in which the analysis takes place. The more one just attends and the less one actually *thinks* during an analytical session the more open one is to learning to trust the intuition which arises from the less rational and cognitive parts of the self, and the more open one is also to a full and direct apprehension of the patient and of what is actually going on. This is not to undervalue or dismiss the great and abiding importance of really knowing one's stuff, being well-grounded in theory and techniques, and capable of applying one's rational mind to problems thrown up by sessions, especially in the intervals between them. Nor do I wish to encourage emotive, self-orientated and wild interventions which are unprofessional and which can be frightening and burdensome to patients. The discipline of meditation practice enhances the discipline of one's contribution to an analytic session which sometimes is, in fact, itself almost indistinguishable from a form of meditation.

I do not teach my patients meditation. It has no role, except for me as analyst as described above, in the carrying out of what my patients come to me for and expect from me, which is that I should use as flexibly as I can the tools of my own trade for their benefit. There are plenty of good meditation teachers around now, both inside and outside the Buddhist tradition, and if patients should reach a point where they recognize in themselves a real hunger to continue their search along that line, which is tangentially angled to ours, then they will begin to look further for themselves. Many patients do not reach that point, and do not wish or need to, and it is not part of my job to encourage them in that direction. I would not expect an experienced Buddhist to start trying to teach psychoanalysis, and nor would he do it as well as I. Equally, I would not feel equipped to teach Buddhism or meditation; if anyone should actually ask, I would point them towards a teacher or even a book, but no more. There are far too many well-intentioned, untrained amateurs springing up in both these fields, who may lead patients and religious seekers into disastrous confusions where, as I said earlier, their last state is worse than their first, and at which point the amateur teachers have no idea about what to do next. Furthermore, such lack of true, hard-won skills is not only dangerously misleading and often a cloak for a shaky narcissism, but it devalues the real worth of both the two great traditions by the sowing of false hopes and erroneous ideas.

To end, I would like to quote the words of a wise and distinguished older Buddhist friend, Maurice Walshe, for many years a Professor of German Studies in the University of London, who also has a long list of translations from Sanskrit, Pali and Latin to his credit; his remark speaks, I think, to all of us who practise either one, or both, of the disciplines to which I have referred. He said: 'I don't really know what enlightenment is or could possibly be; the only thing I hope for, and work slowly towards, is a process of gradual dis-endarkenment.'

12

ATTENTION

It was very pleasing to me to be asked to give the paper tonight for the celebration of the Twentieth Anniversary of the Arbours Association. I have been one of their supporters from the beginning, and for ten years I had the privilege of being on their Training Committee. During that time I had a special function which meant that I came to know a large number of them in a very special way. It linked up directly with one of my other interests which had been the building up and running of a consultation practice at home: nearly thirty years ago now, it struck me that there was a gap in the London scene where it seemed that a sort of broker was needed. There were not as many good psychotherapists around then as there are now, but even so there were quite a few, and quite a few analysts who too often were short of patients. On the other hand, when I was still working in the NHS, I not only discovered that it is almost impossible to do good, detailed, long therapy there, but also that there were plenty of potential patients for such therapists and analysts and that many of these patients could get together the price of a couple of sessions a week, simply by deciding that having some therapy might be more important than two or three nights in the pub or a visit to the movies. So I started the consultation practice to try to bring the two together and 'match' them if possible, a process I became more interested in as time went by. When I worked for Arbours, all the students to

Given as the Arbours Association Twentieth Anniversary lecture and first published in the *British Journal of Psychotherapy*, Volume 7, Part 2 (1990).

be trained were of course carefully selected by members of the Admission Committee; then they would come and see me for a single long discussion, after which I would place them with an analyst for what is the central feature of their three-year training as therapists, the training analysis, which they committed themselves to, three times a week or possibly more, for anything up to eight years. Analysts in training have to do this, too, but have to attend five times a week. In fact, the frequency of sessions is one of the few things that distinguishes full analysis from analytical psychotherapy. From that meeting I took an interest in the various individuals I had met that way, during their trainings, and of course this paid off over the years as they would qualify and start their own practices and I gained a growing pool of good Arbours therapists to whom to refer new patients from the consultation service, who did not need or want full analyses. And I also came to know the senior, pioneering members of Arbours, who were mostly on the Training Committee, very well over a long period and continued to observe the growth of Arbours with great admiration. They built a thorough analytic training for their students, created a low-fee clinic for patients, established and nurtured their community houses, ran the Crisis Centre, and earned themselves a unique and respected place on the London therapy scene.

The capacity for taking for granted what is *there*, which I will speak about more later in a somewhat different context, is so developed in human nature that we are in danger of forgetting that the successful maintenance of community houses for disturbed patients, with resident therapists, and of the Crisis Centre for short-term acute admissions, was a new phenomenon in our world twenty years ago. It had certainly been attempted but on a smaller scale and with less forethought and less skill. Some individual communities had foundered, run down or fragmented from lack of good, professional administration and of consistent discipline amongst the staff. This lacuna Arbours filled and continues to do so, and I would like it to be known more widely how hard they struggled, this handful of dedicated and well-trained pioneer therapists, and against what odds, not least desperate shortages of funds and also the suspicious, almost paranoid attitudes to a new development which I am sad to say often characterizes the outlook of older established professionals such as the psychoanalysts.

Arbours arose originally, like the phoenix, from the ashes of the first Kingsley Hall, Ronnie Laing's own early attempt at a therapeutic community, where Joe Berke and Morty Schatzman – who together we might say *were* that phoenix – had originally worked. The people who worked with Laing brought a stunningly (almost shamingly) original idea to their project, and it was this simple, fundamental idea which was carried forward into the new embryonic organization, the Arbours, and which has continued to infuse it with its own power ever since. It may seem surprising that the revolutionary notion of paying attention to a person who is labelled Mad, and trying to understand him or her, is not much more than thirty years old. When I was taught psychiatry in the early 1950s as a medical student, we were taken in small groups to big psychiatric hospitals, even then commonly known as 'bins' or 'the asylum', and a series of patients was wheeled on before us, sometimes literally, strapped into chairs or strait jackets or both. A consultant would then proudly take them through their paces, demonstrating the signs by which we were meant to learn the nature of madness: one sign I have never forgotten was called *flexibilitas cerea* or waxy passive immobility. A catatonic schizophrenic man was wheeled on, and our consultant pushed and pulled bits of his body into strange unnatural positions where they stayed – eerily – until they were put back. Then another schizophrenic man, who spoke in a cheerful, stream-of-consciousness babble, demonstrated 'word salad', thought-disorder and neologisms. A mute woman with a hysterical psychosis displayed the stigmata, clearly oozing blood from her hands and feet. And so on and so forth. We gaped for a while and went away. No attempt was made to give close attention to a patient as a whole person, to engage in any sort of dialogue, however mad-sounding, not even to establish eye contact. The patients were unfortunate objects and likely to stay that way, since, when I started psychiatry, few of the psychotropic drugs had appeared.

Although Arbours has always tried not to use major drugs, as far as is concomitant with relative stability in the communities, I would like to insert a note here about their value, speaking as one who did psychiatry before their advent. They started to come in

while I was working as the admitting doctor for the acute wards at
the North Middlesex Hospital, and I don't think any psychiatrist
who witnessed what a huge difference they made could sincerely
argue with their value, *if used judiciously*. It was they which
eliminated the hitherto frequent use of the padded cells and the
excessive, random use of ECT, and they produced a reduction in
severe anxiety states, violent schizophrenic disorders, melancholia
and mania which really did provide a good basis to work from.
But having put in my plea not to throw out the baby with the bath
water, I must add that I would not like you to think the new era
of care, understanding and enlightenment has even yet fully
dawned: indeed, American psychiatry recently has shown a regres-
sive tendency to revert to complex classification of signs and
elaborate use of drugs, as its major diagnostic tools.

What was revolutionary about the early work of R. D. Laing,
and people like our Joe Berke and Morty Schatzman, was that
prolonged, careful and humane attention was paid to trying to
make sense, in context, of what was happening to a mad patient. I
am not implying that psychoanalysis did not do this. It was Freud's
greatest contribution to the twentieth century that in 1895 he
started doing just that; but, with very rare exceptions, psychoanalysts have worked with neurotic patients. Psychotic disturbance
has usually been considered to be beyond its scope. The distinctive
innovation which Laing, himself a psychoanalyst by training,
brought to analytical therapy was to direct the attention of the
technique of psychoanalysis to psychotically disordered people, on
a holistic basis. It is to this ideal that Arbours dedicated itself, its
structure and its trainings and treatments, and does to this day.
One of the great strengths of Arbours has always been that it
attracts, most often, and from many walks of life, potentially gifted
therapists who have a strong sense of vocation. The Arbours policy
of not stipulating that applicants must have certain bits of paper
registering them as doctors or psychologists, but of relying on
skilful selection from a wide spectrum of people who *want* to *do*
therapy, means that they continue to attract gifted people. You can
teach a lot of people a lot of things but a first-rate therapist is born,
not made, and many of them train and work at Arbours. I believe
being a good therapist is a vocation; it did not surprise me to
discover that some resident therapists in the communities, who

offer holistic care and treatment for extremely disturbed patients, have been nicknamed 'psychiatric monks'.

In order that this great resource should be used to its maximum advantage, certain supportive features have grown and been maintained in the structure of Arbours. One is that there is a definite hierarchy of authority for purposes of administration, consultation, supervision, regulation, treatment and support. It is no good baulking psychological truth, and one truth is that human beings in groups form hierarchies and need authority. Another source of strength is that many of their therapists, trained in the ordinary, psychodynamic programme which has been constructd for their students, move laterally into the communities or the Crisis Centre to work while they are training and also when they qualify, as well as starting to build up their own part-time private therapy practices. And another is the continued source of inspiration represented by the dedication and hard work of the few at the top, and their ceaseless attention to detail and to the maintenance of professional standards and of the Arbours ethos.

These keys to their success over twenty years bring us to the subject I selected for the Arbours Anniversary celebration: *attention* – a subject extraordinarily neglected or overlooked. In all our vast literature, very little attention has been paid to attention. In clinical discussion, public or private, one finds the same neglect. I think this may be to do with its being so taken for granted – it *must* be there as the invisible, essential ingredient – this seems to be a sort of given. Or perhaps we have not developed any kind of language to speak about it. Or perhaps it verges on the religious. Certainly some of those who do attend to it and write about it with clarity are found in religious fields. And there is little more calculated to stir up anxiety and defensiveness in your average analyst than any hint of religion.

In a paper I first wrote ten years ago called 'Slouching towards Bethlehem' (1986; this volume, Ch. 1), I tried to say something about the faith with a small f that learning to be a therapist requires, and discussed some of the dark passages we have to negotiate, or just plain sit through, when 'not knowing' is a daily experience. Usually not, I am glad to say, with all our patients at once, though there can be days in the early years of running a practice when that is what it feels like. Winnicott used to say that there is a sort of self-regulating ladder among the patients in your practice, and in some extraordinary way they seem to sort themselves out and take it in turns to clamber to the top to be Number 1 mind-blowing problem for a while: to the therapist, that is! This is usually the patient whom you feel you know least about, will never understand and with whom your faith is most severely tested. Then, by dint not so much of thinking – though that certainly has its place in a phase of bafflement – but of perpetual bare attention, light of a sort does eventually dawn, something is unravelled, that patient slides down the ladder and usually, before long, someone else clambers to the top to take that place.

During these extremely testing passages in a treatment when bewilderment and maybe anxiety predominate in the therapist, and despairing feelings, frustration and anxiety in the patient, one's attention is focused sharply with little effort. And it is as a result of this (and we can notice and store away for future reference the sense of inevitability, of cause and effect here) that we begin to understand what is going on. Many of you must know the state directly from within, from times when you have been sitting in a session, with all your skills and experience gathered preconsciously at your sensory and psychological nerve endings, when everything comes together, light begins to shine through the darkness, and you have a brief phase of enlightenment about what is happening between you and your patient; and the gift of communicating an insight in *appropriate language* often suddenly occurs as part of this phenomenon.

So here I am, ten years on from 'Slouching towards Bethlehem', still virtually saying the same thing, or returning to aspects of the subject which I obviously feel can never be stressed too much. It is in the early stages of learning to be analysts and therapists when we are developing our technique, our confidence and our clinical acumen generally that the use of 'bare attention' absolutely has to be the scaffolding of everything else we do. Even when we are doing nothing (or appear to be), sitting in silence, testing our faith in the process – our constant, perhaps I should say *only*, attitude is one of 'bare attention'. In this we try to teach ourselves so continuously to observe, and watch, and listen, and feel, in silence, that this kind of attention becomes – in the end – second nature. It is the bedrock of our day's work. And it is as this bedrock that it becomes forgotten or overlooked.

You will note that I have added an adjective, that I am now calling it 'bare attention'. This is a phrase lifted from Buddhist teaching where it is also the main feature of the meditation practice, which in turn is the essential basis of the whole philosophy. I have been involved in both practices for a long time now and have always found that Buddhism melds harmoniously with the practice of psychoanalysis in every aspect; I want to make use of their concept – 'bare attention' – as I think it says even more clearly something about this skilful capacity which we need to learn than does the single word 'attention'. That after all can become at worst an order – Attention! *Achtung!* – or a reminder, a threat or a warning. And in so doing it becomes a terse command and loses the quality of profound and self-forgetful opening of oneself to another person. A few months ago I happened to hear someone talking about the last novel that Aldous Huxley wrote, which was called *Island* (1962), in which it was said there were birds whose cry was 'Attention!' Thinking my troubles were over and that I could plagiarize Huxley, I managed to get hold of the book and read it eagerly. It does indeed have birds in it which cry out 'Attention', and they also cry 'Here and now, here and now' – with what I must say I came to feel was a deadly monotony. The book as a whole I found dreadfully boring and rather priggish: having only hitherto read some of the wonderful early novels, among them *Brave New World* (1932) to which this was supposed to be a kind of long footnote, I had not fully realized that Huxley's life folded over, as on a hinge, in the late 1930s; at that point he ran away to America to escape the war and embraced Vedanta which, although contaminated by a certain amount of loose occult and theistic embroidery, also contains some of the same philosophy of life as does austere and atheistic Buddhism. Years of drug experimentation mixed with this ill-digested Eastern religious diet ruined Huxley's elegant and witty style. *Island*, his last book, is an attempt to put a great philosophy, which had taken thousands of years to evolve, into a fanciful modern-day fiction. I think it is a failure. Those birds, however, do stick in the mind; they are trained to issue continual reminders to the islanders about focusing their attention on the immediate present. As a religious practice, this is

fundamental to Buddhism and has a strongly therapeutic effect.
This is not surprising since the teaching of Buddhism is what is
called *bhavana* or the cultivation of the mind with the direct aim
of the relief of suffering in all its forms, however small; the method
and the aim are regarded as indissolubly interconnected; so it seems
to me logical that neutral attention to the immediate present, which
includes first and foremost the study of our own minds, should
turn out to be our sharpest and most reliable therapeutic tool in
psychoanalytic technique since there, too, we aim to study the
workings of the mind, our own and others, with a view to relieving
suffering.

Freud said, in a paper in 1912 discussing the technique of
psychoanalysis, that the essential constant attitude is one of
'evenly-suspended attention without which the physician is in
danger of never finding anything but what he already knows'
(pp. 111–12). I quote the founder of psychoanalysis here because,
although substantial developments in theory and technique have
taken place since his time, it is a salutary experience to return to
him occasionally and, on rereading, to come to realize how much
of what he said is still true of psychoanalytic therapeutic practice
today: I quote also to allay any stirrings of anxiety in those who
can receive gratefully what Freud has to offer, but who begin to
quail if I draw on sources which not only long pre-date him but
which are avowedly religious. When analysts become anxious and
defensive at the mention of religious teaching or meditation
practice, I have to say that this most often represents prejudice, an
ugly characteristic which besets psychoanalysts quite extensively,
and which itself, wherever it crops up, deserves attentive study.
Perhaps I should add here that I certainly do *not* consider that
analytical therapists, doing their daily work in the most professional way possible, have any need or right to introduce religious
teachings into that practice; but occasionally, for all our sustained
attempts to preserve our anonymity – in order to provide blank
screens on which the patients' fantasies may play – patients do tend
to discover odd things about us and weave them into their own
communications. And then it is very instructive to observe which
patients, with what psychopathology, exhibit fury, sarcasm and
denigration towards any hint of religious interest in their analysts,
and which are respectful, careful or interested. I need hardly say

that it is invariably those who are ignorant about religion in any form and whose own upbringing was deprived of any religious or philosophical input, who are the most vociferous in their criticism. This goes for attacks made by analysts, too. Many analysts come from secular backgrounds and are still inclined to hold Freud's own view – that all religion is neurosis – which betrays their discomfort and anxiety in the face of what they may regard as competing systems which threaten them.

In fact the aims and practice of bare attention are exactly the same whether taught by a Buddhist meditation master or by an experienced analyst such as Freud, Searles or Bion. One can summarize these aims by saying they are to calm the mind, reduce anxiety and misery, deepen our knowledge and produce a sustained increase in a sense of wellbeing, peace and happiness. If I were to present you with a medley of quotations from such teachings, I would be willing to bet that you would find it hard to distinguish one set, the religious, from another, the psychoanalytic. For example:

> The practice of attention is rooted in pure listening, a listening that becomes deepened by trust. We allow ourselves to be aware of our own pain, or that of others, of darkness, upset, unfulfilled yearnings; an awareness is allowed to grow and should not be unthinkingly forged through idealism. This trust then allows direct experience of ourself and others to grow in silence; we strive for being at ease with all workings of the mind, reached through being silently attentive to its endless wanderings, and non-judgemental about them. The silence that embraces rather than resists has a healing touch. Using the silence as a container for anxiety and sorrow brings its own serenity.

This was said by a Western Buddhist monk (Sucitto, 1989, p. 3) but, especially in its use of the idea of the container, the concepts of becoming more at ease with silence and being non-judgemental, it could as well be any of a dozen good analytic teachers. In my Bethlehem paper, I was concerned to stress the importance of this capacity to sit in darkness, not knowing. Here I am more concerned to identify some aspects of our professional life and work which require continuous attention in order to sharpen our particular skills and also aspects which may, without our conscious awareness, interfere with the development of our capacity to attend.

One of the most important of these is the subtle effect on all we do of our own basic personality – its type, colouring and biases. In our field, of course, the essential background of our training is our own personal analysis and it is hoped that, as a result of this, the worst of our own neurotic excesses is ironed out. I would like to erase the erroneous idea that a training analysis is in any important way different from an ordinary analytic treatment; it most certainly is not. Anyone who trains to be an analyst is, anyway, probably quite disturbed and is as much in need of their own personal analysis as anyone else who is labelled 'patient'. But there is no such thing as a fully analysed person or a fully treated patient, as Freud rather sadly came to admit in his last great paper 'Analysis terminable and interminable' (1937a). We have undertaken to live by what has been called 'the impossible profession'. We emerge from our training analyses, struggle through our lives as analytical therapists with all our own secret inclinations, fantasies, emotions, likes and dislikes, defence systems and residual neurotic tendencies, and it is only by ceaseless attention to ourselves operating *with* ourselves as our only resource that we can more or less make the best of the package.

You *feel* a lot as a therapist – it comes with the job. It is all very well to start off with an idealistic view of oneself as a reflecting mirror or a purveyor of neutral compassionate interest. The every essence of long treatments, which depend entirely on the transference and the countertransference as their main vehicles, is that the coolness of the theory is soon lost in the thicket of day-to-day work where we have to use own own skills, our personalities and all the patients' communications, including their unconscious projections into us – in fact everything that comes to hand in any one session. Only by the most continuous endeavour to focus an evenly hovering attention on all that is going on can we hope to maintain an equilibrium so that we can continue to *work*, to be of therapeutic value to the patient, and not to disintegrate ourselves. It is within the remit of our job not to act out ill-observed feelings, either deep old stuff of our own or projected into us as intolerable by the patient. Learning about the countertransference and projection in student seminars is only part of it. We used to have rather nervous discussions about such papers as Donald Winnicott's 'Hate in the counter-transference' (1947), and tried to think about it all

coolly – at that point – although the very idea that *hate* could
feature as part of the countertransference was thoroughly alarming
to us. We were still struggling to achieve equanimity and benevolence. All that was necessary, of course, as forewarned is
forearmed. But in the day-to-day struggles in the consulting room,
it is pretty disturbing actually to *experience* violent emotions,
although that is the only genuine way to know what your
countertransference is; perhaps, for a while, you may not even
know rightly to whom the emotions belong, you or the patient.
The hallmark of a true projection is that the patient's buried
feelings do somehow get into your own system, and you do learn
about them primarily by *feeling* them first and foremost. Then you
have to sort them from your own. Hence the enormous importance
of knowing yourself well. Sometimes a willed and heroic attempt
to maintain an island of attention in ourselves will keep the
treatment going. I like to think of the capacity for bare attention as
a sort of observatory in our own minds – and I find an image like
this can be a help in times of trouble; even to visualize it briefly
when struggling can send a salutary breath of cool breeze over
one's heated judgement. At times, all we can hang on to is a
recollection of what we know, a sort of flash of memory about the
capacity to be attentive or detached.

While on the subject of the constant attention we need ourselves,
here is an illustration of its necessity – and its difficulty – taken not
from analytic literature, nor from the religious traditions, but from
a novelist. I often think that we are all novelists *manqués*; we live
through life stories of extraordinary intricacy and suffering, and by
participating, change them. For us to pay attention to skilful
novelists also can be a rich source of insights we might never have
gained elsewhere. Occasionally, one encounters people who say
loftily that they 'never read novels', somehow implying that those
of us who do have not got much beyond the stage of *Beano* and
Dandy. Most analytical therapists, however, do read novels as one
of their great relaxations and know just how valuable they can be.
Anna Freud was a mine of information about Agatha Christie –
she could have done a *Mastermind* appearance on her. The
quotation I'm about to give you is from *The Black Prince*, one of
Iris Murdoch's dense, packed and psychologically complicated
novels. I have rarely come across a passage, anywhere, which

tackles so vividly the very subject we are most concerned with: human consciousness and the attention we need to try to give it. Incidentally, she is always deeply concerned with the morality inherent in our task, an aspect I have not even touched on here. Certainly, no analyst has written so vividly and succinctly about it. Here, in doing one of her elaborate digressions on human wickedness, she writes:

I daresay human wickedness is sometimes the product of a sort of conscious leeringly evil intent . . . But more usually it is the product of a semi-deliberate inattention, a sort of swooning relationship to time . . . the space between the stage where the work is too unformed to have committed itself and the stage where it is too late to improve it can be as thin as a needle. . . . most artists, through sheer idleness, weariness, *inability to attend*, drift again and again and again from the one stage straight into the other, in spite of good resolutions and the hope with which each new work begins. This is of course a moral problem, since all art [and I must insert here that I consider the practice of psychoanalysis to be more an art than a science] is the struggle to be, in a particular sort of way, virtuous . . . We ignore what we are doing until it is too late to alter it. We never allow ourselves quite to focus upon moments of decision; and these are often in fact hard to find even if we are searching for them . . . There is thus an eternal discrepancy between the self-knowledge which we gain by observing ourselves objectively and the self-awareness which we have of ourselves subjectively: a discrepancy which probably makes it impossible for us ever to arrive at the truth. Our self-knowledge is too abstract, our self-awareness is too intimate and swoony and dazed. Perhaps some kind of integrity of the imagin-ation, a sort of moral genius, could verify the scene, producing minute sensibility and control of the moment . . . In fact, the problem remains unclarified because no philosopher and hardly any novelist [or analyst, I would insert here] has ever managed to explain what that weird stuff, human consciousness, is really made of. [Here she embarks on an amazing list of the contents of consciousness.] Body, external objects, darty memories, warm fantasies, other minds, guilt, fear, hesitation, lies, glees, doles, breathtaking pains, a thousand things which words can only fumble at, coexist, many fused together in a single unit of consciousness . . . How can such a thing be tinkered with and improved, how can one change the quality of consciousness? Around '*will*', it flows like water round a stone . . . There is so much grit in the bottom of the container, almost all our natural preoccupations are low ones, and in most cases the rag-bag of consciousness is only unified by the experience of great art or of intense love [and to these I would add 'single-minded attention'] . . .
(1973, pp. 154–5; my italics)

I am sure I am speaking for all of us who work in the therapy world when I say that this extraordinary passage expresses better than we can what the daily experience of ourselves in our work is like. I am particularly struck by the image of the will – the continued effort required to keep the will-to-attend functioning, as the crowded waters of consciousness swirl and swirl around.

Tempting as it is to stay with the subject of morality, I think it is too demanding to be part of this paper; the view that in our work we are morally neutral is quite widespread and needs a strong challenge. I think it is quite simply a wrong view; but it deserves a paper in its own right. I would only issue a signal here to say that I think we need to direct attention to the possibility that we are, whether we like it or not, conveying moral judgements in many of the things we say; they derive from our own views, whether thought out or deeply conditioned, and it seems to me that not, at least, to acknowledge this is to be imprisoned within a strait-jacket of denial or to turn a blind eye to important aspects of ourselves, and to what we may be imposing on our patients.

I would however like to comment on the need to study our very use of language and ideas. Much of our hard-won theory and conceptualizing becomes gradually metabolized into our own being so that eventually we hardly know, when we think, decide and speak, from whence it comes. There is nothing wrong with this – indeed, I see it as an aim for young therapists still earnestly acquiring the wherewithal of their trade. The machinery should not be creaking; our aim should be to develop a technique marked by ease and spontaneity, drawing primarily on our own *un*conscious as we work and trusting it, not '*thinking*' about everything we do and say, with a visible effort. But this has its own dangers; we become very accustomed to our own ways of thinking, especially if we have the repeated experience, in practice, that they 'work', that is, effect response and change in the patient. The danger is that we may fall off our own tightropes, which represent the need for continually fresh judgements, down on to one of several rocky places: we may become inordinately self-satisfied with a piece of technique, or an idea, and come to use it almost automatically, perhaps even fail to notice when it misses the target, or produces a negative response. We may also become possessive about it, as if we have been original or clever and invented this manoeuvre, when all we have done is stamp with our own personal style an idea first broached by Freud or one of the other very few true innovators of all time, among whom we ourselves are unlikely to be numbered; and unless we rethink a tired old concept each time for each new use with each unique patient, we will certainly undermine its effectiveness. This is one of my major criticisms of the repetition of clichés when teaching such concepts as 'the patient's anxiety about separation' at holiday breaks; students are taught that this is part of a proper tool-kit; often they have had some experience of it in their own analyses, especially at a point where they were dependent or regressed, or working through some sad old trauma of their own; but to trot it out with mechanical regularity from the very beginning of every treatment seems to me to be a gross error and a neglect of the true state of each patient at that moment; in other words, a failure of attention.

This is linked with the tendency in our profession to overestimate our own importance in an unthinking way. Of course, an analytical therapy is important to a patient and of course, as its agent, we become an important figure in the life of that patient. But there are analysts who teach that the analyst is *always* overwhelmingly important, that the rest of external reality pales into insignificance beside the analysis, and at all costs the sort of 'you mean me' type of interpretation must be forced into every exchange in every session. I have no respect for this so-called technique which seems to me at best meaningless and at worst unreal and insulting to the patient's individual self.

Quite apart from this, there is also the tightrope of the transference to be considered. The transference is a huge feature of our sort of therapy; it takes a lot of learning about in all its complexity, and is ever-present. An experienced analyst teaching about transference interpretation may be so deeply familiar with its use that when he or she dissects a reported session, in supervision, with the subtle insertion of 'you mean me' interpretations, it really is transformed and we are thereby enlightened. Whereas an awkward, ill-digested use of this approach can make it sound as if practitioners really do feel themselves to be all-important and omnipotent. And indeed, one does sometimes hear inexperienced workers being a bit boastful or self-satisfied when a patient is passionately grateful or attached to them; the same therapists would be the first to invoke 'negative transference' as the explanation if patients hated them or were being critical. It does not do to forget that when our patients think that we are wonderful or lovable, this is *just as much transference* as is their hate and fear. Freud himself, that sceptical realist, was of the opinion that no particular credit was attributable to the personal charms of the physician (1914b).

To return to the cliché about agonized separation anxiety at holiday times, I think, for example, it should always be attentively borne in mind that some patients may be glad to get away from us; that the defences *against* dependency may be far stronger than any true sense of need or closeness or fear of loss; and it is these which should be dealt with by the interpretation. We should avoid the danger of brainwashing our patients into submitting compliantly to a technique just because we happen to have learned how to handle it. There is a particular version of this which can be utterly maddening to lay people and which, if it does not bring the whole of analytic work into disrepute, at the very least renders it ludicrous. As a way of defending themselves against criticism of, say, an automatic interpretation about separation anxiety over a holiday, an analyst may say, 'Oh, but the patient is only resisting; *unconsciously* he is very upset, and is just putting up defences.' Thus the inattentive analyst takes refuge in the 'heads I win, tails you lose' argument; if the patient is overtly distressed, fine; if he is not, then the distress is unconscious. This can be not only infuriating but also shows a neglect of the importance of the defences in question. I must put in here another plea for special attention to those significant words 'only' and 'just' and issue a caveat; that if you hear yourself saying that *anything* about a patient's feelings or behaviour is 'only' this or 'just' that, *that* requires instant attention: nothing is *ever* only or just something.

Closely linked with the problem of making assumptions and taking things for granted is a subject that connects with the question of morality. It is one through which our profession overlaps with that of the sociologist, the historian, the teacher of morality on whatever level. I refer to the subject of manners. Some people's first reaction is that manners, good or bad, have little to do with the practice of our impossible profession. I would contend that they have everything to do with it. The study of manners reveals that they convey subtle messages about the whole life-philosophy of a person. Manners are not merely a matter of remembering to say please and thank you; nor are they the fossilized remnants of a few social lubricants learned in the nursery; nor are they a thin, superficial coating of falsity. They are the very stuff of how we are in our being-in-the-world. I would be very suspicious of any analyst or therapist who maintained that his manners were irrelevant to his behaviour in the consulting room. They are not a disposable piece of clothing to be shed in the morning – what do you put on instead? Detached observation is not a manners-substitute. Just after Ronnie Laing died, there was a Channel 4 programme about him (1989) which had been made over a series of visits to his home and consulting rooms. At one point he said:

> Most of the people we meet are very frightened; they are putting up all sorts of defences, consciously and unconsciously. They can, however inexperienced we are, be guaranteed to be more anxious than us. It is therefore required of us that we conduct ourselves with courtesy; the ordinary rules of politeness should be *our* rules; we are harmless, and our intentions are on the whole benevolent; but we have to show it. It is *not apparent* to a frightened person. Don't say 'Trust me', and expect them to. Why should they? It is in the very way we *treat* each other that *treatment* itself lies . . .

And speaking of the ways in which we treat each other, you may have noticed that I have so far not mentioned what is called 'attention-seeking'. The phrase is ubiquitous, pejorative, and is often the only context in which my subject for tonight crops up at all. Children are said to be attention-seeking if they show off or interrupt the grown-ups with demands and complaints. Adolescents are attention-seeking, whether they dress eccentrically and make a lot of uncouth noises, or sulk in their rooms in speechless malaise. Patients, particularly in the 'bins' I was referring to, are called attention-seekers if they ignore the ward-sister's rules, throw their food about, pester other people's visitors, cut their wrists or hang themselves. On the whole the behaviour identified as attention-seeking is unattractive, disruptive and aggravating. The label would be different if you sat down at the piano and played a Mozart sonata from memory; or told a really funny joke at the dinner-table; or even with some confidence pointed to a picture you had just painted, or to how lovely your garden was looking. Attention-seekers in our culture are not only desperately and rather pathetically trying to get someone – anyone, really – to notice them at all, but are also infringing one of the most sacred rules of British society, which approximates to some version of being seen and not heard. Seeking attention is very natural, human behaviour. We all need attention and we all seek it; it is just that most of us are more subtle or more successful. The failures – the people described above – remind us uneasily of our secret selves. I suggest that we put the phrase in a rag-bag marked 'Words and phrases to be avoided if possible' along with 'hysterical', 'manipulative', 'selfish', 'greedy' and 'childish', all of which carry a strong negative moralistic flavour, and should have no place in psychotherapeutic clinical descriptions.

I would like to make, finally, a plea for enjoyment – that we should all attend to the very real and, as we go on, growing possibility that we enjoy what we do. Kit Bollas, in his excellent book *Forces of Destiny* (1989), has a chapter on what he calls celebration, the celebrating of good things in a patient's life, of ground gained and of increased happiness, and shows us how celebration may be permitted between analyst and patient. It is still, I note with regret, a subject which has some shreds of taboo hanging around it. I am not talking directly about humour, though the capacity to laugh and to use humour in our work does come with enjoyment and does grow with experience, and does occur in celebration. I am certainly not talking about making light of suffering, not at all; that would be some sort of manic defence and the sooner dismantled the better. I am talking about the fact that, although it may be easier to groan a bit and be grim about our heavy tasks, these tasks after all are self-chosen, and it was with our eyes open that we entered the impossible profession; and with any luck most of us have the sense, most of the time, that we are round pegs in round holes; or that, to use another notion from Bollas's book, we are creating our own destinies as we work through our lives, rather than being doomed to live helplessly, pushed about by Fate. This is one of the most rewarding things about this life, and I see every reason to be attentively conscious, from day to day, of our enjoyment. The late Dr Bion was a distinguished and in some ways rather awe-inspiring analyst. He was one of the first analysts to teach the use and value of silence, and he could be very intimidating in his way of doing it. He would come into a student seminar and sit down and stare at us in silence. He was a large man with a solemn appearance and penetrating dark brown eyes; he made me think that that was what a basilisk would look like. He tended to provoke anxiety and the seminar frequently turned into something rather more like a therapeutic group, and he would then interpret how we were handling the experience. It was unnerving but it was brilliant teaching and I, for one, have never forgotten what he taught us by this unorthodox method. He was teaching a seminar in Brazil in the 1970s, which fortunately for us was recorded and transcribed, and in it he was being more freely talkative than he often was with us, and he said:

> I wonder if it is within the rules of psycho-analysis to be able to laugh at ourselves? Is it according to the rules of psycho-analysis that we should be amused and find things funny? Is it permissible to enjoy a psycho-analytical meeting? I suggest that, having broken through in this revolutionary matter of being amused in the sacred progress of psycho-analysis, we might as well continue to see where that more joyous state of mind might take us. (1980, pp. 94–5)

And in the television programme I referred to, Ronnie Laing said, towards the end:

> Getting through a day is one of the most difficult things in life – and I have come to the conclusion that you can't be miserable for long if you notice that in some small way you are enjoying yourself. Let us try to celebrate and enjoy ourselves – I am really only interested now in trying to entice people with all the skills at my disposal to live in that sort of way if they possibly can.

And I would like to second that. So am I.

BIBLIOGRAPHY

The place of publication is London unless otherwise stated.

Arlow, J. A. (1961) 'Silence and the theory of technique', *J. Amer. Psychoanal. Assn* 9: 44–55.

Augustine, Saint *Confessions*, H. Chadwick, trans. Oxford University Press, 1991.

Baker, R. (1987) 'Note responding to an article on humour', *Bull. Brit. Psycho-Anal. Soc.*

—(1980) 'The finding "not suitable" in the selection of supervised cases', *Int. Rev. Psycho-Anal.* 7: 353–64.

Balint, M. (1968) *The Basic Fault*. Tavistock.

Bergman, M. (1988) 'Freud's three theories of love in the light of later developments', *J. Amer. Psychoanal. Assn* 36(3): 653–72.

Bettelheim, B. (1950) *Love is Not Enough*. Glencoe, IL: Free Press.

Bible, The Holy (1611) The Old Testament, Job chs. 5, 27, 42: Proverbs ch. 9: 10 ff. The New Testament, St Paul's First Epistle to the Romans chs. 1, 2; I Corinthians, ch. 13: 4–8.

Bion, W. R. (1963) *Elements of Psycho-Analysis*. Heinemann.

—(1970) *Attention and Interpretation*. Tavistock.

—(1980) *Bion in New York and São Paulo*. Perthshire: Clunie Press.

Bloom, H. (1986) 'Freud, the greatest modern writer', *New York Times Book Review*, 23 March, pp. 1, 26–7.

Blum, H. P. (1980) 'The value of reconstruction in adult analysis', *Int. J. Psycho-Anal.* 61: 39–52.

—(1983) 'The position and value of extra-transference interpretation', *J. Amer. Psychoanal. Assn* 31(3): 587–617.

Bollas, C. (1987) *The Shadow of the Object*. Free Association Books.

—(1989) *Forces of Destiny*. Free Association Books.

Boswell, J. (1791) *The Life of Samuel Johnson*. Oxford University Press, 1953.

Boyd, W. (1990) *Brazzaville Beach*. Sinclair-Stevenson.

Brenman, E. (1980) 'The value of reconstruction in adult analysis', *Int. J. Psycho-Anal.* 61: 53–60.

Chasseguet-Smirgel, J. (1985) *The Ego Ideal*. Free Association Books.

Chesterfield, Lord (1774) *Letters to his Son*.

Coltart, N. (1985a) 'The treatment of a transvestite', *Psychoanal. Psychother.* 1(1): 65–79.

—(1985b) 'The practice of psychoanalysis and Buddhism', published under the title 'Freud and Buddhism', *The Middle Way*.

—(1986) 'Slouching towards Bethlehem . . . or thinking the unthinkable in psychoanalysis', in Gregorio Kohon, ed. *The British School of Psychoanalysis: The Independent Tradition*. Free Association Books, pp. 185–99.

—(1987) 'Diagnosis and assessment for suitability for psychoanalytic psychotherapy', *Br. J. Psychother.* 4(2): 127–34.

—(1988) 'The assessment of psychological-mindedness in the diagnostic interview', *Br. J. Psychiatry* 153: 819–20.

—(1990) 'Attention', *Br. J. Psychother.* 7(2): 164–74.

—(1991a) 'The analysis of an elderly patient', *Int. J. Psycho-Anal.* 72(2): 209–19.

—(1991b) 'The silent patient', *Psychoanalytic Dialogues: Journal of Relational Perspectives* 1(3).

Cowper, W. (1782) *Table Talk*, in H. S. Milford, ed. *The Complete Poetical Works of William Cowper*. Oxford University Press, pp. 1–17.

Dante Alighieri (1314) *The Divine Comedy*. Cantica 1: 'L'Inferno'. Harmondsworth: Penguin, 1949.

Diatkine, R. (1968) 'Indications and contraindication for psychoanalytical treatment', *Int. J. Psycho-Anal.* 49: 266–70.

Donne, J. 'Progress of the Soul', in H. J. C. Grierson, ed. *The Poems of John Donne*, vol. 1. Oxford University Press, 1912, pp. 245–6.

Freud, S. (1895a) 'The psychotherapy of hysteria', in James Strachey, ed. *The Standard Edition of the Complete Psychological Works of Sigmund Freud*, 25 vols. Hogarth, 1953–73, vol. 2, pp. 255–305.

—(1895b) *Project for a Scientific Psychology*. S.E. 1, pp. 283–397.

—(1905a) 'On psychotherapy'. S.E. 7, pp. 255–68.

—(1905b) *Three Essays on the Theory of Sexuality*. S.E. 7, pp. 125–243.

—(1909) 'Analysis of a phobia in a five-year-old boy' ('Little Hans'). S.E. 10, pp. 1–149.

—(1911) 'Formulations on the two principles of mental functioning'. S.E. 12, pp. 218–26.

—(1912) 'Recommendations to physicians practising psycho-analysis'. S.E. 12, pp. 111–20.

—(1913a) 'On beginning the treatment'. S.E. 12, pp. 123–44.

—(1913b) *Totem and Taboo*. S.E. 13, pp. 1–161.

—(1914a) 'On narcissism: an introduction'. S.E. 14, pp. 73–102.

—(1914b) 'Observations on transference love'. S.E. 12, pp. 159–71.

—(1915) 'Instincts and their vicissitudes'. S.E. 14, pp. 117–40.

—(1916) 'Some character-types met with in psycho-analytic work'. S.E. 14, pp. 309–36.

—(1917) 'Mourning and melancholia'. S.E. 14, pp. 237–58.

—(1923) *The Ego and the Id*. *S.E.* 19, pp. 12–59.
—(1925) 'Some psychical consequences of the anatomical distinction between the sexes'. *S.E.* 19, pp. 241–60.
—(1927) *The Future of an Illusion*. *S.E.* 21, pp. 5–56.
—(1930) *Civilization and its Discontents*. *S.E.* 21, pp. 57–146.
—(1932a) 'Anxiety and instinctual life'. *S.E.* 22, pp. 81–111.
—(1932b) 'Femininity'. *S.E.* 22, pp. 112–35.
—(1937a) 'Analysis terminable and interminable'. *S.E.* 23, pp. 216–53.
—(1937b) 'Constructions in analysis'. *S.E.* 22, pp. 255–69.
—(1939) *Moses and Monotheism*. *S.E.* 23, pp. 7–137.
Glover, E. (1955) *The Technique of Psycho-Analysis*. New York: International Universities Press.
Greenacre, P. (1953) 'Certain relationships between fetishism and faulty development of the body image', *Psycho-Anal. Study Child* 8: 79–98.
—(1960) 'Further notes on fetishism', *Psycho-Anal. Study Child* 15: 191–207.
Greenson, R. R. (1966) 'A transvestite boy and a hypothesis', *Int. J. Psycho-Anal.* 47: 396–403.
Huxley, A. (1932) *Brave New World*. Chatto & Windus.
—(1962) *Island*. Chatto & Windus.
Keats, J. (1816) 'On First Looking into Chapman's Homer', in H. B. Forman, ed. *The Poetical Works of John Keats*. H. B. Forman, 1914.
Kingsley, C. (1863) *The Water Babies*, in *The Works of Charles Kingsley*, vol. 2. Macmillan, 1980–85.
Knapp, P. H., *et al.* (1960) 'Suitability for psychoanalysis: a review of one hundred supervised analytic cases', *Int. J. Psycho-Anal.* 49: 459–77.
Kuiper, P. C. (1968) 'Indications and contraindications for psychoanalytic treatment', *Int. J. Psycho-Anal.* 49: 261–4.
Limentani, A. (1972) 'The assessment of analysability: a major hazard in selection for psychoanalysis', *Int. J. Psycho-Anal.* 53: 351–61.
McDougall, J. (1986) *Theatres of the Mind*. Free Association Books.
Malcolm, J. (1981) *Psychoanalysis: The Impossible Profession*. New York: Knopf. Karnac, 1988.
Murdoch, I. (1973) *The Black Prince*. Chatto & Windus.
Namnum, A. (1968) 'The problem of analysability and the autonomous ego', *Int. J. Psycho-Anal.* 49: 271–5.
Needleman, J. (1976) 'Psychiatry and the sacred', in J. Needleman and J. L. Lewis, eds *On the Way to Self-Knowledge*. New York: Knopf.
Nietzsche, F. (1882) *Joyful Wisdom*, in O'Leary, ed. *The Complete Works of Friedrich Nietzsche*, vol. 10. N. T. Foulis, 1910.
Order for Morning Prayer (1872) *The Book of Common Prayer*. Oxford University Press.
Rousseau, J.-J. (1781) *Confessions*.
Rosenfeld, H. (1985) 'The relationship between psychosomatic symptoms and psychotic states', in *Yearbook of Psychoanalytic Psychotherapy*, vol. 1. Emerson, NJ: New Concept Press.
Sacks, O. (1973) *Awakenings*. Duckworth.

Searles, H. (1959) 'The effort to drive the other person crazy', in Searles (1965) pp. 254–83.

—(1965) *Collected Papers on Schizophrenia and Related Subjects.* Hogarth.

Shakespeare, W. (1603) *Hamlet, Prince of Denmark.*

Skynner, R. (1976) 'Psychotherapy and spiritual tradition', in J. Needleman and J. L. Lewis, eds. *On the Way to Self-Knowledge.* New York: Knopf.

Steiner, J. (1982) 'Perverse relationships between parts of the self: a clinical illustration', *Int. J. Psycho-Anal.* 62: 241–51.

Stoller, R. J. (1968) *Sex and Gender.* Hogarth.

Stone, L. (1954) 'The widening scope of indications for psychoanalysis', *J. Amer. Psychoanal. Assn* 2: 567–94.

Strachey, J. (1934) 'On the nature of the therapeutic action of psychoanalysis', *Int. J. Psycho-Anal.* 25: 127–59.

Sucitto, The Ven. (1989) *The Forest Newsletter*, Journal of the Amaravati Buddhist Monastery 3.

Symington, N. (1983) 'The analyst's act of freedom as agent of therapeutic change', *Int. Rev. Psycho-Anal.* 10: 283–91.

—(1990) 'Virtue and mental health', *Bull. Brit. Psycho-Anal. Soc.*

Tillich, P. (1949) *The Shaking of the Foundations.* SCM Press.

Trilling, L. (1972) *Sincerity and Authenticity.* Oxford University Press.

Welwood, J. (1985) *Awakening the Heart.* Boston: Shambala.

Winnicott, D. W. (1947) 'Hate in the counter-transference', in Winnicott (1958).

—(1958) *Collected Papers: Through Paediatrics to Psycho-Analysis.* Tavistock.

Wordsworth, W. (1805) *The Prelude*, S. Gill, ed. Oxford University Press, 1970.

Yeats, W. B. (1919) 'The Second Coming', in *Collected Poems.* Macmillan, 1950, pp. 210–11.

Zetzel, E. (1968) 'The so-called good hysteric' *Int. J. Psycho-Anal.* 49: 256–60.

INDEX